CW00554282

KING TORRISMONDO

King Torrismondo

by

TORQUATO TASSO

DUAL LANGUAGE EDITION

Translation, Introductory Essays, and Notes by

MARIA PASTORE PASSARO

Fordham University Press
New York
1997

Copyright © 1997 by Fordham University Press
All rights reserved
LC 96-47133
ISBN 0-8232-1633-0 (hardcover)
ISBN 0-8232-1634-9 (paperback)

Library of Congress Cataloging-in-Publication Data

Tasso, Torquato, 1544—1595.
   [Re Torrismondo. English]
   King Torrismondo / by Torquato Tasso ; with a translation,
introduction, and notes by Maria Pastore Passaro.
     p. cm.
   Includes bibliographical references.
   ISBN 0-8232-1633-0 (hc). — ISBN 0-8232-1634-9 (pbk.)
   I. Pastore Passaro, Maria C. II. Title.
PQ4642.E268P37   1996
851'.4—dc21
                                  96-47133
                                       CIP

Printed in the United States of America

To the memory of my husband,
Vincent J. Passaro

CONTENTS

INTRODUCTION

Tasso's Life and Works

THE YEAR 1995 marked the fourth centennial of the death in Rome of a great poet at odds with himself—an instinctive poet ("nature's child") and a scholar poet, an ideologue and an anti-idealogue, a rationalist and an irrationalist, a hedonist and an ascetic, an authoritarian and a libertarian, a poet who taught that, since art imitates life and is in turn imitated by life, it must therefore present exemplary lives, but whose own life no one would ever choose to imitate, a poet of doomed love and connoisseur of erotic seduction whose own loves seem to have been exclusively platonic, the poet of verisimilitude and the poet of the marvellous, the poet of romance escape and errancy and the poet of *pietas* and epic responsibility, the pope's poet and the poet's poet—but ever the fastidious, rank-conscious aristocrat, haughty and servile by turns, and never for the life of him a people's poet. This paradoxical, elusive chameleon, this master of rhetoric who became rhetoric's slave, this restless wanderer in search of rest, this poetically triumphant and existentially tragic figure was Torquato Tasso. As we will see, there are excellent biographical reasons why Tasso's literary production is uneven. Like the little girl with the little curl, when Tasso was good he was very, very good, and when he was bad he was horrid. Or arid. Those of us who cherish him are willing to overlook his horrid aridities for the sake of the good, which is good as gold.

Torquato Tasso is by far the most important Italian poet born in the sixteenth century. He is also one of the half dozen or so most influential authors Italy has ever produced. His influence transcends his nation's borders and the confines of literature in the strict sense. Not since Petrarch in the fourteenth century had an Italian poet enjoyed such resonance throughout Europe. And never before or since has a literary corpus inspired so many contemporary or later exponents of the other arts, providing texts and subjects for generations of painters and musicians (above all composers of madrigals, and pioneers of the opera such as Claudio Monteverdi and Jean-Baptiste Lully). Characters and episodes from the *Jerusalem Delivered* (the encounters between Tancredi and Clorinda, Erminia among the shepherds, Sofronia and Olindo, Rinaldo and Armida in their Bower of Blysse) were depicted by the most famous Italian and French artists of the seventeenth and eighteenth centuries, from Tintoretto and the Carracci to Poussin, Claude Lorrain, Salvator Rosa, Boucher, Fragonard and Giambattista Tiepolo, to name only a few. And never before or since has a literary life (or legend) been viewed, from Tasso's contemporary Montaigne to Rousseau, Goethe, the Romantic painter Eugène Delacroix (nineteenth-century artists turned from the work to the poet's life), Leopardi, Byron, and Baudelaire, as so quintessentially poetic and so variously and tragically emblematic of the tormented destiny of genius in a hostile, uncomprehending world.

Tasso died at the age of fifty, after a life of acute physical and mental anguish whose external manifestation was a chronic inability to settle down in any one place and a seven-year imprisonment as a dangerously unpredictable "madman." Yet he managed to produce a narrative romance in the traditional eight-line stanza in twelve books, an epic poem in twenty (eventually expanded to twenty-four), a tragicomic pastoral masque, a classical tragedy, a blank-verse poem in seven books on the creation of the world, a number of shorter but substantial poems of a religious or encomiastic nature, a collection of twenty-eight dialogues on a variety of social, ethical, and literary subjects, several major works of literary criticism, to say nothing of a corpus of lyric poetry so extensive, and, since the poems were never collected during his lifetime, so textually problematic, that after four centuries it has not yet had a satisfactory critical edition, as well as an extensive, more or less private correspondence that runs to five volumes in the standard nineteenth-century edition. Only the comic genre or genres seem—significantly—to be missing. Though in the pastoral *Aminta* and even in the epic *Jerusalem Delivered* the author indulges a vein for witty conceits (which irritated Dryden, for one, who, though he once declared that he reverenced Tasso as "the most excellent of modern poets," found this mannerist trait contrary to decorum and to the very nature of heroic verse), the "melancholy" Torquato is basically without a sense of humor, and the recent attempt to attribute to him an anonymous sixteenth-century comedy is anything but convincing. In any case the student of Tasso already has enough on his plate without it.

The years of Tasso's relatively brief life (1544–1595), the years of the Late Italian Renaissance, were years of political, economic, and spiritual crisis and dramatic, even violent, change for Europe generally and Italy in particular. Economically, Italian commercial pre-eminence had withered away as trade shifted from the Mediterranean to the new Atlantic routes along the coasts of Africa and out to the New World. Moreover, the Mediterranean itself, with its Balkan, Asian, and African shores occupied by the Ottoman Turk, was no longer the safe *mare nostrum* of recent tradition. Politically, while the other European countries were consolidating into nation-states, Italy remained divided and conquerable. Moreover, the precarious internal balance of power among the Italian states had broken down in the last decade of the fifteenth century. In the sixteenth century, Italy became a pawn and a battleground, a bone of contention and the chief venue for the conflict for continental hegemony between France and Spain. The states of Italy, unable to form a common front and shortsightedly opportunistic in their individual allegiances, encouraged foreign intervention. The Sack of Rome of 1527, which saw the Eternal City and her icons laid waste by Catholic Spanish and Protestant German troops and the Medici pope Clement VII held virtually in captivity, was an epochal scandal which stunned not only Italy. Charles V's 1530 coronation as Holy Roman Emperor further mortified the papacy and made Charles the most powerful European ruler since Charlemagne. The fate of Italy as a dependency of Spain was henceforth all but sealed. Spanish domination was fully sanctioned in 1559 by the Peace of Cateau-Cambrésis, by which France gave Spain effective carte blanche in Italy.

The treaty was touted, however, as uniting the great Catholic powers against the spread of heresy. The widespread appeal of Luther's 1517 call for an antihierarchical religious Reformation—actually the latest in an ongoing series of protests over the Church's corruption—had quickly divided European Chris-

tendom into two schismatic camps—broadly speaking, the
Protestant north against the Catholic south. The Catholic estab-
lishment seems initially to have seriously underestimated the
challenge; the defensive Counter-Reformation (or Catholic Ref-
ormation, as apologetic historians prefer to call it) did not really
get under way until 1545, the year after Tasso was born, when
Pope Paul III convened the first of the three sessions of the
Council of Trent. The chief Tridentine aspiration—to reunite
confessionally divided Europe in the face of the threat posed
by the Ottoman Turks under Suleiman the Magnificent—was as
much political as it was religious. This goal of a reunited mis-
sionary Europe was not attained, of course, though it was still
devoutly wished by Tasso—often too glibly dubbed "the poet of
the Counter-Reformation"—and it is advanced as the epic's
extra-poetical justification in the opening stanzas of the *Jerusa-
lem Delivered*. The Council was more successful in reforming
the Catholic Church internally: standardizing liturgy and forms
of worship, modernizing church law and organization, redefin-
ing doctrine, and correcting inveterate abuses. The structures
it produced were punitive and authoritarian. During his reign,
Paul III also excommunicated Henry VIII, reactivated the Ro-
man Inquisition (the medieval tribunal designed to root out her-
esy), and established a regime of preventive censorship and an
Index of Forbidden Books. It was Paul who in 1540 approved
the constitution of Ignatius of Loyola's militant Jesuit teaching
and missionary order, whose religious zeal and intransigent de-
votion to papal authority and the bowdlerized pagan classics best
exemplify the new spirit of religious proselytism. Typical, not
merely of their own elitist approach, but of the increasingly hier-
archical view of the state prevalent among the ruling classes,
was the Jesuits' approach to the conversion of the heathen: con-
vert the monarch and you have to all intents and purposes con-
verted his people. As a boy, the future author of the *Jerusalem
Delivered* was one of the Jesuits' first pupils in their upper-class
school in Naples.

   In 1543, the year before Tasso's birth, the Polish canon and
astronomer Copernicus set forth his conclusion that our plane-
tary system was heliocentric—that our universe, in other words,
had the sun and not the earth at its center. Thus Copernicus
innocently called into question the creationist letter of the Bible

and ultimately the so-called Renaissance philosophy of man, which confirmed Christian man's privileged position in the great chain of being as intermediary between the lower creatures and the angels. The full implications of the Copernican theory, however, seem to have taken some time to sink in: it was not until 1616 that it was denounced as a threat to the faith by the Catholic Church. In 1633 Galileo Galilei, who had defended the Copernican system publicly against the geocentric Ptolemaic system, was tried by the Roman Inquisition and forced to abjure his scientific convictions.

The distance that separates Torquato Tasso from the revolutionary science of his day, his zeal indeed to profess and propagate only received doctrine, especially characteristic of his later years, can be best measured by the long poem on the Creation, *Il Mondo Creato* [The World Created or The Creation of the World], an erudite, rambling, and for the most part arid elaboration of the first book of Genesis, filled with curious antique lore derived from the Bible, pagan Greek and Latin sources, and the early Christian fathers. (As a footnote to this paragraph, it is worth pointing out that Galileo, an antimannerist and a partisan of Torquato's predecessor and rival Ariosto, was no admirer of Tasso's. Paradoxically, however, Erwin Panofsky, in his *Galileo as a Critic of the Arts,* suggests that he would have been an even better scientist if he had liked Tasso better, if he had been able, in other words, to liberate his taste from the aesthetic prejudices that went with High Renaissance style.)

Whatever a Freudian might have to say about the poet's melancholia (and one presumes it would run to volumes!), a Wordsworthian with an eye to the formative influence of nature might rejoice in the fact that Torquato Tasso was born shortly before the vernal equinox in March 1544 in an area—Sorrento, at the southern tip of the Bay of Naples—proverbial for its lush natural beauty. In spite of these favorable auspices, however, Torquato's childhood and youth turned out in practice to be an idyll *manqué*. His father, Bernardo Tasso, was a gentleman of excellent family from the far northern city of Bergamo. He was related to the barons Taxis, who had enjoyed a monopoly on postal service in the Empire since the previous century. Bernardo was also a poet of international repute and a courtier by profession (in other words, a "noble servant," and anything but the sine-cure it sounds!) and at that time secretary to Ferrante Sansever-ino, Prince of Salerno. Bernardo had been born a whole half century earlier, in 1493, and would not die until 1569. It is symptomatic that when his second surviving child and only son Torquato was born (the seven-year-older sibling was a daughter named Cornelia; before Cornelia, another Torquato had been born and had died in infancy), Bernardo was away on military and diplomatic missions to Piedmont and Flanders as one of the negotiators between the Habsburg Emperor Charles V and his chief rival, the Valois King of France François I. Bernardo's loy-alty to a series of princely masters would make of him a mostly absent father.

In 1552 Ferrante Sanseverino, the ringleader of the Neapoli-tan barons in revolt against the Spanish viceroy and his plan to introduce the Spanish Inquisition to Naples, was forced to take refuge in France, and the loyal Bernardo accompanied him into exile, thereby forfeiting whatever property he had accumulated. In 1554 the ten-year-old Torquato was summoned from Naples to join his father in Rome, where he would study for the next two years. He left behind his sister Cornelia and his young mother, whom he would never see again, since she would die suddenly and mysteriously two years later, perhaps poisoned by her brothers, who had steadfastly refused to pay her dowry. Years later, in a famous *canzone,* Torquato would ring the Oedipal changes on the scene, evoking a blown-up detail, as it were, from some print or painting of that favorite sacred subject, "The Massacre of the Innocents," with himself in the role of the zoomed-in-upon Innocent:

> Me from the bosom of my mother
> cruel Fortune snatched while still a babe in arms.
> Oh! those sweet kisses bathed with fretful tears,
> those ardent prayers the swift winds bore away,
> with sighs I now remember them; for never
> more was I to lay my cheek upon her cheek,
> clasped in those arms with knots so close and clinging.

The following year, 1557, Torquato followed his father to the court of Urbino—fifty years previously the brilliant setting for Castiglione's *Cortier* and currently a focal point for pro-Spanish sentiment—where he became companion of studies to the Duke's son, the young prince Francesco Maria Della Rovere. In the spring of 1559 he once more joined his itinerant father, this time in Venice. This protracted stay in Venice and the nearby university city of Padua, where the budding poet came into contact with some of Italy's most prominent scholars and men of letters, marks his first decisive encounter with the academy and the official beginning of Torquato's brilliant literary career. It was in Padua that he met the young prince Scipione Gonzaga, later to become a cardinal, who hosted the meetings of the private academy of so-called Ethereals in his residence. Tasso's *Discourses on the Art of Poetry* have Scipione Gonzaga as their addressee, and his earliest lyrics would be first published in 1567 in a collective volume of verse by the academy's members.

In Venice, under the influence of older poet and sculptor Danese Cattaneo, Tasso, a precocious fifteen-year-old with a growing reputation as a lyric poet, wrote the initial fragment (only 116 stanzas, though a surprising number of them would survive practically unchanged into the definitive version) of an epic poem based on the events of the First Crusade, preached by Pope Urban II in 1095. These unpublished stanzas, rediscovered in the eighteenth century, turned out to be the hesitant first seeds of what was destined to blossom into the poet's major work, the *Jerusalem Delivered*. At this early stage, however, though he can strike the note of communal religious enthusiasm, the poet has not yet hit upon a generative narrative strategy. He has not figured out how to postpone the inevitable denouement, how to tie some narrative knots.

For the time being, then, young Tasso's epic ambitions were temporarily set aside, as was the study of law urged on him by his father—in the latter case, the shelving was permanent—as he set about composing another narrative poem, this time in a chastened version of the sprawling and at the time extraordinarily popular genre of the chivalric romance. Not until 1560, when he had reached the age of sixty-six, had Tasso senior finally published in Venice his magnum opus, much heralded and long-awaited by the literary world and an immediate *succès d'estime,* but in hindsight dull and labored (and, with its record 100 cantos, interminably long to boot), *Amadigi di Gaula,* which retold in Italian verse the adventures of the worthy knight

Amadis of Gaul. Barely two years after his father's *Amadigi,* in 1562, Tasso junior (all of eighteen!) published, also in Venice, his own first full-length romance (full-length, though a tenth the length of Bernardo's!), the *Rinaldo,* dedicating it to young Don Luigi d'Este, his father's current patron and already a cardinal at the age of twenty-four. The dedication would earn Torquato a place, a year or two later, in the cardinal's household. Don Luigi was a member of the ruling family of Ferrara. Tasso's best work would be done at Ferrara under the Este family's increasingly gingerly protection.

The *Rinaldo* is, of course, eponymously titled for its hero, one of Charlemagne's legendary paladins and the chief rival of his cousin Orlando (the Italian form of Roland), and is, so to speak, a prequel to his better-known later adventures. It recounts the champion's pre-history, the exploits by which he acquired his early fame (a kind of "Enfances Renaud"). Rinaldo can be seen as an alter ego of the young Torquato and the personification of both his eagerness for emulation and his anxiety of influence, especially in light of the fact that the Great Italian Romance of his father's generation, Ludovico Ariosto's *Orlando Furioso,* had been named, like the romance by Boiardo which it continued, for Rinaldo's archrival Orlando. Ariosto (1474–1533) had been dead for almost thirty years, but his influence on poetic narrative had been immediate, decisive, and lasting. The bookshops well beyond mid-century were full of imitations of the *Orlando Furioso.* It is no accident, then, given the defiant autobiographical associations of the name, that one of the key figures of the *Jerusalem Delivered,* the young savior of the Christian cause, will also be called Rinaldo, although the character has in fact no connection with the hero of the early poem. Nevertheless, despite the fact that the *Jerusalem Delivered*'s Rinaldo (a figure comparable in his hyperbolic pursuit of honor to Shakespeare's Hotspur) purports to be historical rather than fictional, his ties to the world of romance, particularly during his period of errancy, before he is shamed into returning to the field of battle, are undeniable and symptomatic. There is no Rinaldo in the chastened *Jerusalem Conquered.*

Though the episodic variety of the romance genre continued to delight and entertain, and romances to proliferate, the critics' expectations of modern literary narrative (however hypothetical those expectations might be for the moment) were becoming more and more demandingly classical. The sixteenth century in Italy has been labelled the Age of Criticism. It rediscovered Aristotle's incomplete *Poetics,* which it read not in a *descriptive* but a *prescriptive* sense, with the consequent enthronement of the two genres discussed in the surviving fragment: epic and tragedy. Homer (and his follower Virgil) and the Greek tragedians (filtered in part through their would-be follower Seneca) became the great models. Their styles, structures, and ethos, as analyzed by the rationalist Aristotle, were to be imitated by the poet. Moreover, the poet's moral responsibility became staggering, since, for his earnest reader, in addition to being a faithful imitation of life, serious literature ought to be a school for life. Tragedy portrayed nobility with a flaw; the epic, flawless nobility. The heroes and heroines of both were socially exalted (and therefore potentially morally perfect), and their conduct was negatively exemplary in tragedy and positively exemplary in the epic. Tragedy taught by default, as it were, showing the dire consequences of moral imperfection or error; the characters of epic taught by example, showing the triumph of heroic integrity. The moral atmosphere of the Counter-Reformation, sternly paternalistic and authoritarian, no doubt favored this second Catholic apotheosis of Aristotle, literary and morally didactic this time around and not, or not exclusively, as with Thomas Aquinas and the schoolmen, theological.

Fortunately, the Age of Criticism, like our own, was not short of explainers. The reader who expects to be enthralled by this literary scholasticism will find a solid guide in J. E. Spingarn's 1899 *Literary Criticism in the Renaissance,* and, once his appetite has been whetted, he can progress to the 1,200 pages of Bernard Weinberg's 1961 *History of Literary Criticism in the Italian Renaissance.* Among the countless subtle theoreticians and exegetes whose contributions Weinberg analyzes, he will find Torquato Tasso. What distinguishes Tasso from the rest, however, is that he actually wrote the epic and tragedy he theorized, probably because consciously or unconsciously he allowed for a margin of error or inspiration. In all fairness, it should be stated that another theorist and commentator, Giangiorgio Trissino (1478–1550), also wrote both a tragedy, *Sofonisba,* and an historical epic, *L'Italia Liberata dai Goti* [Italy Delivered from the Goths], whose title is echoed in the vulgate title of Tasso's *Jerusalem Delivered*. (If Tasso had published the poem himself, there is a strong possibility he would have entitled it *Goffredo or Gotifredo*.) Trissino's tragedy, based on an incident from the Roman historian Livy, is still read as part of the (very short) history of Italian tragedy; his epic is scarcely read at all.

After publishing the *Rinaldo*, in which he had offered a specious solution to the problem of unity of plot by giving the poem a single hero, Torquato must have returned almost immediately to the critical and narrative problems posed by the true epic. In his *Discorsi dell'arte poetica* [Discourses on the Art of Poetry], the generic gap between epic and romance is minimized by drawing the romance into the sphere of the epic.

It had become more and more urgent for the young Tasso to define just what it was he was aiming for. And it is of capital importance for us to observe that, far from falling an unwilling victim to critical Aristotelianism, as is often asserted, Tasso's allegiance to the Greek philosopher's *Poetics* at this stage in his career was wholly spontaneous. In order to articulate his own poetic theory, he needed well-defined literary parameters, a system founded upon authority which would supply categories and concepts, in which the basic issues had been clearly brought into focus, leaving him free to choose in each case, in the light of his experience as a practitioner, and with lucid critical intelligence, the solution most apt to liberate his creative energies. Tasso embraced Aristotle's categories with enthusiasm, he avidly attended the humanist Carlo Sigonio's lectures in Padua, he was a frequent visitor to authoritative critic and would-be poet Sperone Speroni's private apartments. These were exciting months. The mood in which the *Art of Poetry* was composed is reflected in the brisk, businesslike attack ("Anyone proposing to write an heroic poem has three things to watch out for . . . ."), in the coherence and perspicuity of the argument, in the vitality that sets it apart from run-of-the-mill sixteenth-century critical writing. Above all, we feel in it the eager *élan*, which culminates in the justly famous passage celebrating the *concordia discors* of unity in variety, with Tasso's Platonic vindication of the godlike qualities of the poet as maker or demiurge, and his transport before the epic world as microcosm. His commitment to his poetic partakes of the sustained ardor and intensity that characterized Tasso as a poet. That is why it is misleading in this early phase to distinguish sharply theory from practice. In the young Tasso there is between poem and principles a relationship at once dialectical and symbiotic. This is a working poetic. It seeks a balance between contemporary critical speculation and pre-scription and what the poet feels is right. The theory acts as midwife to the *Jerusalem Delivered;* it does not dictate it. In Tasso's Aristotelian view, epic, like tragedy, though it may con-tain a variety of episodes dialectically related to the central ac-tion, must tell a single story, and that story must be both believable (though it may strain belief) and paradigmatic, and it must be told in the noblest of styles. Furthermore, epic and tragedy are in a sense an ethically superior—because less purely contemplative—form of history. Poetry's truth is a more effec-tive ethical persuader, since, through "imitation," it brings his-tory dramatically to life, making it happen again now, re-enacting heroic and tragic events, involving the spectator or reader, and producing a salutary catharsis or emotional release.

After the poem's completion, after the carping of its revisors and the cruel attacks of Tasso's literary enemies, the harmoni-ous and reciprocally nourishing coexistence of poetry and poet-ics would be destroyed. In the years following his breakdown, Tasso's wandering and declining years, an odd disassociation occurs. His defense of his masterpiece is carried forward on two fronts: the practical and the theoretical. On the one hand, he feels compelled to defend his contingent practical choices, on the other he upholds the permanent and unique validity of the principles that guided them. The mode of dependence of poem on poetic theory is made to seem far more peremptory than it ever was in fact. The principles are credited with an independent existence, anterior to and apart from the poem; and with each restatement they become less flexible and vital, more sclerotic and intransigent. In defending the authority of Aristotle and, in the second place, his own interpretation of the Master, Tasso imagined he was defending his poem. In fact, he was defending an abstraction. A poetic which had been functional and adaptive, a permitting cause, became an end in itself. Moreover, the rela-tive importance accorded to the theory grew with the poet's growing alienation from his own empirical judgment. It was probably inevitable that the poem should at last be modified to fit the reified theory and that, while the matter of the poem was if anything reduced, the twenty "cantos" (with all the lyric overtones of that designation) of the *Liberata* should become the twenty-four portentous "books" of the *Conquistata*. Whatever their representative value as indicators of the concerns of Late Renaissance literary criticism, of the "Italian sixteenth century *ethos*" (the phrase is Saintsbury's), in terms of Tasso's own career, the *Discourses on the Art of Poetry* are inseparable from the *Jerusalem Delivered*, while the revised *Discourses on the Heroic Poem* must be paired with the *Jerusalem Conquered.* And the *Jerusalem Conquered* evokes the poignant imperfect of Baudelaire's *Albatros*—"l'infirme qui volait." But we are getting ahead of ourselves.

In 1572 in Ferrara Tasso passed from the service of the cardinal to that of the Duke Alfonso II, and in the spring of 1573 he offered his new patron the *Aminta,* an exquisite generic hybrid in the recently revived tradition of the pastoral. The name of the protagonist Aminta (in English Amyntas) and the names of other characters such as Tirsi (Thyrsis) and Mopso (Mopsus), like Spenser's and Noel Coward's Corydon, Milton's Lycidas, or Matthew Arnold's Thyrsis, are signals of the pastoral convention and go back to Latin Virgil and beyond him to the Greek poet Theocritus, though the pastoral was originally a lyric and not a narrative or dramatic tradition, and Aristotle has nothing to say about it. Tasso's play was given its first and only court performance in the summer of that year on the island of Belvedere in the Po River, where the Este family had their summer residence. The island pleasance and the holiday season provided a perfect setting for a work like the *Aminta*—as they might have for Shakespeare's *Tempest*—which, for all its smiling or ambiguously polemical allusions to the Ferrara court, and in spite of the fact that several of its secondary characters are identifiable courtiers in disguise, takes place in a timeless Arcadian Never Never Land. Its *carpe diem* message is muted and tinged with nostalgia for an unspoiled primitive Golden Age—perhaps recapturable, more likely not—of mythic innocence. Thus the mood, despite the play's anxious vicissitudes, is by and large golden, but a memorable chorus at the end of the first act poignantly laments the passing of that age of unguilty pleasures (the Freudian overtones need no underlining) and the advent of the tyrant

Honor and his Age of Shame (the Civilization of the Renaissance surprised by Sin). But for its happy ending, the *Aminta* follows the narrative conventions of classical tragedy (the three so-called unities, the division into five acts, the introduction of a chorus, on-stage narration of offstage action, peripeteia; critics have even looked for catharsis). Aside from its strictly pastoral genealogy, one of its models is in fact Sperone Speroni's tragedy *Canace,* whose free alternation of long and short lines it puts to more appropriate lyric use. This seemingly spontaneous masterpiece of lyric musicality, suspenseful plotting, sensibility, persuasion, wit, and delicate sensuality, whose theme is the anguish and joys of adolescent love, how love can separate and how love can unite, is a miracle of balance and a perfect example of art concealing art.

Much traditional criticism of the play has been devoted to fleshing out the nineteenth-century scholar-poet-critic Giosuè Carducci's dictum that the *Aminta* is a miracle, although recent critics have tended instead to play down the ineffability and stress instead its consummate literary awareness and its sophisticated Alexandrian intertextual play of citation and allusion. The plaintive young swain Aminta, whose character more than any other is a dramatic extension of the lyric madrigal form in which Tasso excelled, declares his predicament to his more experienced companion Tirsi: he is in love with the recalcitrant nymph Silvia, a devotee of Diana and the hunt, who has no time for sentiment or boys. In vain Tirsi's ally and Aminta's self-appointed go-between, the mature and knowing Daphne, attempts (in a hymn to the eros of ecology) to demonstrate to the froward Silvia the *naturalness* of love and the *unnaturalness* of her own indifference to it. It will take a series of dramatic incidents and reversals to bring the intractable Silvia (her name, cognate, for instance, with the adjective "sylvan," bespeaks her wildness) out of the woods and into the arms of her devoted Aminta. But she will come round in the end.

Like his father, Torquato was a courtier poet who relied on the hospitality and patronage in cash and in kind of his patrons. The protégé's role had become less administrative and more exclusively literary and decorative as the century advanced, there was no longer any question of their telling their prince the truth, and patrons were extremely jealous of their catches. Strictly speaking, even the act of publishing was unnecessary and chiefly intended to reflect credit on the dedicatee. In addition, Torquato seems to have inherited, in a far more acute and neurotic form, his father's perfectionism and reluctance to publish. Almost none of Torquato's works was printed when it was first completed, but instead circulated promiscuously in manuscript, often in several different versions at the same time. Add to this the poet's seven-year imprisonment, his well-known distraction, and his compulsive restlessness, as well as the difficulties faced by the sixteenth-century traveler and the consequent restrictions on what he could carry with him, and you will begin to have an inkling of the confusion that reigns among his books, manuscripts, and papers.

In the absence of a datable manuscript, we can only speculate that it was in the fall of that same year 1573 that Tasso began to compose the fragmentary tragedy which was published without his consent in 1582. This untitled work, a first venture in the second of the two most ambitious avant-garde genres alongside the epic, has traditionally been named for its royal protagonist, *Galealto re di Norvegia* [Galealto King of Norway]. The preposterous plot claims to be based on history, and the ever-scrupulous Tasso will wind up combing Olaus Magnus's recently published history of Scandinavia for documentary plot-hooks, local color, and customs. But tragedy, unlike epic, though it too involves the great, involves their private affairs and emotions more than their public roles.

Even when completed, Tasso's "tragic poem" (to borrow a subtitular cop-out from Gabriele D'Annunzio) can barely aspire to the weight of a single episode in the plot of the epic. For the moment, like the *Gierusalemme,* the narrative fragment previously mentioned, and presumably in the same kind of impasse, the composition of the tragedy was interrupted. The version printed by Aldus Manutius Jr. several years later, in 1582, breaks off in fact in the second scene of Act II. The play would later be taken up again, rewritten, completed, and published by Tasso himself with a new title, *Il re Torrismondo* (King Torrismondo). This completed version is of course the work presented in translation in the present volume. We shall have something more specific to say about it in the second part of this introduction.

The first draft of his epic poem, which Tasso had been toiling over for a good ten years, was terminated and read to the Duke of Ferrara and his sister the Duchess of Urbino in April 1575. If it had not been before, the epic now became an obsession. The poet was becoming increasingly anxious, however, and beset by suspicion of his fellow courtiers, as well as by compulsive doubts as to his own religious and poetic orthodoxy. He submitted his poem for their private approval to a number of the most distinguished religious and literary figures of the day (a "committee" which among others included his former mentor Sperone Speroni and another friend from his student days in Padua, Scipione Gonzaga). He also appeared voluntarily before the Inquisitors in Bologna and Ferrara to confess his doctrinal uncertainties and defend himself against the supposed spies who had accused him of heresy. The protracted revision of the poem (in a sense never completed) placed a tremendous strain on Tasso's already vulnerable and schizophrenically over-subtle mind. His intense correspondence, in which he pits his wits against the literal-mindedness of the individual revisors, shows him apparently accommodating but in reality stubborn and defensive, and possessed of a desperate casuistry capable of fabricating any number of hair-splitting arguments in defense of every choice and its opposite. To defend what were, if anything, salutary transgressions against slavish orthodoxy, he even composed an elaborate moral *Allegory* of the poem, a "darke conceit" indeed, as circumstantial as it was spurious, in which even the "naughty bits" were explained away by being burdened with an alleged ulterior symbolic meaning. It is a further savage irony that, while its author was being held incommunicado, the *Jerusalem Delivered* would eventually find its way into print in several different unsatisfactory editions, none of which had the author's approval and none of which brought him the slightest profit or advantage.

In the *Jerusalem Delivered,* Tasso was able to resolve and to make brilliantly productive (and expressive of his most profound mental tensions, and his age's, and perhaps our own) a central critical dilemma. He succeeded in turning to remarkable creative account a by now traditional critical opposition—the

dichotomy between the classical Aristotelian epic and the ver-
nacular pastoral romance. Whatever lip service Tasso may have
paid to the Aristotelians in his preface to the *Rinaldo,* whatever
practical gestures he may claim to make in the direction of epic
structure by simplifying the action of his poem and concentrat-
ing on a single protagonist, the *Rinaldo* had remained pure (per-
haps we should say "impure") pastoral romance. Eminently
readable, its convenient length had avoided the problem of lon-
gueurs—an important consideration for a debutant poet writing
from the point of view of a hedonistic, reader-oriented poetic
in which the final criterion is the reader's delight. The earlier
Gierusalemme had been pure epic—albeit epic run aground.

The structure of the *Rinaldo* is strictly romance, starting out
with two practically contiguous points and excogitating narrative
strategies designed to keep them apart. The points in question
are the knight Rinaldo and his lady Clarice, whose paths con-
verge and diverge at the start of the action, providing the motiva-
tion for his ensuing feats, but who do not come definitively
together, in marriage, till the end. This serial structure is of
course infinitely expandable by the addition and interpolation
of episodes—adventures, quests, errancy, obstacles, and chal-
lenges—narrative digressions without much inner character-
ological motivation. This is a world ruled by chance; and Tasso
in the *Rinaldo* falls in behind the imitators of Boiardo and Ari-
osto in passive mechanical allegiance to a superannuated con-
vention in which *virtù* vies with *fortuna* and triumphs without
any particular conviction. On the teenage Tasso's other table, we
found the interrupted first book of the *Gierusalemme.* Straight
epic without a chaser. The problem with this rigid distinction
of genres—and the problem concerns the narrative strategies of
the *epic* world—is how to find an alternative motive force, an
alternative structure capable of generating teleological pur-
posive and deliberate narrative diegesis, a structure other than
the eternal departure, arrival, and re-departure (in a word, er-
rancy) of which the romance "plot" is woven. For here too—in
the epic, that is—destination tends to coincide with starting
point. But here the drive is not erotic (nor "thanatotic," as it
might be at certain points of the *Aminta*). The two points are
not a man and a woman but a man and a ritually sacred place
enslaved, the protagonists Goffredo (or Gotifredo) and Jerusa-

lem. (Tasso had trouble deciding which name to use in his title.) The goal (in other words, narrative closure) was attained, they were brought together, in the trial balloon of the *Gierusalemme*, by stanza 30 of Book I. And this was supposed, to quote Pound, to be "a poem of some length"! Breaking the stasis, that was the first heave—a heave Tasso at fifteen years of age had not been capable of. The impasse was the direct result of his inability to transcend the terms of the literary debate as he found it.

What happens in the *Jerusalem Delivered* is a radical reinvention of epic structure, the creation and maintenance—against all odds—of a threatened epic center ("Things fall apart. The center, can it hold?"), a center encircled and entoiled by a perverse and pulling romance periphery. Errancy must now be viewed, not simply, as in the *Rinaldo* and the pastoral romance tradition in general, as tending *toward what,* but we must be simultaneously aware of *away from what.* In such a world, the new Rinaldo can no longer merely follow the libidinal call of "desire for glory and the heat of love"; he must be made to feel the full guilt of his error, expiate it, and learn to redirect his libidinal economy, to submit in order to be free, as civilization exacts of our several discontents. I know of no work that enacts more dramatically than the *Jerusalem Delivered* the struggle with the angel and the triumph of its own creation. The psychomachia is the psychomachia of the poet's creative throes, the mapping of the Holy Land and its environs the pre-Freudian mapping—or, better, the *sounding*—of the character's and the creator's psychic depths, Tasso's great contribution to the psychology of literary narrative. All of those great and minor characters—Tancredi, Erminia, Sofronia and Olindo, Clorinda, Rinaldo, Armida—have a fundamental instinctive impulse toward the world of pastoral romance. (Less so Goffredo and the pagan heroes Argante and Solimano, who, in their very attachment to the center, are rooted in and representative of the purely epic dimension.) When Tasso attempted, against the strictures of his puritanical censors, "to save"—as he so inadequately put it—"the loves and the enchantments," he was fighting to defend the most intimate structure of his poem, the mannerist tension between center and periphery, between centrifugal and centripetal fields of force, between the harsh but needful task of the epic and the soft lure of pastoral romance.

Against the suasive consolations of the pastoral and the hedonistic rewards of romance, the *Jerusalem Delivered* bears inconsolable witness to the tragically incalculable *costs* of achievement (or *achèvement*), the inevitable mortification of any and all aspiration toward a personal felicity, a small private peace, in the face of the stern and unbending exigencies of the inexorable Other, call it fate, guilt, duty, mission, war, or public history.

In retrospect, 1575 would be seen by Tasso as a watershed year, the year between wellness and misery, and the trip to Rome and Florence he made at the end of it as marking "the cause and onset of all his ills." His negotiations for a place with the Medici, Alfonso D'Este's chief political and dynastic rivals, and the possibility that he might dedicate his poem to them when he finally made up his mind to publish it, were not calculated to set his current patron's mind at ease. Tasso was becoming a problem. His absences from court became more frequent, his confrontations with other courtiers, even with servants, more shrill and more violent. More than once he had to be locked up for his own good and placed in what then passed for treatment. Despite his physical exhaustion, he would escape, whenever he could, from Ferrara to scour the length and breadth of the peninsula. Apocryphal or not, the incident related by biographer Giambattista Manso, which has Torquato, disguised as a pilgrim, knocking on his sister's door in Sorrento with the news that her brother is dead, just to see how she would react, is a neat emblem of his state of mind.

In March 1579 Tasso returned to Ferrara from an absence at the Savoia court in Turin just in time for the celebration of Duke Alfonso's third marriage, to Margherita Gonzaga of Mantua. In the midst of the festivities he seems to have felt neglected. It was at this point that his behavior became so abusive and unpredictable that it was thought best to chain him up in solitary confinement. His segregation in the convent hospital of Sant'Anna was to last for seven long years, until 1586, when the heir to the Duchy of Mantua, Vincenzo Gonzaga, had him released into his custody. After the initial months, the poet was allowed books and writing materials, and he continued to compose new works and to revise those already written.

The twenty-eight pseudo-philosophical Platonic *Dialogues*, for instance, were for the most part composed during the Sant'Anna years. Abstract discussions of a broad assortment of fashionable moral, social, and aesthetic—in a word, courtly—norms and values: nobility, virtue, courtesy, pleasure, piety, jealousy, dignity, precedence, the consolations of philosophy, clemency, emblems, masks, idols, and epitaphs—the list, which could not help including discussions of love and friendship, the conflicting loyalties of *King Torrismondo,* reads like an index to Montaigne's or Bacon's *Essays.* Many of the dialogues introduce an authorial spokesman—significantly dubbed "Il Forestiere Napoletano," which might be rendered "The Outsider from Naples"—to whose preachy erudition most of the other characters defer. As dramatic evocations of actual conversations, these didactic fragments fail to convince. We regret the wit, verve, repartee, and relevance of the comparable but less one-sided discussions of Castiglione's High Renaissance *Courtier.* Moveover, notwithstanding the autobiographical presence, the ideas expressed, the positions espoused and defended, and the ethical and aesthetic lore exhibited are conventional and conformist, the received ideas of contemporary society (Tasso as Polonius) more interesting from the point of view of cultural history than from that of Tasso's life or personal convictions. It is as though their author were displaying his academic (and rational) credentials, the perfection of his cultural literacy.

Meanwhile, the first pirated editions of the *Jerusalem Delivered* were being published. (There would never be an officially approved one.) Camillo Pellegrino's exaltation of Tasso over Ariosto in his 1584 dialogue on epic poetry, *Il Carrafa o vero dell'epica poesia,* sparked the ire of the representatives of the Florentine Crusca Academy and ushered in one of the most virulent literary battles of the century. Poor Tasso himself intervened with a dignified *Apology* and began reinforcing his defenses by rewriting the *Discourses.* At the same time, he began his own revision of the poem, and the change of heart is evident in the speaking epithets—Jerusalem is no longer *Delivered* or Made Free but *Conquered.* He also tore up his tragedy again and rewrote it, with the title *King Torrismondo.* He would finish it in Mantua shortly after his release.

Tasso's stay in Mantua, which lasted in theory until 1592, was interrupted by protracted trips to Rome, Naples, and Florence.

Even after his release, his symptoms persisted. In a letter of October 1587 to Scipione Gonzaga, we read: "I am not well, and so melancholy that I am judged mad by myself as well as others, when, unable to keep hidden so many thoughts and so many anxieties and cares typical of a sick and disturbed mind, I launch into interminable soliloquies." In 1592 he returned once again to Naples, where he was the house guest of his biographer Manso (whom Milton visited on his own Grand Tour). There he began the composition of the *The Creation of the World*. Later the same year, in Rome, he was welcomed by Pope Clement VIII. The rewritten version of the epic, *Jerusalem Conquered,* published in Rome in 1593, was dedicated to the Pope's nephew Cinzio Aldobrandini. In Naples the following year Tasso finally managed to print the *Discourses on the Heroic Poem.*

Two hundred and fifty years had gone by since 1341, when Petrarch, in imitation of the ancient poets, had been crowned with a wreath of laurels on the Capitoline Hill in Rome. And now Pope Clement VIII invited Tasso to come to Rome to receive the poet's crown. This papal endorsement should have set Torquato's mind at ease at last, but when he got to Rome, he was already terminally ill. He died on April 25, 1595, in a narrow convent cell in the Hieronymite monastery of Sant'Onofrio (founded, fittingly enough, as a hermitage, a refuge from the world, in sight of but remote from *orbem et urbem*) on the slopes of the Janiculum Hill. He is buried in the beautiful little church with its fifteenth-century cloister that still stands there. Downriver, across the Tiber, at the foot of the Aventine, lie the dust of John Keats and Shelley's heart. Tasso's Oak, actually an evergreen live oak which stood close by, under which the nineteenth-century imagination liked to place the poet, looking down upon the city and the world in a suitably contemplative pose, is now a stump. Tasso's long-suffering patron Alfonso II d'Este died without an heir two years after Tasso himself, in 1597, whereupon Pope Clement VIII took advantage of the extinction of the male line to annex Ferrara to the Papal States. Ferrara, long the home of one of Renaissance Italy's most brilliant courts, was to become a provincial city of "grass-grown streets." Torquato Tasso, however, who knew all about transience and "mutalibitie," speaks to us just as passionately and painfully of what is freed and conquered, lost and won, as he did four hundred years ago; his heart—like yours and mine—is just as finite and as yearning.

KING TORRISMONDO

Few authors have combined greatness and fragility in the same degree as Torquato Tasso. Few have been so precocious or have declined so precipitously. We have seen how the career of his most ambitious project, an epic poem (part history, part fiction) based on the events of the First Crusade, is bracketed between the eager enthusiasm of the youthful fragment, *Il Gierusalemme*, begun in 1559, when the poet was barely sixteen (and set aside, probably in 1561, while he composed the romance *Rinaldo*), and the stubborn and anxious orthodoxy of the final revised and approved version, the *Jerusalem Conquered*, published in 1593, two winters before his death in April 1595. In between stands his masterpiece, the *Jerusalem Delivered*, the first (pirated) edition of which appeared in 1581. By that time the unstable Tasso was about to enter the third year of what would prove to be a seven-year period of protective custody in Ferrara. Tasso's imprisonment obviously represents a watershed. In happier days, in 1573, before his breakdown, he had made his dramatic debut with the pastoral tragicomedy *Aminta,* a mannerist work of such delicate dawning erotic verve and suspenseful elegance that we can only echo the enchantment of the nineteenth-century poet-critic Carducci: "L'*Aminta è un portento!*" The *Aminta* is a miracle.

When Carducci came to discuss the poet's tragedy, *King Torrismondo,* it was all too easy for him to reprise, with the nonchalant addition of a negative, the opening sentence of the *Aminta* essay: "Non è un portento!" *King Torrismondo* is not a miracle.

The 3,340-line tragedy—*pace* Carducci, for better or for worse the closest sixteenth-century Italy seems to have come to producing the Great Italian Tragedy—actually represents the correction and completion of a previous fragmentary redaction. This earlier 1,197-line fragment (a draft of Act I and the opening of Act II) was published for the first time by Aldus Manutius, Jr. in 1582, with the designation *Tragedia non finita* (Unfinished Tragedy), as part of the second volume of Tasso's collected lyric poetry *Delle Rime del Signor Torquato Tasso Parte seconda.* The first of the four documented references to the existence of this earlier experiment—no manuscript of which is extant— occurs in a letter of June 11, 1581 to one of Tasso's correspondents, Maurizio Cattaneo.[2] The assignment of the work's composition to 1573–74, though completely without documentary foundation, has since become something of a critical commonplace. Nor is the title usually assigned to it, *Galealto re di Norvegia* (Galealto King of Norway), in any sense authorial. In his few epistolary references, Tasso never gives the work a title, and the title under which it was first published by Manutius (during Tasso's confinement) is the noncommittal, reticent, generically descriptive one previously cited: *Tragedia non finita.*

Tasso was to take up his tragedy again sometime around September 1585 while still a prisoner-patient in the Sant'Anna hospital in Ferrara, to which he had been relegated, practically on his thirty-fifth birthday, in March 1579, and he continued to work on it during his last few months there. He was provisionally released into the custody of Vincenzo Gonzaga, future Duke of Mantua, on July 12, 1586. On December 14, 1586, the completed manuscript (which already contained extensive corrections) was sent from Mantua to Ferrara to Tasso's friend Antonio Costantini so that he could make a fair copy for presentation to Eleonora de' Medici, "la signora prencipessa serenissima," the second wife of Vincenzo Gonzaga.[1] Tasso got back the fair copy twenty-six days later, on January 9, 1587, and immediately (and typically) set about introducing further corrections. He continued to do so even after the presentation copy was in the hands of the duchess. We have letters to her asking if he could get it back for a few hours, to add the finishing touches.

Sometime before August 1587, his original draft copy was also returned by Costantini, and Tasso proceeded to make further corrections in that copy, subsequently taking it with him toward the end of August to Bergamo, where it would serve as the basis for the first printed edition, printed by Comino Ventura & Conpagni. A copy of the *editio princeps,* with additional autograph corrections added by Tasso, served as the basis for a second edition, published by Ventura before the end of 1587. This second Ventura edition ought, then, to be the critical copy text, though it appears that additional copies annotated by the author may have served as the more or less authorized basis for other subsequent editions printed independently in 1587 and 1588. The tragedy appears to have enjoyed phenomenal contemporary success, going through as many as fourteen separate printings between 1587 and 1588. At least one edition came out in practically every northern Italian capital (Mantua, Venice, Genoa, Ferrara, Verona, Cremona, Bologna, Turin, in addition to the first and second Bergamo editions previously mentioned). It is not surprising or without significance, given her perfectly commensurable status with Torrismondo as heroine or as victim, that one of the two extant indirect manuscript copies of the autograph bears the title *Alvida,* derived, as is indeed the case for most classical Italian (and, later, French) tragedies, from the name of the female protagonist.

The plot of *King Torrismondo* is of course absurd.[2] Or rather, the foreplot. It doesn't have much of an actual plot, since, as is customary in classical or classicizing tragedy, everything important has already happened before the play begins. All that happens onstage (one might say, in the closet, this being, in every conceivable sense of the word, a closet drama) is that the chief characters discover the full extent and implications of what has in fact occurred already. But even the perfection of this knowledge doesn't really change anything. This is a tragedy, a double tragedy, and in the end the two protagonists will die. But they have been hurtling toward death since they first appeared onstage—first Alvida, then Torrismondo himself. Nothing was ever more inexorable or less arbitrary than the absurdity of their final double suicide. To my mind—and this statement, as anyone who has attempted or attempts to read the play will readily concede, is to be taken with an enormous pinch of salt—this is what makes the play so extraordinarily modern. In the first place, the professional student of sixteenth- and seventeenth-century drama cannot fail to be struck by a remarkable circumstance: the complete absence of any credible transcendental superstructure, of any sacred or religious apparatus. It is hard to take seriously the oracle or Macbeth-like witch's prophecy (which we do not learn about in any case until Act IV of five acts) that is supposed to have set the foreplot in motion. It belongs, like so many of the background details, more to the world of pastoral romance and melodrama than to that of tragedy, and raises questions of verisimilitude that are quite impossible to swallow.

Instead—and here the play really does invite comparison with its Sophoclean model, or with its Shakespearean quasi homonym, *King Lear,* or with Racine's masterpiece *Phèdre*—what destroys the principal and princely characters, what drives them to their doom, is something inside them. This is the furious compulsion to know what cannot and should not be known, to achieve a perfect epistemology of love and friendship, to find a key to the universe of signs, and especially the signals emitted by the soul (the mind's construction in the face?): the soul of the other, but also one's own soul, which is an Other. It is a play about being human, as Tasso in his late years conceived of that experience, a play about irrational guilt, anxiety, and neurosis of almost unbearable intensity. It is a play, Pirandello might have said, about the simultaneous lucidity and obscurity of madness, and certainly about its Pirandellian compulsion to monologue. Like you and me, only more so, the characters are insane. From the start they carry such an incredible burden of guilt—they *are* their guilt—that, even though they may be rightly accused, or accuse themselves, of an error (in Torrismondo's case premarital sex with his best friend's girl; in the case of Alvida premarital sex only, as she doesn't know she is his best friend's girl!), nevertheless, the guilt of which they are the bearers is hopelessly incommensurate with any possible imaginable transgression. Even the ultimate but predictable transgression they eventually discover themselves to be guilty of, namely incest, is a transgression in any case so hackneyed in the tragic genre as to have lost, for jaded audience and practitioner alike—much of its power to shock. Here incest seems to stand for the state of being—or feeling—*unnatural,* for an existential sense of alienation from nature. The imagery of the play keeps the idea of an unnatured nature constantly before us.

It has been customary in Tasso criticism to read *King Torrismondo* in the context of the supposedly descending parabola of the poet's total literary production, and to see it as the beginning of the end, a sign of the involution of his later years, after the "happy season" of the *Aminta* and the fruitful tensions of the

Jerusalem Delivered. For those critics (and they are many) for whom the art of the Renaissance is ultimately an art of affirmation, Tasso is somehow felt to have let his readers down. But another context in which the play could be read is the generic context, that of the evolving sixteenth-century Italian revival of classical tragedy. This is the context which the most useful recent criticism has emphasized. I would like to suggest that it is possible to reconcile both these exegetical approaches to the considerable advantage of a dialectic and dynamic reading of the poet's career. Let us first review summarily the options offered the would-be tragedian by the recent tradition of the tragic genre.

The most influential exponent of that genre at Ferrara was Giambattista Giraldi Cinthio, a theorist as well as a practitioner and the author of an impressive number of tragedies, of which his *Orbecche* (1541)[3] can be taken as paradigmatic. The Giraldian model is a truculent Senecan enactment of horrors, with a running commentary of sententious apodictic reflections, couched in resonant hendecasyllables and intended to stimulate catharsis as he understood it. One of Giraldi's chief polemical targets is Sperone Speroni's tragedy *Canace* (1542), which, like the *Torrismondo,* has at its center an incestuous brother and sister. According to Giraldi, however, the *Canace* lacks all tragic decorum because it is written, not in sublime hendecasyllabic blank verse, but in an elegant and decorative "mannerist" admixture of long and short metrical lines interspersed with rhymed couplets and triplets.

Tasso's *King Torrismondo* could be said to combine the technique and the tone of two traditions, the "public" and the "private," the grimly didactic and the introspectively lyrical, keeping the sublime regularity of Giraldi's somewhat wooden lockstep of meter and diction, while at the same time exploiting—though screwed to an unbearably shriller pitch—the subjective resonance of Petrarch's obsessive wandering in the verbal labyrinth ("Il lungo error in cieco labirinto"). Metrically speaking, apart from the rather extraneous moralizing choruses in the *canzone* form placed at the end of each of the first four acts, Tasso reserves the short line for the climactic "recitative" into which several of the play's victims melt at the end of Act V.

There is, however, some justice to the fact that Tasso's tragedy has survived in the common critical memory by being reduced to its much admired and anthologized final lyric chorus. The chorus tells us it is time to read the tragedy again backwards, that the lumbering and logorrheic (in)action of the previous five acts was all part of an elaborate theorem designed to lead us by the hand to this negative epiphany, to the vision of a universe in which not only is the god hidden, but any attempt to identify a system of values, indeed to name a single value, is doomed to ruin.[4]

Tasso's literary career, like anyone else's, had been a search for values and authority. The plot and characters of the *Jerusalem Delivered* have, as we have seen, an important didactic and exemplary dimension. The insistent elative adjectives (*alto* ["high"] and the extended paradigm of its variants), which have often been pointed out as an important and stylistically motivated feature of Tasso's version of the Grand Style, are the textualization of the author's spontaneously over-awed posture before the greatness and nobility of his subject matter.

The characters of *King Torrismondo* are high, too—high and mighty, and hopelessly remote. They dwell on ontological heights utterly unscalable by their humble confidants. In the very first line of the play, Alvida is greeted reverently by her Nurse with the distancing vocative, "alta regine" ("high queen"). By contrast, the opening words of the previous version the *Tragedia non finita,* the Nurse's address to Alvida ("Figlia e signora mia") ["My daughter and my lady"]) had been more sentimentally ambivalent. Besides situating her higher in the social hierarchy ("signora" ["lady]), they also stressed Alvida's emotional dependence ("figlia" ["daughter"]), but even more important, the possessive "mia," which covered both nouns, anchored Alvida, in either role, securely in the affection of her Nurse. This, Tasso came to realize, was the wrong note to strike. The "alta regina" of *King Torrismondo* belongs to nobody. The possessive and the dependent kinship term are withdrawn, the appellation "signora" moves up to the top of its paradigm ("regina"); once there it is pushed up even higher by the elative adjective "alta," while the vocative phrase is programmatically isolated, not at the beginning, but at the ending of the line. Isolated and exposed, vulnerable, one of the destructible elect, exalted only to be crushed, because each height must be made low ("ogni altezza s'inchina" ["each height's made low"])—this is the real meaning of height ("your highness") in the tragedy. Thus, the same stylistic tic acquires a radically different significance in the epic and the tragic genres. Is it, then, merely a question of genre? The question would demand a longer discourse. All I can say here is that I believe it is a question of genre, and then of something else. I think that in Tasso's generic "experimentation" there is decisive existential component. Ripeness is all. At the time of the *Galealto,* Tasso wanted to write a tragedy; at the time of *King Torrismondo,* he was ready to write *his* tragedy.

Allow me in closing to tax your patience a moment longer by reminding you of a more discursive English poem, also much anthologized, but no less magnificent on that account, first published in 1867, almost three centuries after Tasso's *King Torrismondo,* but perhaps the masterpiece of what its author would no doubt have been incensed to hear me dub "the Victorian baroque." I shall resist the temptation to quote the whole poem, citing only the closing lines. In defense of what may seem an anachronistic citation, let me draw your attention to the setting: like *King Torrismondo,* the poem is set on the shores of a "distant northern sea," evoked in the opening lines in the metapoetical scansion of the waves and echoed in the flux and reflux of the poem's meter. Other things we may note are how it too harks back to Sophocles ("Sophocles long ago / Heard it on the Ægaean"); the crucial rhyme-pair, "seems" and "dreams," a yoking which epitomizes the quintessence of the baroque vision; and finally the orthographic swallowing of the rhyme-word "light" in the rout of "flight," followed by its engulfment and extinction in its Manichean rival "night":

> The Sea of Faith
> Was once, too, at the full, and round earth's shore
> Lay like the folds of a bright garment furl'd.
> But now I only hear
> Its melancholy, long, withdrawing roar,
> Retreating, to the breath
> Of the night-wind down the vast edges drear
> And naked shingles of the world.
>
> Ah, love, let us be true
> To one another! for the world, which seems

> To lie before us like a land of dreams,
> So various, so beautiful, so new,
> Hath really neither joy, nor love, nor light,
> Nor certitude, nor peace, nor help for pain;
> And we are here as on a darkling plain
> Swept with confused alarms of struggle and flight,
> Where ignorant armies clash by night.

Now this is a pretty dismal view of things. And quite similar, I think you will agree, to Tasso's final chorus. Only, Tasso's diagnosis is more pessimistic. Matthew Arnold contemplates at least some variant of the traditional notion of religious salvation still to be derived from interpersonal relationships; if not from Faith, from Love. Tasso's desolate rhetorical question posits no such bulwark against the ravages of an aging world: "Che giova amicizia? Che giova amore?" ("What good is friendship, what does love avail?") "Ahi lagrime," *indeed,* "ahi dolore!"

ANTHONY OLDCORN
Provincetown, Massachusetts

NOTES

1. In dedicating the first edition of the tragedy to Vincenzo, Tasso praises him as a "perfettissimo principe" ("most perfect prince") who "nel flor degli anni suoi giovenili dimostra tanta gravità di costumi e tanta prudenza" ("in the flower of his youth displays such gravity of behavior and such prudence"). This is the same Vincenzo who, only four years earlier, on the night of July 3, 1582, had waylaid on the streets of Mantua and stabbed to death the Admirable James Crichton. Moreover, in order to marry Eleonora, Vincenzo had been forced to provide a practical demonstration before the ecclesiastical authorities and her father's doctors, with a woman "of no account" supplied by them for the occasion, that he was capable of erection and penetration and therefore not the one responsible for his former wife's sterility. One wonders what a man with similar recent memories would make of the anguish of Alvida and Torrismondo. Of course, he may well have taken it in his stride.

2. Sixteenth-century Italian tragedians tend to be long on plot and short on characterization. This may be partly because plot and its management seemed to them to be a major concern of Aristotle's *Poetics* and partly because of the give-and-take between the tragic genre and the narrative devices of the serious *novella*.

3. See P. R. Horne, *The Tragedies of Giambattista Cinthio Giraldi* (London: Oxford University Press, 1962).

4. Our second reading will hardly have begun ("backwards" was only a rhetorical ploy!) before we recognize in Alvida's first speech the terms of the ephemeral vision of the final chorus: "Quante promesse e giuramenti a l'aura / tu spargi, Amor, qual fumo oscuro od ombra!" (80–81). Or take the Nurse's sententious fussing to herself at the close of this first encounter: "Non so ch'in terra sia tranquillo stato / o pacifico sì, che no 'l perturbi / o speranza, o timore, o gioia o doglia; / né grandezza sì ferma, o nel suo merto / fondata, o nel favor d'alta fortuna, / che l'incostante non atterri o crolli, / o non minacci" (203–209). The catalogue could of course continue. It would no doubt prove fruitful to compare the values impugned or deflated in the tragedy with the long list of moral abstractions discussed and extolled in the poet's dialogues. That laboriously constructed edifice, too, is cast down by the wrecker's ball.

5. Compare the conformist Providential message of Battista Guarini's exactly contemporary and enormously successful tragicomedy *il pastor fido* (composed in a genre made popular by Tasso's own *Aminta*), which might be paraphrased: "God casts people down only to lift them up," with the diametrically opposed conclusion of *King Torrismondo*: "God lifts people up only to cast them down." What a difference a genre makes! We find the same tragic commonplace, more commonplacely and programmatically expressed, in the manneristically witty opening scene of Act I of Luigi Groto's 1578 *Adriana:* "Cader non può se non colui, ch'ascende. / La saetta celeste altro non tocca, / per lo più, che materia alzata ad alto" ["Only he who ascends can fall. The Heavenly arrow is wont to strike only what is elevated and high"].

6. I realize that it might have been more appropriate, both formally and chronologically, to cite, say, the well-known *Chorus Sacerdotum* ("Oh wearisome Condition of Humanity! / Borne under one Law, to another bound") from Fulke Greville's *Mustapha,* published in 1609, or the somewhat later negative litany of the famous "dirge" from James Shirley's 1659 *Contention of Ajax and Ulysses* ("The glories of our blood and state, / Are shadows, not substantial things, / There is no armour against fate, / Death lays his icy hand on Kings, etc."). but it has such a distant, superior, schoolmasterish, Augustan tone, and the conceit of Death as the ultimate democrat ("Scepter and crown / Must tumble down, / And in the dust be equal made / With the poor crooked scythe and spade.") was not something the unreconstructed aristocrat Tasso could have gotten his mind around. And let us not forget Shirley's reassuringly consolatory conclusion: "Only the actions of the just / Smell sweet, and blossom in their dust."

TASSO, A PROTOTYPE OF THE ROMANTIC POET

In the history of European literature as much significance has been attached to the life and legend of Tasso, the man, as to the work of the poet. Elizabethan England soon learned to admire Tasso.[1] The legend of Tasso's hopeless love for Leonora d'Este was known in England while the poet was still alive. John Eliot refers to it in his *Orthoepia Gallica,* published in 1593,[2] and Scipio Gentile acknowledged it in his Latin translation of the *Gerusalemme Liberata* (1594). During the summer of the same year (August 1594), a play entitled *Tasso's Melancholy* was performed in London and subsequently revised on a number of occasions in the succeeding months. It is interesting to note that in 1602, when *Hamlet* was first produced at the Globe theater, Thomas Dekker revised *Tasso's Melancholy* for still another run.[3]

Seventeenth-century writers accepted Tasso's love legend, and by the eighteenth century a varied and extensive body of fiction developed in Italy and soon crossed the Alps. The vicissitudes of Tasso's life attracted considerable attention throughout Europe during the period 1750–1850. The Romantics saw in him a forerunner of their own ideal of the unhappy creative artist at odds with society. In England, the author of *Childe Harold* had a deep admiration for Tasso.[4] In visiting Ferrara, Lord Byron had himself shut up in Tasso's cell in order to relive the poet's feelings. The English poet imagines the gloom of Tasso's solitary confinement and its effect on the poet's sensitive mind in the memorable monologue *The Lament of Tasso.*[5] For Byron, Tasso's was a romantic and hopeless love: "A princess was no love-mate for a bard" (124). The poet's feelings, however, were so strong as to live beyond the grave: "No power in death can tear our names apart, / As none in life could rend thee from my heart" (244–

245). The English Romantic poet proclaims Tasso's dungeon a shrine for future generations: ". . . and I shall make / A future temple of my present cell / Which nations yet shall visit for my sake" (219–221). Byron even confirmed Rousseau's claim to have heard Venetian gondoliers quote verses from Tasso's epic poem.[6]

In Germany, the Romantic poet who contributed most to Tasso's legend was Goethe. In *Dichtung und Wahrheit,* the author of *Faust* tells us that Tasso was a favorite poet of his father, and that he himself in his boyhood had read the *Jerusalem Delivered* in Kopp's translation.[7] Goethe began his drama *Torquato Tasso* on March 30, 1780 and completed the first two acts in rhythmical prose by the spring of 1781. He left his drama as a fragment until 1786, only to complete it in 1789.[8] Published in 1790, his *Torquato Tasso* was performed with success at Weimar in 1808. Goethe's drama illustrates the "Überwindung" of his *Sturm und Drang,* and his mastering of classicism.[9] The play can be seen as a "dramatic portrait" of Tasso and of his relations with his patron and the court circle, including the Princess whom he loves. Goethe depicts Tasso's character from a psychological angle: his hero is as happy as a child when he is writing his poems, or when he is in love; he is as triumphant as a king when he is crowned with the wreath of laurel by the Duke, but he is also a man in whom genius poses a permanent problem in his relation to the world.[10]

Following the distressing story of Tasso's life, Goethe portrays our poet in a romantic vein. *Torquato Tasso* has a link with *Werther* and with *Egmont.* The analogies between Goethe and Tasso were many and striking: they both experienced the perturbations of a poet's heart, they were familiar with the rules and conflicts of court life. In Eckermann's "Conversation with Goethe" (May 6, 1827), we learn Goethe's own opinion of the drama he had written:

> I had the life of Tasso, and I had my own life, and putting together these two singular figures with their peculiarities, I obtained my *Tasso.* To him, by way of prosaic contrast, I opposed Antonio, for whom I also had models. As for the rest, the general situation was the same in Weimar as in Ferrara; and I can truly say of my delineation, that it is bone of my bone and flesh of my flesh.[11]

In Italy, Goldoni saw in Tasso a reflection of himself.[12] In the vast production of the Venetian playwright, three of his comedies in verse stand apart from any prose comedies in that they treat of the lives of classic poets.[13] *Il Torquato Tasso* gave Goldoni the opportunity of creating "an Italian Hamlet or an Alceste."[14]

Ugo Foscolo saw in Tasso the poet who enacted the agony of his own tortured spirit. Foscolo preferred Tasso's *Gerusalemme Liberata* to Dante's *Divina Commedia* because, in the epic tradition, it joined a national theme to a serious religious subject. In his essay "Lyric Poetry of Tasso" he concluded that Tasso's poetry was the "last great flowering of Italian Renaissance literature,"[15] and that "Tasso is worthy of being placed by the side of Dante and Milton. Like them, his erudition was unbounded, his character was dignified; and he adhered to literature despite every misfortune which can afflict human nature."[16]

Moved by the sight of Tasso's humble tomb, Vittorio Alfieri expresses his outrage in a sonnet, "Per il sepolcro del Tasso" (On Tasso's Tomb).[17] Alfieri is irate against Rome for denying to the sublime epic poet the only place worthy of his tombstone: the center of Saint Peter's Church:

> Là, nel bel centro d'esso ei sia locato: degno d'entrambi il monumento quivi Michelangelo ergeva al gran Torquato.

> (There, at the center, let him be placed: worthy of both, now soars the dome, which Michelangelo raised for great Torquato.)

Tasso's life and works greatly influenced some of Giacomo Leopardi's writings. In *Operette Morali,* Leopardi imagines a dialogue between "Tasso" and his "Genio."[18] In a letter written from Rome to his brother Carlo, Leopardi says:

> Friday, February 15, 1823 I went to visit Tasso's tomb and wept. This is the only pleasure I felt in Rome. Many visitors experience indignation on seeing Tasso's ashes covered and marked by nothing more than a stone approximately a span and a half in width and height, and placed in a narrow corner of a small church. By no means would I want to find these ashes under a mausoleum. You understand what a multitude of feelings rises from the consideration of the contrast between Tasso's greatness and the humility of his burial. But you cannot imagine another contrast, that is, that which is felt by one

whose eye is accustomed to the infinite magnificence and vastness of the Roman monuments, when compared to the meanness and bareness of this sepulcher.[19]

Among other Italian plays and dialogues dealing with Tasso's life are Girolamo Brusoni's *La gondola a tre remi* (1657), Pier Paolo Martello's *Il Dialogo della Vana Gloria* (1722),[20] and Francesco De Sanctis' *Torquato Tasso* (1849).[21] In England, in 1762, was published *Il Tasso* (*A Dialogue: John Milton and Torquato Tasso*). The author is unknown, but I have reasons to believe that the play was written by Richard Hurd, an enthusiastic admirer of Tasso.[22] In Paris, as late as 1908, a French play by Paul Souchon followed the traditional legends, and, in 1914, the *Veglie del Tasso* were republished as authentic work.

In art history, Tasso's life and poetry inspired Delacroix,[23] Morelli, Reni, and Hayez. In the field of music, we must remember Monteverdi's *Il Combattimento di Tancredi,* Gluck's opera *Armide,* Handel's *Rinaldo* and *Armida Abbandonata,* Rossini's *Tancredi* and *Armida,* Verdi's *I Lombardi alla Prima Crociata,* Listz's tone poem *Tasso,* and Donizzetti's three-act opera *Torquato Tasso.*[24]

In conclusion, it is interesting to note that the term "romantic poetry" was first used in connection with Ariosto and Tasso. Hurd speaks of Tasso as "trimming between the Gothic and the Classic."[25] How close to truth was Tasso's love legend? The answer is not important; its end result, however, had the magic of his poetry: it created a symbol which the Romantics adopted.

NOTES

1. Queen Elizabeth had committed to memory many stanzas of the *Gerusalemme Liberata;* she considered the Duke of Ferrara, for having "his praise sung by such a poet," as lucky as Achilles "for having had the great Homer." See Mario Praz, *The Flaming Heart* (Gloucester, Mass.: Peter Smith, 1966), 310.

2. Returning from a trip to Italy, John Eliot sums up his view of Tasso for the English reader: "Torquato Tasso, a fine scholar truly, who is yet living, the last Italian Poet who is of any great fame in our age, but worthie of the first honour, besides that he is a divine Poet, he is also a most eloquent Oratour and Rhetoricyan as his massive Epistles

do shew very well. This youth fell mad for the love of an Italian lasse descended of a great house." He goes on to mention Tasso's works among which "a Tragedie," and the heroic poem "where in all the riches of the Greekes and Latines are gathered. . . ." John Eliot finds in Tasso the "grace, brevitie, gravitie, learning, liveliness and vivacitie" that was in Virgil, "Prince of Latine Poets." See *Godfrey of Bulloigne: a critical edition of Edward Fairfax's translation of Tasso's Gerusalemme Liberata, together with Fairfax Original Poems* (Oxford: Clarendon, 1981), 28.

3. The author of the play is unknown; the play itself is lost. See E. K. Chambers, *The Elizabethan Stage* (Oxford: Clarendon, 1923), 11, 13, 168, 181.

4. Ugo Foscolo collaborated with John Cam Hobhouse on the illustrations of Byron's *Childe Harold*. See E. R. Vincent, *Ugo Foscolo, An Italian in Regency England* (Cambridge: Cambridge UP, 1953), 87.

5. Lord Byron, *The Complete Poetical Works,* edited by Jerome J. McGann, Vol. IV. (Oxford: Clarendon, 1986), 116–24. "The Lament of Tasso" offers a model for Browning's and Swinburne's lyrical monologue. See Mario Praz, *The Flaming Heart,* 343.

6. Mario Praz, *The Flaming Heart,* 332 and John Black, *Life of Torquato Tasso,* with an historical and critical account of his writings, Vol. I (Edinburgh: John Murray, 1810), 332. Besides Rousseau, other well-known poets who greatly admired Tasso were Dryden, Voltaire, Wordsworth, and Alexander Pope. See C. P. Brand, *Torquato Tasso* (Cambridge: Cambridge UP, 1965), 209, 225, 256, 260. It is interesting to note that in 1833, Antonio Buttura included Tasso in *I quattro poeti italiani, con una scelta di poesie italiane dal 1200 sino ai nostri tempi.* (Paris: Lefevre, 1836.)

7. How deep and lasting an impression the poem made upon Goethe's mind can be seen in the seventh chapter of the first book of *Wilhelm Meister* (1777). See introduction to Calvin Thomas, *Goethe's Torquato Tasso* (Boston: D. C. Heath, 1906), XXII.

8. Kopp's German translation of the *Jerusalem Delivered* was prefixed with a sketch of Tasso's life, based on Manso's biography. Serassi's *Vita di Torquato Tasso* (1785) was probably read by Goethe while he was in Italy (see Calvin Thomas, *Goethe's Torquato Tasso,* XXXVI; also Ronald Peacock, *Goethe's Major Plays* [Manchester: Manchester UP, 1959, 95]). It is interesting to note that Goethe was writing his "tragödie" *Torquato Tasso* exactly two hundred years after the date in which Tasso was returning to his unfinished "tragedia" *Il Galealto,* later completed as *Il re Torrismondo.*

9. Peacock, *Goethe's Major Plays,* 145.

10. Ibid., 104.

11. Thomas, *Goethe's Torquato Tasso,* V.

12. Goldoni was criticized for the impurity of his Italian; Tasso's epic had been censured by the academicians of La Crusca. See H. C. Chatfield-Taylor, *Goldoni: A Biography* (New York: Duffield & Co., 1913), 436.

13. The three comedies in verse are: *Il Molière, Terenzio,* and *Torquato Tasso.* See *Tutte le Opere di Carlo Goldoni,* a cura di Giuseppe Ortolani (*Il Molière in the Third Volume, Terenzio and Torquato Tasso* in the Fifth Volume [Milan: Mondadori, 1941]).

14. Chatfield-Taylor, 437.

15. Glauco Cambon, *Ugo Foscolo: Poet of Exile* (Princeton, N.J.: Princeton UP, 1980), 204.

16. Ugo Foscolo, *Saggi di Letteratura Italiana,* Parte Prima, edizione critica a cura di Cesare Foligno (Florence: Le Monnier, 1958), 195.

17. Vittorio Alfieri, *Rime,* a cura di Rosolino Guastalla, nuova presentazione di Cesare Bozzetti (Florence: Sansoni, 1963), 133–34. For a translation of the sonnet see: *From Marino to Marinetti: an Anthology of Forty Italian Poets,* Translated into English Verse and with an Introduction by Joseph Tusiani (New York: Baroque, 1974), 85.

18. Giacomo Leopardi, "Dialogo di Torquato Tasso e del suo genio familiare," in *Tutte le Opere* con introduzione e a cura di Walter Binni, Volume Primo (Florence: Sansoni, 1983), 110–14.

19. Leopardi, *Tutte le Opere,* 1150.

20. Brand, *Torquato Tasso,* 223–24.

21. Francesco De Sanctis, *Torquato Tasso* (Rome: Dell'Oleandro, 1995). In 1849, during his stay in Calabria, De Sanctis felt a lack of affection and the same sense of injustice that Tasso found at the Court of Ferrara. In his drama *Torquato Tasso,* the critic portrays the poet in deep sorrow, while strong remains his desire for glory. In Act IV, Scene I, De Sanctis recalls Tasso's visit to his sister Cornelia in Sorrento. Disguised as a shepherd, the poet echoes the lament of the final chorus in *King Torrismondo.*

22. See "Un momento della 'fortuna' del Tasso in Inghilterra. Il dialogo settecentesco *Il Tasso,*" in my translation, with an introduction by G. Baldassarri (Bergamo: *Studi Tassiani,* No. 39, 1991) 97–117. This dialogue further demonstrates Tasso's popularity in England. The author researched the lives and the works of the two epic poets. As in *Reason of Church and Government,* in the dialogue, Milton praises the *Gerusalemme Liberata* and places Tasso next to Virgil and Homer.

23. Delacroix's painting "Le Tasse en Prison" inspired Baudelaire's sonnet on the painting. See C. P. Brand, *Torquato Tasso,* 220.

24. For a more detailed list see footnote 4 in the introduction of:

Torquato Tasso, *Jerusalem Delivered,* translated into verse and with an introduction by Joseph Tusiani (Cranbury, N.J.: Associated UP, 1970), 15–16.

25. Rene Wellek, *Concepts of Criticism* (New Haven: Yale UP, 1963), 128.

KING TORRISMONDO,
A RENAISSANCE TRAGEDY

At the beginning of 1582 the first, incomplete draft of Tasso's version of *Galealto re di Norvegia* was published as *Tragedia non finita* in the *Seconda Parte* of the Aldine Edition of Tasso's *Rime and prose.*[1] In 1586, as soon as he was released from St. Anna's hospital,[2] Tasso resumed his *Galealto;* he reworked the tragedy and brought it to a conclusion with a new title: *Il re Torrismondo* (*King Torrismondo*).[3] The tragedy enjoyed phenomenal contemporary success. The 1587 edition (Edizioni Bartoli, published in Bergamo and dedicated to Vincenzo Gonzaga), was reprinted fourteen times in the sixteenth century.[4]

The popularity of *King Torrismondo* is proved by its performance at the Teatro Olimpico of Vicenza in 1618 and at the San Luca Theater of Venice (with a performance by the famous actor Luigi Riccoboni).[5] Although no translations were as yet available in English or Spanish, Tasso's tragedy influenced other seventeenth-century works in both England and Spain.

Tasso's contemporaries praised *King Torrismondo* for its allegiance to neo-Aristotelian principles. Tasso's only tragedy follows the classical rules and the standard models of both ancient and modern drama: Sophocles' *Oedipus Rex* and Seneca's *Oedipus* and *Phaedra;* in his own century, Giraldi's *Orbecche* (1541) and Speroni's *Canace* (1542).[6] Tasso's sense of the tradition, however, cannot be circumscribed within this conventional perimeter of "influences." It is a mistake, for instance, to believe that of Giraldi's works, his *Orbecche* alone shapes the substance and form of Tasso's own tragic text. It is a fact, which Tasso's specialists have not yet taken sufficiently into account, that Giraldi's theoretical musing on tragedy—his *Discorso attorno al comporre delle commedie e tragedie* (1543)—deeply mark the contour of Tasso's reflective and textual practice. Giraldi's sense of man's "condizione laberintica" (labyrinthine condition), his

"Ariostesque" view of the randomness of human experiences, and his distance from the balanced and classical view of either Bembo or Castiglione affect Tasso's *King Torrismondo* at least as much as some of his novellas affected sections of Shakespeare's *Othello* and *Measure for Measure.*

It is not surprising that, because of Tasso's linguistic texture, the rigor of his structure, and the consistency of his tragic articulation of the text, his work should have aroused the critical interest of nineteenth-century writers as well. Carducci noted that "Italian men of letters spoke extensively about Torrismondo."[7] According to Crescimbeni, Tasso's tragedy "greatly shines among the most selected tragedies"[8] and for Tiraboschi, "it is rightly among the the best tragedies of the sixteenth century."[9]

Although much of the critical writing devoted to *King Torrismondo* has sought to demonstrate that, as a tragedy, the play is only a partial success, in the past thirty years we have seen a gradual upswing in the critical evaluation of *King Torrismondo,* from Sozzi's erudite and sensitive evaluation to the studies of Getto, Ramat, Renda, Di Benedetto, and Venturini, all of whom find in Tasso's tragedy the unity of content and form that the author envisioned.[10] Other recent studies see in the play a novel and original approach to tragedy, or a study of the dilemma of late-Renaissance man entangled in the restrictions of the Counter-Reformation, and, more importantly, a "text" which withstands the same close analysis of symbolic, lexical, prosodic, and phonetic features that have been applied to the *Gerusalemme Liberata.*[11] An approach frequently used is a comparative study of the play's earlier, incomplete version, *Galealto re di Norvegia,* with the completed, mature play of 1586–1587.[12]

King Torrismondo reflects Tasso's theory of tragedy as an autonomous literary genre. In the *Discorsi dell'arte poetica* (1564–1565), Tasso argues that a tragedy normally borrows its subject from history,[13] in the name of verisimilitude: "The matter, which we may call the subject, is either feigned, in which case the poet seems to partake not only of his choice but also of his invention; or is taken from history. But, according to my judgment, it is much better that it be taken from history."[14]

In 1553 Olaus Magnus had published, in Rome, his *Historia de gentibus septentrionalibus.*[15] This work provided Tasso with an historic subject and with the harsh and mysterious setting of the remote northern countries, for the effect of awe and horror needed for his tragedy. As a matter of fact Tasso mentions in his dialogue having read the work: "And I read in Olaus Magnus' history of Gothland that men turn into wolves."[16]

For Tasso, tragedy, like epic, deals with actions that are noble and illustrious, but its methods are different: it represents those actions instead of narrating them, and has the use of rhythm as well as harmony (i.e., the Chorus); but more important is the sudden change of fortune which arouses pity and terror: "The tragic actions move to horror and compassion; and, wherever they are missing, that which is awful and that which is pitiful is no longer tragic."[17]

Tasso bases his opinion on Aristotle: "To rejoice in the punishment of the wicked, in spite of how pleasing this may be to the audience, is not in keeping with the tragic fable, whereas in the heroic one its praise is unquestionable."[18] He goes on to explain that the actions of the tragedy and the epic do not present high matters in the same fashion; their concern with great affairs is diverse in nature and form. Since tragedy consists of the "unexpected and sudden change of fortune as well as of the greatness of the events that rouse compassion and terror,"[19] consequently, the persons introduced in the two types of poem are not of the same nature, though both deal with kings and noble princes. Whereas the epic requires characters of exceptional virtue, the dramatis personae of the tragedy should be "neither good, nor bad, but of a middle condition: such are Orestes, Electra, Jocasta, Eteocles, Oedipus, a character held by Aristotle as highly suitable for a tragic play."[20] Thus, Tasso subscribes substantially to the neo-Aristotelian dramatic theory fashionable in the second half of the Cinquecento.

The Italian high Renaissance had failed to produce an acknowledged tragic masterpiece in spite of Trissino's *Sofonisba* (1524),[21] Giraldi's *Orbecche* (1541),[22] and other works by Rucellai,[23] Aretino,[24] Alamanni,[25] Dolce, and others.[26] Actually, it was Giraldi's tragedy and Speroni's *Canace* (1542)[27] which gave the principal debating points to critics of the late sixteenth century. While Giraldi proposed an Aristotelian imitation of Seneca, Speroni aimed to produce a drama based on strict Aristotelian principles, thus providing a model of peripeteia. *King Torrismondo* was written in the midst of the controversy over these two contemporary tragedies. Tasso was concerned with composing a tragedy that could and would avoid the pitfalls into which other writers had erred. As a result, *King Torrismondo,* tempered by the new spirit of his age and incorporating into the dramatic genre elements of the epic and lyrical poem, tries to equal, or even surpass, the tragedies of ancient Greece and Rome.[28] In accordance with Aristotelian principles, there are pity and terror, no death on the stage, the use of a known theme (that of *Oedipus Rex*), and an incestuous relationship such as Speroni had treated.

With the aid of his own inventiveness, Tasso devised a complex and original plot. *King Torrismondo* starts as a tragic betrayal of friendship and ends as a sheer tragedy of incest. All the main characters suffer tragic consequences; thus, it is not only Torrismondo's tragedy, but also that of Germondo, Rosmonda, the Queen, and indeed Alvida, who commits suicide, not because of incest (she does not believe that she is Torrismondo's sister), but because of what she deems to be unrequited love. Alvida can be seen as the heroine of the play. Her love for Torrismondo is parallel to that of the shepherd Aminta for the nymph Sylvia, the would-be Christian scapegoat Olindo for the chaste Sofronia, and the African princess Erminia for the Christian knight Tancredi.

The love story has reminiscences of Dante's Paolo and Francesca. The language that Alvida uses in confiding to the nurse the first impact of her love for Torrismondo, "Io del piacer di quella prima vista / così presa restai" (I was so taken with the pleasure of that first sight) (I, i, 82–83) is an echo of Francesca's "Amor, ... / mi prese del costui piacer sì forte" (Love, ... / took hold of me so strongly through his beauty) (*Inferno,* V, 103–104). The account of the seduction scene is modelled on canto V of the *Inferno:*

> ... Il tempo largo,
> e l'ozio lungo e lento, e 'l loco angusto,
> e gl'inviti d'amor, lusinghe e sguardi,
> rossor, pallore e parlar tronco e breve,
> solo inteso da noi, con mille assalti
> vinsero alfin la combattuta fede.
>
> Ahi ben è ver, che risospinto Amore
> più fiero e per repulsa e per incontro
> ad assalir sen torna, e legge antica
> è che nessuno amato amar perdoni.
>
> . . . .
>
> Questo quel punto fu che sol mi vinse.

(. . . The time on hand,
the long slow idleness, closeness of space,
love's invitations, flatteries and glances,
blushing, blanking, and brief and broken words
that we alone could hear, with a thousand sorties
at last overcame my long-embattled faith.
Oh, how true it is! Love, if repelled,
returns to the attack more fierce
for being fended off or parried,
for it is an ancient law that no one who is loved
is absolved from not loving.

. . . .

This was the one moment that won me over.)
(I, iii, 488–564)

In Torrismondo's words, ". . . Ma troppo accresce/questa dolce memoria il duolo acerbo" (But this sweet memory / too much augments the sharpness of my pain) (I, iii, 313–314), we recall Francesca's

. . . Nessun maggior dolore
che ricordarsi del tempo felice
nella miseria; . . .

. . . (There is no greater sorrow
than thinking back upon a happy time
in misery; . . .)
(*Inferno,* V, 121–123)

Nature and Tasso's reading of the classics play an important part in the consummation of Torrismondo's and Alvida's love. The tent recalls the cavern of Dido and Aeneas (*Aeneid,* IV). The description of the storm, "e diventò di nembi e di procelle / il mar turbato un periglioso campo;" (and the sea, whipped up, became / a perilous battlefield of squalls and storms) (I, iii, 513–514) echoes Virgil's "Eripiunt subito nubes caelumque diemque / Teucrorum ex oculis; ponto nox incubat atra." (Suddenly the clouds blotted sky and daylight / from the Trojans' eyes; bleak night descends on the sea) (*Aeneid,* I, 88–89). Moreover,

parte inghiotinne ancor l'empia Caribdi
che l'onde e i legni intieri absorbe e mesce:
son rari i notatori in vasto gorgo.

(other ships were swallowed, still,
    by pitiless Charibdis
who absorbs and sucks down the waves
    and entire ships:
rare are the swimmers in the vast vortex.)
(I, iii, 542–544)

is a reminder of

Dextrum Scylla latus, laevum
    implacata
Charybdis obsidet atque barathri
    ter gurgite vastos
sorbet in abruptum fluctus,

(Scylla holds the right; insatiable
Charybdis keeps the left, and three
    times she sucks the vast waves in
    the deepest whirlpool
within her vortex,)
(*Aeneid,* III, 420–422)

and "apparent rari nantes in gurgite vasto" (scattered, the ship-wrecked men are seen in the vastness of the billows) (*Aeneid,* I, 118)

Echoes of Petrarch's *Rime* can be singled out beginning with the nurse's first words: "vi sono in vece di pietosa madre" (take the place of a tender mother) (I, i, 11), a reminder of "Né mai pietosa madre al caro figlio" (Nor did a pitying mother to her dear son) (*Rime,* CCLXXXV, 1). Alvida's "Bramo e pavento" (I yearn and dread) (I, i, 23) echoes "dolce et acerbo, ch'i pavento et bramo"(sweetness and gall, which I both dread and crave) (*Rime,* CLXXXI, 6); moreover, "di stelle congiurate; e temo, ahi lassa" (conspiring stars; and, woe is me, I fear) (I, i, 29) is reminiscent of "o stelle congiurate a 'mpoverirme!" (O stars, you conspire to ruin me!) (*Rime,* CCCXXIX, 2). Other echoes of Petrarch include Alvida's "m'arde e strugge" (it burns and consumes me) (I, i, 60),[29] "che s'aspetti non so, né che s'agogni" (I do not know what we are waiting for, nor what we crave;) (I, i, 118),[30] and Torrismondo's "grave pondo" (grievous burden) (I, iii, 269),[31] "le squille" (the morning bells) (I, iii, 276),[32] "tutta lontana dal camin del sole" (far far away from the course of the sun) (I, iii, 354).[33] These are only a few instances of Petrarchan influence on the language of *King Torrismondo*. Other works that influenced *King Torrismondo*'s language include Ariosto's *Orlando Furioso*,[34] Seneca's *Phaedra*,[35] Ovid's *Metamorphoses*,[36] and Olaus Magnus's *Historia de gentibus septentrionalibus*.[37]

Tasso's epic language is easily recognized in the fatalistic romantic love of Torrismondo and Alvida. The tragedy is pervaded by an aura of lugubrious omens and spiritual inquietude by which Tasso so often seems to identify himself in his characters. From the very beginning of the play the lovers appear to be inwardly tormented: Torrismondo because he has betrayed his friend Germondo, and Alvida because she believes that Torrismondo does not love her any longer. Their sense of guilt is heightened not only by their awareness of having fallen victim to their own desires, but, in Alvida's case, by the fact that she has become oblivious to her brother's memory, and, in Torrismondo's case, because he has deceived his friend as well as the woman he loves. Alvida's fears and forebodings are typical of Tasso's work:[38]

> e temo, ahi lassa
> un non so che d'infausto o pur d'orrendo
> ch'a me confonde un mio pensier dolente,
> lo qual mi sveglia e mi perturba e m'ange
> la notte e 'l giorno.

> (and woe is me, I fear;
> I know not what ill-omened or appalling thing
> that an anguished thought instills in me,
> which wakes, confounds me, and gives me pain
> both night and day.)
> (I, i, 29–33)

Such a gloomy, pessimistic attitude recalls the poet's letter from St. Anna: "Poverty, exile and other risks, and pale deaths, and long illnesses, sides, stomachs, fevers" (I, 1247).[39]

Tasso's own experience and melancholy nature seem to find their best poetic utterance in his characters. Rosmonda, "vergine bella" (beautiful virgin) (IV, iii, 2281), a reminder of Petrarch's "Vergine bella, che di sol vestita" (Beautiful Virgin, who, dressed with sunshine) (*Rime* CCCLXVI, 1), can also be seen as the counterpart of Sofronia "Vergine . . . di già matura / verginità" (Virgin, of an already mature virginity) (*Gerusalemme Liberata*, II, 14).

Her desire "di viver vita solitaria e sciolta" (to live an unattached
and solitary life) (II, iv, 1146) and

> Ed a me gioveria lanciare i dardi
> tal volta in caccia e saettar con l'arco,
>
> . . . .
>
> poiché non posso il crin d'elmo lucente
> coprirmi in guerra, e sostener lo scudo
>
> . . . .
>
> come un tempo solean feroci donne
>
> (It would please me more at times to cast the spear
> in the hunt, and draw the bow,
> since in battle I cannot hide my hair
> beneath a shining helmet, . . .
> just as, in ancient days, those fearsome women did)
> (II, iv, 1297–1307)

remind us of Sylvia (*Aminta*) and Clorinda (the fierce woman
warrior of the *Gerusalemme Liberata*). Through Rosmonda's
words (II, iv) we learn about the advantages and disadvantages
of marriage—a controversial theme of the Counter-Reformation
and also a theme dear to the poet.[40] The Queen's monologue
deals with maternal joy: "Infelice non è dolente donna / se ne'
suoi figli il suo dolor consola" (A grieving woman is not un-
happy / if she can find comfort for grief in her children) (II, V,
1343–1344).

In his perfection, Germondo, the true friend, who sighs:
"Oimè, qual grave colpa / non perdona amicizia o non difende?"
(Alas, is there such grievous fault / that friendship cannot forgive
or excuse?) (V, 3137–3138) reminds one of the dignity of "pio
Goffredo" (pious Godfrey).[41] It is, however, less in the character
of Torrismondo than in the figure of Alvida that Tasso vents his
innermost emotions in a fashion that recalls the figure of the
tragic lover Tancredi, and that of tearful Erminia. The romantic
lovers express the psychological aspect of the situation.

The conflict between the duty of friendship and love remains
unabated in Torrismondo's soul even after he has possessed his
beloved; it is, rather, augmented by the pangs of his conscience,
which Tasso lays bare whenever the protagonist appears on the

scene. Torrismondo abhors his princely title and position and would like to escape the situation in which he finds himself: "Lasso, io ben me n'andrei per erme arene / solingo, errante;" (Alas, readily would I go through lonely sands, / alone and wandering;) (I, iii, 258–259). He would like to flee from people's sight, from the sun, from the stars. His conscience is at war with itself: it rebels, is overcome with disgrace and shame, resounds and roars within him (I, iii, 275), while the sweet memory greatly augments the sharpness of his pain (I, iii, 313–314). In Torrismondo, feelings of "love" and "friendship" fight for supremacy. Alvida, dominated by "love" alone, dramatically shows the raptures, the doubts, the torments and contradictions of that love. Love conquered her like the classic thunderbolt;[42] she says: "e prima quasi fui che sposa, amante / e me n'avidi a pena." (and I was almost a lover before being a bride, / though almost unawares.) (I, ii, 92–93). It is love that causes her to forget the vow she has made to her father, and makes her ready to surrender her royal pride and her own personality. Torrismondo's pleasures will be her only pleasures, his joy her only joy: "Posso io, s'a voi dispiaccio, odiar me stessa, / posso, se voi l'amate, amar Germondo." (I can, if I displease you, hate myself, / I can, if you too love him, love Germondo.) (III, iv, 1698–1699). Alvida provides another example of Tasso's natural tendency to delve into the psychology of his female characters.[43]

Another distinctive note is Tasso's penchant for sexual details. As a result, while *King Torrismondo* follows the Sophoclean theme, it reflects late sixteenth-century attitudes.

King Torrismondo has been seen as a tragedy of incest, and of "love and friendship,"[44] but it is also a great tragedy of love. We are kept unaware of the incest until Act Four; Alvida's death occurs before she becomes cognizant of the incestuous nature of her love, and Torrismondo's suicide is determined by his inability to survive his beloved (V, iv, 3028–3031). The themes of love and death, favorite ones in Neo-Latin poetry,[45] are equally important in Tasso's tragedy. In dealing with the romantic love of princely characters, *King Torrismondo* becomes innovative in tragedy as a genre, foreshadowing as it does the romantic love of Shakespeare's *Romeo and Juliet.*

King Torrismondo invites comparison not only with its Sophoclean model, but also with Shakespeare's *King Lear,* with

Corneille's *Héraclius,* with Racine's *Phèdre, Athalie,* and *Britannicus,* and with Calderón's *La vida es sueño* and *La Devoción de la Cruz.*

One of the most highly praised features of *King Torrismondo* is Tasso's handling of language. A pertinent example is Torrismondo's description of the storm (Act One, Scene Three). Tasso's model is obvious, judging by the closeness of the Italian hendecasyllabic line "son rari i notatori in vasto gorgo" (rare are the swimmers in the vast vortex) (I, iii, 544), which echoes Virgil's hexameter "apparent rari nantes in gurgite vasto." It seems to me that this "gurgite," with the ominous, lugubrious sound of its first vowel, inspires Tasso's masterly use of onomatopoeia in his description of the mounting billows, which he compares to "minacciose rupi" (threatening reefs) (I, iii, 535). As with "gurgite" in *Aeneid's* Book One, 118, the sound of "rupi" in Tasso's tragedy is prolonged and therefore strengthened by the fierceness of its own echo: "sempre can*u*te, ove risona e m*u*gge, / mentre combatte l'*u*n con l'altro fl*u*tto." (forever white, where the sea resounds and roars / while one wave fights with the other.) (I, iii, 538–539)

But, masterly though it be, such a passage should not divert our attention from what may constitute this work's most conspicuous characteristic: the lyrical beauty of the Choruses at the end of the five acts and in the action of certain scenes.[46] The combination of seven- and eleven-syllable lines recalls the metrical variety of the *Aminta* and *Rogo Amoroso.* While the dialogue does not depart from "endecasillabi sciolti" (blank endecasyllables) until the end of Act Five, the meter of the Choruses concluding the acts employs the metrical scheme of the medieval "Canzone," complete with an "Envoi." The Chorus at the end of Act One, for example, in each stanza shows the intricate rhyme-scheme ABbCACcADEeDDEfF, whereas the Envoi, with a considerable "rallentando," has the scheme aBBAcC. Where the Chorus participates in the dialogue, blank verse is retained. The change of metre coincides with the catastrophe: in the final scene of the last act we find in the dialogue seven-, five-, and three-syllable lines.[47]

All of the Chorus's speeches are most effective, especially those which conclude each act. The tone is lyrical, detached from the immediate persons and situations, commenting on events and bewailing the inevitable tragic denouement, like an echo of the spectator's shifts of emotions. So authentic is Tasso's lyric voice in his Choruses that the final commentary upon each Act can be read separately as a Canzone (or as a Madrigal), similar to those collected in his *Rime*. Thus the Chorus becomes a necessary element in the overall aesthetic and ideological composition of the tragedy. Its final lament identifies human misery with the cold Scandinavian setting (winter, ice, mountain torrent):

> Ahi lacrime, ahi dolore:
> passa la vita e si dilegua e fugge,
> come giel che si strugge.
>
> . . . .
>
> E come raggio il verno, imbruna e more
> gloria d'altrui splendore;
> e come alpestro e rapido torrente,
> come acceso baleno
> in notturno sereno,
> come aura, o fumo, o come stral, repente
> volan le nostre fame, ed ogni onore
> sembra languido fiore.

> (Oh, tears, oh, grief:
> life passes, vanishes and flies,
> like melting ice. . . .
>
> And as a wintry beam, the glory
> of man's radience darkens and dies.
> And like a swift alpine torrent,
> like lightning
> on a clear night,
> like a breeze or like smoke, or like an arrow, swiftly
> our reputations fly and every honor
> seems like a wilting flower.)
> (V, 3320–3329)

NOTES

1. Tasso wrote the *Galealto re di Norvegia* toward the end of 1573 or the beginning of 1574. The 1197 line fragments represent the draft of Act I and the opening of Act II of the *Tragedia non finita* (Unfin-

ished Tragedy) published by Aldus Manutius, Jr. in Vinegia, MDXXCII. See *Il teatro italiano II—La tragedia del Cinquecento* (Tomo Secondo) (Turin: Einaudi, 1977), 427.

2. In a letter to his sister Cornelia, Tasso announces his release from St. Anna: "I am free through the intercession of his lordship the prince of Mantua." The letter is dated July 1586 and was sent from Mantua to Sorrento. See Letter LXXV in Torquato Tasso, *Prose*, a cura di Ettore Mazzali (con una premessa di Francesco Flora) (Milan: Ricciardi, 1959), 980.

3. In a letter to Antonio Costantini, in Ferrara, Tasso says: ". . . today I finished my tragedy." This letter is dated December 14, 1586. (Torquato Tasso, *Prose*, 999.) Antonio Costantini, secretary to don Cesare and later to the Gonzaga family, became a dear friend and amanuensis of Tasso. At least 29 out of the 213 published letters of Tasso are addressed to Costantini. The poet's last letter, written from the monastery of Sant'Onofrio, dated April 10, 1595, was addressed to Costantini in Mantua: "Che dirà il mio signor Antonio, quando udirà la morte del suo Tasso? . . . Mi sono fatto condurre in questo munistero di Sant'Onofrio, non solo perchè l'aria è lodata da' medici più che d'alcun'altra parte di Roma, ma quasi per cominciare da questo luogo eminente, e con la conversazione di questi devoti padri, la mia conversazione in cielo." (What will my lord Antonio say, when he'll hear about the death of his Tasso? . . . I asked to be taken to this monastery of Saint Onofrio, not only because the air is praised by physicians more than in any other place in Rome, but almost to begin from this eminent place, and with the conversation of these devoted friars, my own conversation in Heaven.) Torquato Tasso, *Prose* (Letter CCXII), 1142. (Tasso died in the monastery of Sant'Onofrio in Rome, on April 25, 1595.)

4. "Tasso's fame was so great, and the curiosity of the public so strong, that, in the course of five months, at least eleven editions of *Il re Torrismondo* were published in different cities of Italy." (See John Black, 204.) For a complete list of the editions of *Il re Torrismondo* see: Solerti, *Torquato Tasso, Opere minori in versi, III: Teatro* (Bologna: Zanichelli, 1895), CXXVII–CXXXIII.

5. B. T. Sozzi, *Studi sul Tasso* (Pisa: Nistri-Lisci, 1954), 93. Luigi Riccoboni was known in France by the name Lelio. He translated Racine's *Andromaque* and *Britannicus*. He also wrote a history of the Italian theater in French. See *Teatro di Torquato Tasso*, edizione critica a cura di Angelo Solerti con due saggi di Giosuè Carducci (Bologna: Zanichelli, 1895), XLIV–XLV.

6. Guastavini remarks that Tasso's tragedy until now, in everybody's opinion, has kept the sceptre of as many tragedies as have been

written in any language. See Giovanni Getto, "Dal Galealto al Torrismondo," in *Interpretazione del Tasso* (Naples: Edizioni Scientifiche Italiane, 1967), 171. Also see Guastavini's introduction to the *Torrismondo* (Genua: Bartoli, 1587).

7. Torquato Tasso, *Teatro,* ed. di Solerti (Bologna: Zanichelli, 1895), XLVI. "Gl'italiani letterati discorsero del Torrismondo assai." Carducci adds that *Il re Torrismondo*'s elocution and style are a notable event in the development of the play. Giosuè Carducci, *Opere* (Bologna: Zanichelli, 1954), 349.

8. ". . . tra le più scelte tragedie largamente risplende." See *Istoria della volgar poesia* (Tomo Secondo) (Venice: Basegio, 1730), 444. According to Venturini, *Il re Torrismondo* was a sincere and original work that Tasso worked on constantly, giving Italy one of the few tragedies which is still read, along with Alfieri's *Saul* and Manzoni's *Adelchi*. G. Venturini, *Saggi Critici* (Cinquecento minore: O. Ariosti, G. M. Verdizzotti e il loro influsso nella vita e nell'opera del Tasso) (Ravenna: Longo, 1970), 149.

9. ". . . ha luogo a ragione tra le migliori tragedie del Cinquecento." *Storia della letteratura italiana* (Tomo VII) (Modena: Società tipografica, 1792), 1292–93.

10. B. T. Sozzi, *Studi sul Tasso* (Pisa, 1954), 69–202; and also his "Il Torrismondo," in *Nuovi studi sul Tasso,* 116–20; Arnaldo Di Benedetto, "Per una valutazione del Re Torrismondo," in *Stile e Linguaggio* (Rome, 1974), 136–41; Giuseppe Venturini, "Il Torrismondo," in *Saggi critici* (Ravenna, 1970), 143–57.

11. See Ariani, and Jacques Goudet's essay, "La Nature du tragique dans *Il Re Torrismondo* du Tasse," in *Revue des etudes italiennes* 7 (1961), 146–68.

12. Giovanni Getto, "Dal Galealto al Torrismondo," in *Interpretazione del Tasso,* 171–209.

In Tasso's "Dialogo II" there is mentioned "Galealto re delle isole" (Galealto king of the islands), the one who "fra Lancilotto suo amico e Ginevra pose maggior concordia di quella che ponesse mai alcun giudice fra' litiganti" (between Lancelot his friend and Guinevere he placed a greater harmony than any judge ever placed between litigants). See Torquato Tasso, *Opere,* a cura di Bruno Maier IV (Milan: Rizzoli, 1964), 547.

It is interesting to note that in Spanish and Portuguese the name Noruega is a symbol of obscurity. See A. Castro, "Noruega simbolo de oscuridad," in *Revista de filologia española*, VI (1919), 184–85; and L. Spitzer, "La Norvège comme symbole de l'obscurité" (Norway as symbol of darkness), Ibid, IX (1922), 316–17.

13. In the history of the fourth to the eleventh centuries there are

at least three kings named Torrismondo: the son of king Unimondo (and grandson to Ermonarico, who fought with success against Sweden); the son of Torisindo; and the son of Teodorico, king of the Visigoths. See *I Barbari, Testi dei secoli IV–XI scelti*, tradotti e commentati da Elio Bartolini (Milan: Lagonesi 1970), 517–35, 545, 905–907.

In Giangiorgio Trissino's *L'Italia Liberata dai Goti* we find the name Turrismondo. He is a famous and brave king (Books X and XV); his death is decided by a celestial council (Book XVIII). See Filippo Ermini, *L'Italia Liberata di Giangiorgio Trissino* (Rome: Tipografia Editrice Romana, 1895), 36–43.

14. "La materia che argomento può chiamarsi, o si finge, ed allora par che il poeta abbia parte non solo nella scelta, ma nella invenzione ancora; o si toglie da l'istorie. Ma molto meglio è, a mio giudicio, che l'istoria si prenda." See Torquato Tasso, "Discorsi dell'arte poetica," in *Prose,* a cura di Ettore Mazzali, 351.

15. In the sixteenth century, two histories of the Northern people were published by two brothers, both archbishops: Olaus Magnus, *Historia de gentibus septentrionalibus* (1555) and Johannes Magnus, *Gothorum Suenonumque Historia* (1558).

For Tasso's description of his readings on the Northern countries, see Tasso's Dialogue "Il Massaggiero" in *Prose,* 21–23.

16. "Ed io ho letto ne l'istoria di Gotia d'Olao Magno che gli uomini si trasformano in lupi." See C. P. Brand, *Torquato Tasso: A Study of the Poet and of His Contribution to English Literature* (Cambridge: Cambridge UP, 1965), 176; or see E. Terza, *Una pagina da rivedere nel "Messaggiero" di Torquato Tasso,* in "Propugnatore," III (1890), 235–37.

17. "Le azioni tragiche movono l'orrore e la compassione; ed ove lor manchi questo orribile e questo compassionevole, tragiche più non sono." See Torquato Tasso, "Discorsi dell'arte poetica," in *Prose,* 359–60.

18. Torquato Tasso, *Prose,* 544.

19. Torquato Tasso, *Prose,* 545.

20. Torquato Tasso, *Prose,* 545. For quoted Discourses, see Allan H. Gilbert, *Literary Criticism: Plato to Dryden* (Detroit: Wayne State UP, 1982), 484.

21. Giangiorgio Trissino's *La Sofonisba,* written and published in Rome in 1515, was performed for the first time in Vicenza in 1562. *La Sofonisba* is considered Trissino's masterpiece and the first "modern" tragedy, in that it breaks away from the tradition of the "sacra rappresentazione" and follows the principles of the Greek models (Sophocles and Euripides). *La Sofonisba* was the first tragedy to be written in the

Italian language and, perhaps, the first work written in free verse. See Francesco Flora, *Storia della Letteratura Italiana,* Volume Secondo (Il Quattrocento e il primo Cinquecento) (Milan: Mondadori, 1972), 647–50.

Tasso was familiar with Trissino's tragedy. He read *La Sofonisba* and noted in the margins of his copy the sources for Trissino's lines (i.e., "similitudine tratta da Omero e ben appropriata" (a well appropriated similitude taken from Homer) or "imita Cicerone veni, vidi, vici") (he imitates Cicero [*sic*]: I came, I saw, I conquered), the weakness of some verses (i.e., "Orazio lo chiamerebbe sermo pedestris di cui ne fa l'autore troppo abuso") (Horace would call it sermo pedestris, which the author abuses), the beauty of others (i.e. "parla il poeta con il linguaggio degli antichi, si mostra discepolo et appare pittore da la natura") (the poet speaks with the language of the ancients; he declares himself to be a disciple of nature yet he seems to be its painter). See *La Sofonisba di Giangiorgio Trissino* con note di Torquato Tasso, edite a cura di Franco Paglierani (Bologna: Gaetano Romagnoli, 1884).

22. Gianbattista Giraldi (1541) follows the Senecan example of dismemberment and horror. The subject is taken from one of his *novelle* (Orbecche, daughter of Sulmone, king of Persia, secretly marries Oronte and goes to Armenia. Two children are born to the couple. Sulmone, pretending to forgive his daughter and nephews, invites them to his house and presents to Orbecche the heads and hands of Oronte and the children, on a platter. The woman kills her father and herself). *Orbecche* is considered the first regular tragedy of the Cinquecento. Giraldi's novelle and also Matteo Bandello's novels provided the plots for some of Shakespeare's tragedies. Among the plays that owe their themes to Matteo Bandello's novels are Shakespeare's *Much Ado About Nothing, Twelfth Night,* and the story of *Romeo and Juliet,* which is also based on Luigi Da Porto's novel. Giraldi's *Epitia* had a theme that we can find in *Measure for Measure,* and his novel *The Moor of Venice* became Shakespeare's *Othello.* See Francesco Flora, *Storia della Letteratura Italiana,* Volume Secondo (Milan: Mondadori, 1972), 650–51. See also Ernest Hatch Wilkins, *A History of Italian Literature* revised by Thomas G. Bergin (Cambridge, Harvard UP, 1978), 231–32, 251–52.

23. Giovanni Rucellai's *Rosmunda* was almost contemporaneous with Trissino's *Sofonisba.* The subject is taken from early medieval history (Rosmunda, daughter of Comundo, king of the Gepidae, had been about to marry Almachilde, king of the Lombards. Almachilde slays Comundo and marries Rosmunda, but at the wedding feast, he forces his bride to drink from a cup made of her father's skull; and

Almachilde wreaks due vengeance). Rucellai is also remembered for his *Oreste.* See Francesco Flora, 652; Ernest Hatch Wilkins, 239–40.

24. Pietro Aretino wrote the tragedy *Orazia* (1546), Senecan in its general character. "The tragedy of the Horatii" attains a considerable degree of tragic dignity. The relentless patriotism of Orazia foreshadows Alfieri's tragedies. See Flora, 693–95; Wilkins, 240–41.

25. Luigi Alamanni is remembered for the didactic poem *La Colti- vazione* and for two epics: *Gyrone il cortese* and *L'Avarchide.* Some of his best lyrics are those that express his love for Italy. See Flora, 323–25; Wilkins, 246, 248.

26. Lodovico Dolce wrote *La Marianna.* Among other tragedies of the Cinquecento should be noted: Federico della Valle's *La Reina di Scozia,* Antonio Decio's *Acripanda,* Lodovico Martelli's *Tullia,* Nuzio Manfredi's *Semiramide,* Pomponio Torelli's *Merope, Vittoria, Poli- doro, Tancredi,* whose political theme influenced the French theatre and Alfieri's tragedies. See Flora, 652; Wilkins, 289.

27. Sperone Speroni's *Canace* (1542) was a notable tragedy because of its innovations: its choice of a mythological subject, its mingling of seven- and eleven-syllable lines, and its extensive use of peripetea. See Flora, 349–53; Wilkins, 253–54.

28. Giosuè Carducci, *Il Torrismondo, Opere* (Bologna: Edizione Na- zionale, 1905), 491.

29. See Francesco Petrarca's *Rime,* XVIII, 4

30. Petrarca, LII, 4

31. Petrarca, CCCXXXVIII, 4

32. Petrarca, CIX, 6

33. Petrarca, XXXVIII

34. "Quante promesse . . . Amor" (I,i, 8081) reminds us of "L'amante . . . / aviluppa promesse e giuramenti, che tutti spargon poi per l'aria i venti" (*Orlando Furioso,* X, 5), and "Questa . . . mira" (I, i, 80–81), or "Questa . . . mira" (II, iv, 1083–1086), modelled after Angelica's lament (VIII, 42).

35. ". . . quando . . . potrian lavar occulta e 'ndegna colpa / che mi tinse e macchiò le membra e l'alma?" (when will they ever wash the hidden and unworthy guilt / that stained and soiled my flesh and soul?) (I, iii, 237–238); the theme of guilt which can never be washed by earthly water is a reminiscence of Seneca's *Phaedra*: "Quis eluet me Tanais aut quae barbaris Maeotis undis Pontico incumbens mari? Non ipse toto magnus Oceano pater tantum expiarit sceleris." (Who will be able to cleanse me with the waves of the Don or with the barbaric waters of the Maeotis battling the Pontic sea? Not even the great father could expiate so great a crime with the entire Ocean.) (715–718), an idea which will be echoed in Shakespeare's *Macbeth* ("Will all great

Neptune's ocean wash this blood / clean from my hand?" (Act II, Scene ii).

36. ". . . a' sette . . . Trioni" (I, iii, 353), used by Ovid as "Triones" (II, 171) and by Tasso in the *Gerusalemme Liberata* (XI, 25).

37. ". . . lungo giorno . . . lunga notte;" (long day . . . lengthy night;) (I, iii, 350–51) follows Magnus's description of a phenomenon of the northern regions when one half of an entire year is only an artificial day, and the other half a night (I, I). For the Latin text, see *Historia De Gentibus Septentrionalibus,* autore Olao Magno Gotho Archiepiscopo Upsalensi, Romae M.D.LV. (Westmead, England: Gregg International, 1971), an illustrated text of 815 pages. The text is available also in German, Swedish, and French, and in the Italian translation: *Storia D'Olao Magno Arcivescovo D'upsali, De' Costumi De' Popoli Settentrionali,* tradotta da Remigio Fiorentino (Turin: Vincenzo Bona, 1958), a text of 323 pages, with illustrations reproduced from the original. From Olaus Magnus' work Tasso derived the names for the geography of *Il re Torrismondo* (i.e., Tile, i Moschi, i Biarmi, and Olma). Germondo is the name of one of the kings in *Storia D'Olao Magno,* while Alvida is the name of a princess-pirate, who married king Frontho of Denmark; also, in the same work, we find the names of Rusilla, Aldano, and Araldo, in Chapter (XXIII): "D'alcune donne, che facevano l'arte del Corsaro." (Of certain women, who practiced the trade of the Corsair.) (See *Storia D'Olao Magno,* 102–103).

38. C. P. Brand, *Torquato Tasso,* 174

39. "La povertà, l'essiglio e gli altri rischi, e le pallide morti, e i lunghi morbi, fianchi, stomachi, febri." See C. P. Brand, 175.

40. Getto, "Dal Galealto al Torrismondo," 185. Donadoni sees Rosmonda as a Virgilian Camilla. See Eugenio Donadoni, *Torquato Tasso* Vol. II, (Florence: La Nuova Italia, 1921), 88.

41. See Tasso's *Gerusalemme Liberata,* I, 20.

42. Umberto Renda, "Il Torrismondo di Torquato Tasso e la tecnica tragica del Cinquecento" in *Rivista Abruzzese di Scienze, Lettere ed Arti,* 371–74.

43. Torquato Tasso, *Jerusalem Delivered,* translated into verse and with an introduction by Joseph Tusiani (Cranbury, N.J.: Associated UP, 1970), see introduction, 18–20.

44. Getto, 192 and 204. Carducci says that Tasso was the first in tragedy to contrast friendship and love in the same character. See *Teatro di Torquato Tasso,* edizione critica a cura di Angelo Solerti con due saggi di Giosuè Carducci (Bologna: Zanichelli, 1895), LXV.

45. Fred J. Nichols, ed. and trans., *An Anthology of Neo-Latin Poetry* (New Haven: Yale UP, 1979); see Nichols's introduction, 1–89.

46. Act two, scene one; act four, scenes four and six; act five, scenes four and six.

47. Brand, 176–77.

KING TORRISMONDO BEYOND THE ALPS

The popularity of the *Aminta* and the *Gerusalemme Liberata* assured Tasso's international renown. Soon his works were to prove influential on French,[1] English,[2] and Spanish[3] literature. Although *King Torrismondo* remains a minor work in comparison with his two masterpieces, Tasso's famous name made even this tragedy known throughout Italy and beyond the Alps, where Torrismondo was to influence Racine, Corneille, Milton, and Calderón.

The popularity of Tasso's *Torrismondo* in France is evidenced not only by Dalibray's translation and its reprints, but also by the two performances of the tragedy at the Théâtre du Marais in Paris.[4] In his preface to *Le Torrismon,* Dalibray points out that Tasso's tragedy (and Cremonini's play, which he also translated into French)[5] formulated the tendencies of the period. At this time the French theater closely followed the classical drama and its contemporary genres, the pastoral play and the tragi-comedy, both of which sprang from Italian models of the previous century. It seems most likely that Tasso's tragedy was read by Racine, Corneille, and other French dramatists, if not in Dalibray's popular translation, then surely in the original. We can safely deduce it from the manner in which, in his *Athalie,* Racine introduces the Chorus—in a fashion, that is, which recalls Tasso's *Torrismondo.* The four choral songs divide the five-act play of the French tragedy. The Chorus is not continually present on the stage, but comes on "to punctuate with lyric interludes the otherwise uninterrupted progress of the action."[6]

Secrecy and mystery, a dual characteristic of Tasso's tragedy, is, indeed, one of the themes of Racine's best plays (*Phedre, Athalie, Britannicus*). Another important theme in Tasso's tragedy is the concept of time: "Quel che ricopre, al fin discopre il tempo" (That which is hidden, time finally uncovers) (IV, III, 2267), says Torrismondo to Rosmonda, and "Quetate il duol, che tutto scopre il tempo" (Calm your grief, for time uncovers all.) (V, VI, 3270), says Germondo to the lamenting Queen. In Racine's *Britannicus,* Narcissus says to Nero: "Il n'est point de secrets que le temps ne revele;" (There is no secret that time does not unveil;) (IV, iv, 1404),[7] which reads like an echo of Tasso's *Torrismondo,* though the concept is classical.

In the case of Corneille, the same parallels that we draw between *Theodore* and the *Aminta* can be applied to *Héraclius* and *Torrismondo.* Characters in both plays are substituted for each other and the tragedies make obeisance in the direction of historicity. In *Torrismondo* the principal characters are members of the ruling families of Scandinavian kingdoms. Corneille preserves the real imperial succession that linked Tibere to Maurice and to Héraclius.[8] Both plays have plots that deal with a double substitution of infants and a series of complications years later. *Héraclius* assumes a similar set of exchanges, but of male instead of female infants. To the theme of mistaken identities, *Torrismondo* and *Héraclius* both also add the theme of incest.[9] While Tasso allows the lovers to consummate their passion, Corneille stops short and merely flirts with the idea of incest.

Corneille's remarks on *Héraclius* echo Dalibray's preface to *Torrismon.* He readily grants the over-complication of the plot and, by way of help to the reader, provides a list of the true and assumed identities of the essential characters.

Tasso's popularity in England was such that Giuseppe Baretti tried to contest his supremacy by making the English understand that Italy had in Dante a greater poet, and that Ariosto's reputation had been too long overshadowed by Tasso's.[10] While the pastoral play *Aminta* was being performed in Reading,[11] the *Gerusalemme Liberata* found its first translator.[12] Through Spenser's imitation, in the *Fairie Queene,* Tasso entered English literature. Although Spenser is the most often cited example, echoes of Tasso's "heroic poem" can be traced in Browne, in Dryden, in Hoole, in Cowley, and in Tennyson.[13] Milton's *Paradise Lost,* however, reflects not only the influence of the *Gerusalemme Liberata,* which critics have often dealt with, but also

Tasso's *Le Sette Giornate del Mondo Creato* and *Il re Torrismondo.*

Five years after the first publication of the tragedy, Tasso began to write *Il Mondo Creato*[14] at the suggestion of Donna Vittoria Loffredo, mother of Gian Battista Manso, the Marquis of Villa, Tasso's Neapolitan patron. To Manso, Milton addressed a Latin poem in which he refers to Tasso as "mighty."[15] Milton, who knew Italian well enough to compose perfectly in the language,[16] was able, during his stay at Manso's house, to familiarize himself not only with Tasso's *Torrismondo,* but also with his last work, *Il Mondo Creato.* Consequently, while Tasso's Catholic poem foreshadowed the blank verse of *Paradise Lost,* Tasso's *Torrismondo* set the meter of the English poem.

Mario Praz demonstrates *Torrismondo*'s influence on Milton's epic verse. He quotes a passage toward the end of the Second Act, when Torrismondo orders military games to celebrate King Germondo's arrival:

> Ora a voi, cavalieri, a voi mi volgo,
> Giovani arditi. Altri sublime ed alto
> Drizzi un castel di fredda neve e salda,
> E 'l coroni di mura intorno intorno:
> Faccian le sue difese, e faccian quattro
> Ne' quattro lati suoi torri superbe;
> E di candida mole insegna negra,
> Dispiegandosi a l'aure, e 'l ciel s'innalzi;
> E vi sia chi 'l difenda e chi l'assalga.
>
> . . . .
>
> L'altre diverse mie lucenti squadre
> A cavallo ed a piè frattanto accolga
> Il mio buon duce intorno a l'alta reggia,
> E i destrier di metallo, onde rimbomba
> La fiamma ne l'uscir d'ardente bocca
> Con negro fumo, e' miei veloci carri;
> E lungo spazio di campagna ingombri
> Sotto vittoriosa e grande insegna.
> (VI, 1398–1470)

The rhythm of these lines "seems actually to be the model of the metre of *Paradise Lost*":[17]

> Nigh on the Plain in many cells prepar'd
> That underneath had veins of liquid fire

Sluc'd from the Lake, a second multitude
With wondrous Art founded the massie Ore,
Serving each kinde, and scum'd the Bullion dross:
A third as soon had form'd within the ground
A various mould, and from the boyling cells
By strange conveyance fill'd each hollow nook,
As in an Organ from one blast of wind
To many a row of Pipes the sound-board breaths.
(I, 700–717)

As when to warn proud Cities warr appears
Wag'd in the troubl'd Skie, and Armies rush
To Battel in the Clouds, before each Van
Prick forth th'Aerie Knights, and couch their spears
Till thickest Legions close; with feats of Arms
From either end of Heaven'n the welkin burns.
(II, 533–541)

Magnificence and gravity were Milton's constant guidelines; he followed them in his sentences "variously drawn out from one verse into another," which seems a translation of Tasso's words: "i versi spezzati, i quali entrano l'un nell'altro . . . fanno il parlar magnifico e sublime."[18]

Tasso's popularity in Spain is shown by his influence on Spanish poetry. But was Calderón familiar with Tasso's tragedy? His knowledge of the Italian language and his trips to Italy lead me to believe that he not only read *Torrismondo,* but that he was influenced by the tragedy.

Torrismondo is a tragedy of fate. The sinister predictions that the baby girl would cause Torrismondo's death prompted the king of the Goths to rid himself of his daughter. In Calderón's *La Vida es sueño,*[19] King Basilio's terrible interpretation of Segismundo's future forces him to imprison his son. Both father-kings, in the attempt to escape a future calamity, fulfill fate's decree: Alvida, unaware of her true identity, turns fraternal love into passion; Segismundo, deprived of his humanity, becomes a commixture of man and beast. Both plays are set in a remote, exotic place: Tasso chooses the Scandinavian countries; Calderón chooses Poland.

In conclusion, while Tasso's tragedy can be seen as a revelation of Alvida's identity, Calderón's play unscrambles the puzzle of Eusebio's. Both tragedies deal with pathos, discovery, and a revelation of kinship-love mistaken for passion because of an ignorance of true identity.

NOTES

1. Joyce Simpson, *Le Tasse et la littérature et l'art baroque en France* (Paris: Librarie A. G. Nizet, 1962).

2. Lytton A. Sells, *The Italian Influence in English Poetry (from Chaucer to Southwell)* (Bloomington: Indiana UP, 1955).

3. Joaquín Arce, *Tasso y la poesía española* (Barcelona: Editorial Planeta, 1973).

4. Leo Spitzer, "L'effet de sourdine dans le style classique: Racine" (The effect of a sordine in the classical style: Racine) in *Etudes de style* (Paris, 1970), 208–335, translated from the German, first published in 1931.

5. The French translation by Charles Vion Dalibray (*Le Torrismon du Tasse Tragédie,* Paris: Denis Houssaye, 1636), with reprints in 1640 and in 1646.

The production of the tragedy was successful with the interpretation of Montdory in the role of Torrismondo (1635).

6. Before the translation of *Le Torrismon,* Dalibray had translated *L'Aminte du Tasse* (1632) and Cremonini's *La Pompe funebre ou Damon et Cloris* (1634).

7. Umberto Renda, "Il Torrismondo e la tecnica tragica del Cinquecento," in *Rivista Abruzzese,* Anno XX, Fasc.X, Ottobre 1905, 536–37. See also Jean Racine, *Britannicus,* edited by H. J. Chaytor (Cambridge: Cambridge UP, 1950), 51.

8. Some twenty years before the play's opening, Phocas the tyrant killed the emperor Maurice and ordered that the emperor's infant son, Héraclius, also be put to death. To upset the plan a lady, Leontine, had played a double trick on the tyrant. First she had substituted her own son for Héraclius, allowing her own child to be murdered in order to save the future emperor. Later, for precaution she managed to exchange Héraclius for the tyrant's infant son, Martian. As a result of these exchanges, the child raised by Leontine was in fact the tyrant's son, and the young man who is presumed to be the tyrant's son is in fact Héraclius, the legitimate heir to the throne. See *The Best Plays of Racine,* translated by Lacy Lockert (Princeton, N.J.: Princeton UP, 1964), 303.

9. At times in the play, the action is headed in the direction of Héraclius's being married to Pulcherie, his sister.

10. Mario Praz, *The Flaming Heart* (Gloucester, Mass.: Peter Smith, 1966), 336.

11. The *Aminta* was performed by Italian actors in Reading during July 1574. The pastoral play had been produced at Ferrara the year before.

12. The first complete translation of the *Gerusalemme Liberata* into English was in 1600, by Edward Fairfax. See *Godfrey of Bolloigne* (A critical edition of Edward Fairfax's translation of Tasso's *Gerusalemme Liberata,* together with Fairfax's Original Poems edited by Kathleen M. Lea and T. M. Gang) (Oxford: The Clarendon, 1981), 1–24; also in Mario Praz's *The Flaming Heart,* 315.

13. Praz, 309–320.

14. Critics identify Tasso's *Le Sette Giornate del Mondo Creato* by the title *Sette Giornate* (see Black, 469–476), or *Il Mondo Creato* (see Praz, 324); for this study I am using the title *Il Mondo Creato.*

15. John Milton, *The Latin Poems* (New Haven: Yale UP, 1930), 152.

16. Milton's poetical works include poems written in Italian: five "sonnets" and a "canzone." See *The Poetical Works of John Milton,* Volume II (Oxford: The Clarendon, 1966), 146–49 and 232–34.

17. Praz, 326. "That Milton had read attentively the *Sette Giornate,* has more than once been observed, . . ." (see Black, 469–76). Raphael's story of the Creation of the World (lines 243–547) in book VII of *Paradise Lost* has been called "The Italian element in Milton's verse" (see Praz, 325–326). There are striking similarities between the 9,000 lines of Tasso's *Il Mondo Creato* and Milton's 304 lines dedicated to the Creation of the World. A comparative study of Tasso's Catholic poem and Book VII of *Paradise Lost* has been made easier by the translation of *Il Mondo Creato* into English: *Torquato Tasso, The Creation of the World,* translated by Joseph Tusiani (Binghamton, N.Y.: Medieval and Renaissance Text and Studies, 1982).

18. Ibid., 326, and Torquato Tasso, "Discorsi dell'arte poetica" in *Prose diverse* (Florence: G. Guasti, 1875), 219.

19. It is interesting to note that the Italian version of the name of Calderón's hero, Segismundo, is found in the history of the fourth to the eleventh centuries, along with Torrismondo's name. Segismondo is son of the great Unimondo; since one of the three kings named Torrismondo is also the son of Unimondo, this leads me to believe that, in fact, the two kings were brothers. (See *I Barbari,* 545, and p. 38 in my introduction "*King Torrismondo,* a Renaissance Tragedy").

A BRIEF OUTLINE OF TASSO'S TRAGEDY

King Torrismondo combines the three styles that Tasso speaks of in his essay: "il magnifíco, il mediocre, l'umile"[1] (the magnificent, the mediocre, the humble). The poet distributes the 'ante-fatto' in three parts: the first narration justifies the violence of the drama tormenting Torrismondo, who tries to find a device to save his love and his honor; the second establishes the motif of Alvida's downfall, and the third determines the impossibility of reaching a happy ending. The action of the tragedy is impelled by psychological motives. The interest of the drama is never lost; if at times it seems to slacken, soon it revives and stays alive until the end of the play. There is unity in the tragedy: all actions revolve around the unhappy love of the royal couple. The unity of time and place is observed by Tasso: the action starts in the late morning hours (II, i, 932) and continues into the late evening hours of the same day (IV, i, 2132 and V, ii, 2909). The scenes take place outside the royal palace on a balcony or in the gardens.

While Trissino's *L'Italia Liberata dai Goti* had inspired the title of Tasso's *Gerusalemme Liberata,*[2] the "Goti" gave him the setting for his tragedy. Torrismondo is king of the Goths. The action takes place in Scandinavia and involves the countries of Sweden and Norway.

The tragedy is divided into five acts,[3] with the appearance of Choruses at intervals[4] and at the end of each act.

ACT ONE

In a scene that recalls Seneca's *Phaedra,*[5] the first act sets the stage: Alvida, a Norwegian princess, confides her fears and doubts to her nurse—it is now three weeks since Torrismondo, king of the Goths, has brought her to his home. Torrismondo had gone to Norway to claim her hand from her father, but had insisted that the marriage should be celebrated, in the presence of his mother, in Arana. During the journey, Alvida was as alluring as possible, and Torrismondo's fidelity was shaken. The king might probably have resisted had not a storm forced the ships to stop at a deserted island. It was there, in the intimacy of their tent, that the couple, unable to curb their passion, consummated their love. Since that night Torrismondo has avoided Alvida, whose love for him has meanwhile grown stronger. In the third scene of the first act, Torrismondo confides to his counselor the reason for his torment: he had been led to ask for Alvida's hand out of friendship for Germondo, king of Sweden. Germondo, who was in love with the Norwegian princess, was debarred from marrying her because of the historic hostility between the countries of Norway and Sweden, and because Alvida's father blamed Germondo for the death of his only son. According to the pact between the two friends, Torrismondo was to bring Alvida to his home and hand her over to Germondo. During the voyage, however, the king of the Goths fell in love with the Norwegian princess, thus betraying his friend's trust. The Counselor suggests that Germondo might be persuaded to marry Torrismondo's sister, Rosmonda, whom some might find more beautiful than Alvida.

ACT TWO

The tension reaches its peak when the messenger announces Germondo's arrival. While Torrismondo is in a state of despair, Rosmonda is worried by the Queen's anxiety that she should welcome Germondo and consider him as a husband-to-be. The action becomes relaxed as we witness a discussion of marriage between mother and daughter. The projected marriage of Rosmonda and Germondo is accepted by Torrismondo as a solution to his dilemma. He cannot offer to Germondo the girl he has defiled, and who, perhaps, will bear his child; thus, if Germondo will accept Rosmonda, he will be free to marry Alvida.

ACT THREE

When faced by Germondo, Torrismondo cannot bring himself to make the treacherous suggestion to his friend, but, instead, urges Alvida to receive the Swedish king graciously. To please Torrismondo, Alvida accepts rich gifts from Germondo. Meanwhile, in a soliloquy, Rosmonda hints at her secret—she is herself in love with Torrismondo—and declares her intention of revealing her true identity.

ACT FOUR

On behalf of Torrismondo, the Counselor urges Germondo to accept Rosmonda as his wife, and Germondo, the faithful friend, seems disposed to comply with whatever the king of the Goths should wish. There follow, however, many disclosures of identity which precipitate the catastrophe. Threatened with being forced to wed Germondo, Rosmonda reveals that she is not Torrismondo's real sister: the latter was taken away following a sinister prediction that she would cause her brother's death. Rosmonda is the daughter of a nursemaid and, as a child, was substituted for the princess; even the Queen was not aware of Rosmonda's true identity. Meanwhile, Rosmonda was vowed to chastity by her real mother. At this point, a question is raised: where is Torrismondo's real sister? The tragedy takes on a Sophoclean flavor[6] as a messenger appears with the news of the Norwegian king's death, thus providing the missing link in the chain of events. We learn that Torrismondo's real sister was entrusted, as a child, to a servant who handed her over to others, and that she was eventually brought up at the Norwegian court as the Norwegian king's daughter. Consequently, Torrismondo learns that Alvida is the true Rosmonda and his real sister. The anguished king is forced to change his plans and offers Alvida to Germondo.

ACT FIVE

The last act returns to a setting similar to that of the first scene of the first act: Alvida talks to her nurse about her confusion and dismay. She does not accept the story of her new identity. She thinks instead that only a lack of love can explain Torrismondo's desire that she should marry Germondo. Believing herself to be scorned by Torrismondo, Alvida commits suicide. After persuading the dying Alvida that she is, indeed, his sister, Torrismondo writes a letter bequeathing his kingdom and his mother to Germondo; he then takes his own life rather than live without the woman he loves. The Queen, still expecting to witness a double wedding, suddenly learns instead of the true identity of Rosmonda and Alvida and of the death of both her children. Germondo is left commiserating with the bewailing mother. Had he known, the faithful friend would have pardoned all.

NOTES

1. See "Discorso Secondo" in Torquato Tasso, *Prose,* a cura di Ettore Mazzali, con una premessa di Francesco Flora (Naples: Riccardo Ricciardi, 1959), 392.

2. Ernest Hatch Wilkins, *A History of Italian Literature* (Cambridge, Mass.: Harvard UP, 1974), 27.

3. Act One is divided into three scenes and has a total of 911 lines. Act Two is divided into seven scenes with a total of 495 lines. Act Four is divided into seven scenes with a total of 767 lines. Act Five is divided into six scenes with a total of 561 lines.

4. Torquato Tasso, *Il re Torrismondo,* III, i; IV, iv; IV, vi; V, vi.

5. Seneca's *Phaedra* (Act One, Scene ii) in *The Complete Roman Drama,* edited and with an introduction by George E. Duckworth (New York: Random, 1942), vol. II, 627.

6. Sophocles, *Oedipus the King* in *The Complete Plays of Sophocles* (New York: Bantam, 1982), 99.

ABOUT THE TRANSLATION

The present translation, the first from the Italian into English, is intended to help readers understand the original text. I have aimed to produce a version as faithful to the letter and spirit of the original as modern literary English allows. Tasso's chief concern is linguistic decorum: his characters are royals and more than aware of their stylistic responsabilities. My main concerns have been accuracy, clarity, and readability. These desiderata were not always easy to achieve (indeed, they may have not always been achieved), given the sustained and complex rhetoric of the sixteenth-century original.

To transform "endecasillabi" (eleven-syllable lines) and "settenari" (seven-syllable lines) into iambic pentameters, I would have had to work within severe limitations and would have been forced to make omissions or additions. In order to avoid unnecessary interpolations, I decided to translate *Il re Torrismondo* into English prose. Nevertheless, I have tried to convey a sense of the original poetry by keeping the prose as rhythmical as accuracy and taste would allow. I have tried also to recreate most faithfully Tasso's images, his sensory-emotional overtones, his puns, his classical as well as his baroque visions.

Most of the problems I encountered dealt with the expressive language of the period: often ambiguous and difficult. I was also confronted with the basic problems of the two languages: the Italian tends to be polyvalent whereas English is clear and precise (as in verbs and nouns); yet Italian can be precise where English is vague (as in prepositions and conjunctions). I therefore translated literally whenever possible. However, when the word order required a shift, or when an additional word would help clarify the meaning, I have taken the liberty of sacrificing faithfulness to fluency.

One example will perhaps suffice to illustrate the numerous

instances of textual difficulties which I had to face in the course of my translation. In Alvida's first, lengthy address to her Nurse (Act One, 87–90) we read:

Ma poiché meco egli tentò parlando
d'amore il guado, e pur vendetta io chiesi:
chiesi vendetta, ed ebbi fede in pegno
di vendetta e d'amor; . . .

I was, first, confronted with the semantic value of "poiché," obviously meaning, in this case, "quando" or "dopo che," and not "perché." By translating it as "when," I felt that the meaning of the original term had been respected and faithfully preserved. The second difficulty I encountered was in the metaphorical expression "tentare il guado," literally "to seek a spot where a stream can be forded," that is, to find a safe passage in the crossing of a stream. This fluvial analogy, of which a famous example is found in the last stanza of Petrarch's "Canzone alla Vergine," posed, in turn, another difficulty: it would have become unintelligible to the English reader if left in its original garb. I debated, consequently, between "winning love" and "entering into love," and finally opted for "to cross the ford of love," which seems to suggest, and preserve, something of the original metaphor. The last difficulty of the brief passage was posed by the repetition of "chiesi" at the beginning of the new line. The mere translation of the same verb would not have stressed the clear chiasmus implicit in Tasso's text; therefore, it seemed to me that something else was needed to bring the same device to the fore. Thus I introduced a "Yes," spiritually in keeping with the dramatic tone of the sentence.

This is, then, the translation of the passage in question:

But when he tried, by talking to me,
to cross the ford of love, I asked for vengeance.
Yes, revenge I craved, and was assured a pledge
of revenge and love; . . .

I have based this translation on the Italian text of *Il re Torrismondo* in *Torquato Tasso, Opere II* a cura di Bruno Maier (Milan: Rizzoli, 1964), 723–871. Costantini's sonnet "Nel ritratto di Torquato Tasso" and Tasso's dedication letter "Al Serenissimo Signor Don Vincenzo Gonzaga Duca di Mantova e di Monferrato, etc" were quoted from the *Opere di Torquato Tasso* a cura di

Bortolo Tommaso Sozzi (Unione Tipografico Editrice Torinese, 1964), Volume Secondo, 13 and 275–76. The translations of the sonnet and of the dedication letter are mine.

I must express my gratitude to friends and mentors at the City University of New York who read my translation of *Il re Torrismondo.* Professor Joseph Tusiani, whose classes inspired me to admire and love Tasso's works, helped me understand verses often heavy and ponderous in the original. Professor Fred J. Nichols read the manuscript and made many valuable suggestions. Professor Frederick Goldin and Professor Frank Rosengarten offered their comments when I first began the translation in 1987. Finally, my gratitude goes to Professor Anthony Oldcorn, who read the entire manuscript and made valuable comments and suggestions, to my friend Ada Ricci for looking over proofs of the Italian text, to Loomis Mayer for his editorial revisions, and to Dr. Mary Beatrice Schulte for believing in my work.

If this translation will succeed in making more students fall in love with Tasso's *King Torrismondo,* and if, in comparative studies courses of late Renaissance tragedy, Italy can be represented by a play from the pen of a poet of first rank, I am sure that Tasso's labor of love, and my humble English rendering, will be rewarded.

SONNET

In a letter to Antonio Costantini in Mantua, dated February 13, 1593, Tasso writes:

> Nel leggere il sonetto di V.S. sovra il mio ritratto, non ho saputo riconoscere me stesso; perché m'adorna in guisa col pennello gentilissimo della sua eloquenza, ch'io mi veggio tutto trasformato. M'è piaciuto molto più il delineamento delle mie sciagure, che delle virtù; perché di queste ha detto molto più di quello che doveva: di quelle molto meno di quello che poteva. L'ho ritoccato in alcuni luoghi, acciocché mi rappresenti più al vivo: di che la prego a non isdegnarsi.

> (In reading the sonnet of Your Lordship on my portrait, I have not been able to recognize myself, because you so adorn me with the very kind brush of your eloquence, that I see myself all changed. Much more I liked the description of my misery than that of my virtues, since, of the latter, you said much more than you should; of the former much less than what you could (have said). I touched it up here and there, so that you may represent me more truthfully; for this I beg you not to grow angry.)

The sonnet Tasso refers to is the following:

NEL RITRATTO DI TORQUATO TASSO
SONETTO D'ANTONIO COSTANTINI
RITOCCATO DAL TASSO

Amici, questi è il Tasso, io dico il figlio,
che nulla si curò d'umana prole,
ma fe' parti più chiare assai del sole,
d'arte, di stil, d'ingegno e di consiglio.

Visse in gran povertade e in lungo esiglio,
ne' palagi, ne' tempi e nelle scuole;

fuggissi, errò per selve inculte e sole;
ebbe in terra ed in mar pena e periglio.

Picchiò l'uscio di morte, e pur la vinse,
or con le prose, or con i dotti carmi,
ma fortuna non già, che 'l trasse al fondo.

Premio d'aver cantato amori ed armi
e mostro il ver che mille vizi estinse
è verde fronda: e ancor par troppo al mondo!

ON THE PORTRAIT OF TORQUATO TASSO
A SONNET BY ANTONIO COSTANTINI
RETOUCHED BY TASSO

Friends, this is Tasso, I mean the son,
who did not care for human offspring
but gave birth to children (his works) brighter than the sun
In art, in style, in genius and in wisdom.

He lived in great poverty and long exile,
in palaces, in temples and in schools;
he fled, he wandered through untrodden, lonely woods;
sufferings and perils on land and sea were his.

He knocked on death's door, conquered it,
now with prose, now with learned songs,
but not with fortune, which dragged him to the bottom.

The reward for having sung of loves and arms
and shown the truth that extinguished countless vices
is but a verdant wreath: and yet it seems too much to the
    world!

DEDICATION

Tasso dedicated *Il re Torrismondo* to Don Vincenzo Gonzaga, son of the Duke of Mantua, who, in 1586, had interceded to have the poet released from Sant'Anna. Here, reproduced, is the letter in its original Italian:

Al Serenissimo Signor
DON VINCENZO GONZAGA
Duca di Mantova e di Monferrato, etc.

La tragedia per opinione di alcuni è gravissimo componimento; come ad altri pare, affettuosissimo, e convenevole a' giovenetti: i quali, oltre tutti gli altri, par che ricerchi per uditori. E benché queste due opinioni paiano fra sé contrarie e discordi, ora si conosce come possano amichevolmente concordare: perché V. Altezza nel fior de gli anni suoi giovenili dimostra tanta gravità di costumi e tanta prudenza, ch'a niuno altro principe par che più si convenga questo poema. Oltre a ciò, la tragedia per giudizio d'Aristotele ne l'esser perfetto supera ciascuno altro. E voi sete principe dotato d'altissimo ingegno e d'ogni perfezione, sì come colui al quale non mancano l'antiche ricchezze, né le virtù e la gloria de gli antecessori, né i nuovi ornamenti accresciuti dal padre a la vostra nobilissima stirpe, né il proprio valore e la propria eccellenza in esercitar l'armi e le lettere, né l'azione, né la contemplazione, e particolarmente né la poesia, ne la quale ancora può essere annoverato fra' principi che nobilmente hanno scritto e poetato. A V. Altezza dunque, ch'è perfettissimo principe, dedico e consacro questo perfettissimo poema, estimando che 'l dono, quantunque minore del suo merito, non sia disdicevole a la sua grandezza, né a la mia affezione, che tanto cresce in me, quanto il saper in lei si va accrescendo. In una cosa solamente potrebbe alcuno estimar ch'io avessi avuto poco risguardo a la sua prospera fortuna. Io dico nel donare a felicissimo principe infelicissima composizione; ma le azioni de' miseri possono ancora a' beati servire, per ammaestramento: e V. Altezza leggendo o ascoltando questa favola troverà alcune cose da imitare, altre da schivare, altre da lodare, altre da riprendere, altre da rallegrarsi, altre da contristarsi. E potrà col suo gravissimo giudizio purgar in guisa l'animo, ed in guisa temprar le passioni, che l'altrui dolore sia cagione del suo diletto; e l'imprudenza degli altri del suo avedimento; e gli infortunii, de la sua prosperità. E piaccia a Dio di scacciar lontano da la sua casa ogni infelicità, ogni tempesta, ogni nube, ogni nebbia, ogni ombra di nimica fortuna o di fortunoso avenimento, spargendolo non dico in Gotia, o in Norvegia, o 'n Suezia, ma fra gli ultimi Biarmi, e fra i mostri e le fiere e le notturne larve di quella orrida regione, dove sei mesi de l'anno sono tenebre di continova notte. Piaccia ancora a V. Altezza ch'io sia a parte de la sua felicità, poich'ha voluto farmi parte de la sua casa, accioché il poeta non sia infelice come il poema, né la mia fortuna simil a quella che si descrive ne la tragedia: ma se le poesie ancora hanno la rea e la buona sorte, come alcuno ha creduto, questa, essendo di mia divenuta sua, può sperare lieta e felice mutazione, e fama perpetua ed onore e riputazione fra gli altri componimenti, perché la memoria de la cortesia di V. Altezza fia immortale, ed intesa e divolgata per varie lingue ne le più lontane parti del Settentrione.

Di Bergamo il primo di settembre 1587.

Di V. Altezza Sereniss.
Affez.mo e devot.mo ser.re

TORQUATO TASSO

To the Most Serene Lord
DON VINCENZO GONZAGA
Duke of Mantua and Monferrato, etc.

Tragedy, as some people believe, is a very serious composition; as it appears to others, it is a most pathetic one, most suitable for the young whom it seems to prefer as spectators. And, although these two opinions appear to be opposite and discordant with each other, it is presently known how they can favorably agree, because Your Highness, in the prime of your life, shows such gravity of customs and such prudence that this poem seems to be more fittingly dedicated to no other prince. Moreover, in Aristotle's judgment, tragedy surpasses any other composition in perfection. And you are a prince gifted with high genius and every perfection, as one who does not lack ancient wealth, nor the virtue and the glory of your predecessors, or new ornaments added by your father to your most noble origin, or your own worth and your excellence in the exercise of arms and letters, or action or contemplation, particularly in poetry, in which you can still be numbered among princes who have nobly written verse. To Your Highness, then, to a most perfect prince, that is, I dedicate and devote this most perfect poem, considering that the gift, though less in its own worth, is not unbecoming to your might, nor to my affection, which grows in me as much as knowledge increases in you. In one thing only is someone likely to believe that I may have shown little regard for your prosperous fortune. I mean in dedicating a very unhappy work to a very happy prince; but the actions of the wretched can be a lesson to the blissful; and, in reading or listening to this tale Your Highness will find some things to imitate, others to shun, others to praise, others to blame, others to rejoice at, others to grieve for. Thus, in your great judgment, you will be able to purify your soul, and so temper your passions that the pain of others will be a reason for your joy; and other people's rashness, for your awareness; and others' misfortunes, for your prosperity. And may God drive away from your house all unhappiness, every storm, every cloud, every fog, every shadow of hostile fate or fateful incident, scattering it not in Gothland, or in Norway, or in Sweden, but among the last Biarmians, and among the monsters and wild beasts and the nocturnal ghosts of that awful region where for six months of the year there is continuous, dark night. May it also please Your Highness that I be part of your happiness, since you wanted to make me part of your household, so that the poet may not be as unhappy as his poem, nor my fate be similar to the one described in the tragedy: but if poems are still subject to evil and good fortune, as some have believed, this, then, which was mine and now is yours, can hope for a joyous and happy change, for perpetual renown and honor and reputation among my other works, so that the memory of Your Highness's kindness may be immortal, and known and carried upon many tongues to the farthest regions of the North.

From Bergamo the first day of September, 1587.

Of Your Most Serene Highness
the most affectionate and devoted servant

TORQUATO TASSO

KING TORRISMONDO

INTERLOCUTORI

NUTRICE

ALVIDA

TORRISMONDO RE DE' GOTI

CONSIGLIERO

CORO

MESSAGGERO PRIMO

ROSMONDA

REGINA MADRE

GERMONDO RE DI SUEZIA

CAMERIERA

INDOVINO

FRONTONE

MESSAGGERO SECONDO

CAMERIERO

CHARACTERS

NURSE

ALVIDA

TORRISMONDO, KING OF THE GOTHS

COUNSELOR

CHORUS

FIRST MESSENGER

ROSMONDA

QUEEN MOTHER

GERMONDO, KING OF SWEDEN

A MAID

SOOTHSAYER

FRONTONE

SECOND MESSENGER

STEWARD

ATTO PRIMO

SCENA PRIMA

NUTRICE, ALVIDA.

[NUTRICE]

Deh qual cagione ascosa, alta regina,
sì per tempo vi sveglia? Ed or che l'alba
nel lucido oriente a pena è desta,
dove ite frettolosa? E quai vestigi
5   di timore in un tempo e di desio
veggio nel vostro volto e ne la fronte?
Perch'a pena la turba interno affetto
o pur novella passion l'adombra,
ch'io me n'aveggio. A me, che per etate
10   e per officio e per fedele amore
vi sono in vece di pietosa madre,
e serva per volere e per fortuna,
il pensier sì molesto omai si scopra,
ché nulla sì celato o sì riposto
15   dee rinchiuder giamai ch'a me l'asconda.

ALVIDA

Cara nudrice e madre, egli è ben dritto
ch'a voi si mostri quello ond'osa a pena
ragionar fra se stesso il mio pensiero:
perch'a la vostra fede, al vostro senno
20   più canuto del pelo, al buon consiglio,
meglio è commesso ogni secreto affetto,
ogni occulto desio del cor profondo,

ACT ONE

SCENE ONE

NURSE, ALVIDA

[NURSE]

O noble queen, what is the hidden reason,
that makes you rise so early? Now that the day
in the bright east has barely dawned,
where are you rushing to? And what traces
5   of fear and desire at the same time
do I see in your face and on your brow?
For no sooner does an inner feeling trouble it
or a new passion cloud it
than I am aware of it. To me—who by my age,
10   and duty and most faithful love
take the place of a tender mother,
though servant by desire and destiny—
let your vexatious thoughts now be disclosed,
for there should be nothing so concealed or secret
15   as ever to hide itself from me.

ALVIDA

Dear nurse and mother, it is but right
that I should tell you what my mind
dare hardly formulate within itself:
for to your trust and to your wisdom
20   more reverend than your white hair, to your good counsel,
each secret affection is better trusted,
each hidden longing of my deepest heart,

ch'a me stessa non è. Bramo e pavento,
no 'l nego; ma so ben quel ch'i' desio;
25　quel che tema, io non so. Temo ombre e sogni,
ed antichi prodigi e novi mostri,
promesse antiche e nove, anzi minacce
di fortuna, del ciel, del fato averso,
di stelle congiurate; e temo, ahi lassa,
30　un non so che d'infausto o pur d'orrendo
ch'a me confonde un mio pensier dolente,
lo qual mi sveglia e mi perturba e m'ange
la notte e 'l giorno. Oimè, giamai non chiudo
queste luci già stanche in breve sonno,
35　ch'a me forme d'orrore e di spavento
il sogno non presenti; ed or mi sembra
che dal fianco mi sia rapito a forza
il caro sposo, e senza lui solinga
gir per via lunga e tenebrosa errando;
40　or le mura stillar, sudare i marmi
miro, o credo mirar, di negro sangue;
or da le tombe antiche, ove sepolte
l'alte regine fur di questo regno,
uscir gran simolacro e gran ribombo
45　quasi d'un gran gigante, il qual rivolga
incontra al cielo Olimpo e Pelia ed Ossa,
e mi scacci dal letto, e mi dimostri,
perch'io vi fugga da sanguigna sferza,
una orrida spelunca, e dietro il varco
50　poscia mi chiuda: onde, s'io temo il sonno
e la quiete, anzi l'orribil guerra
de' notturni fantasmi a l'aria fosca,
sorgendo spesso ad incontrar l'aurora,
meraviglia non è, cara nutrice.
55　Lassa me, simil sono a quella inferma
che d'algente rigor la notte è scossa,
poi su 'l mattin d'ardente febre avampa:
perché non prima cessa il freddo gelo
del notturno timor, ch'in me s'accende
60　l'amoroso desio che m'arde e strugge.
Ben sai tu, mia fedel, che 'l primo giorno
che Torrismondo a gli occhi miei s'offerse,

than it is to myself. I yearn and dread,
I'll not deny it: but I know what I desire;
25   what frightens me, I know not. Shadows and dreams I fear,
and ancient portents, new monstrosities in nature,
old promises and new ones, or better, threats
of fortune, heaven, hostile fate,
conspiring stars; and, woe is me, I fear
30   I know not what ill-omened or appalling thing
that an anguished thought instills in me,
which wakes, confounds me, and gives me pain
both night and day. Alas, no sooner do I shut
these eyes already wearied in a little sleep,
35   than does my dream unveil
shapes of horror and of fright; and now it seems
that from my side my dear spouse
is forcibly taken, and, without him, alone,
I seem to wander on a long and gloomy road;
40   now I gaze, or seem to gaze, at dripping walls,
at the marble sweating with dark blood;
now, from the ancient sepulchres,
where the high queens of this kingdom were entombed,
rises a mighty effigy and a loud roar,
45   like a great giant, turning
Olympus, Pelion and Ossa against the heavens,
and drives me from my bed, revealing to me,
that I may flee there from a bloody scourge,
a frightful cave, and then shuts off behind me
50   the way I came; wherefore, it is no wonder,
dear nurse, if I fear sleep
and rest—rather, the dread assault
of the nocturnal specters in the dark,
and if I often rise to meet the dawn.
55   Poor me, I'm like an invalid,
shaken at night by shivers of deep cold,
burning with fever the morning after:
for no sooner does the icy frost
of nocturnal fear cease, than the amorous desire
60   that burns and consumes me is enkindled in me.
Full well you know, my loyal nurse, that the first day
when Torrismondo offered himself to my eyes,

detto a me fu che dal famoso regno
de' fieri Goti era venuto al nostro
65 de la Norvegia, ed al mio padre istesso,
per richiedermi in moglie: onde mi piacque
tanto quel suo magnanimo sembiante
e quella sua virtù per fama illustre,
ch'obliai quasi le promesse e l'onta.
70 Perch'io promesso aveva al vecchio padre
di non voler, di non gradir pregata
nobile amante o cavaliero o sposo,
che di far non giurasse aspra vendetta
del suo morto figliuolo e mio fratello;
75 e 'l confermai nel dì solenne e sacro
in cui già nacque e poi con destro fato
ei prese la corona e 'l manto adorno,
e ne rinova ogni anno e festa e pompa,
che quasi diventò pompa funèbre.
80 Quante promesse e giuramenti a l'aura
tu spargi, Amor, qual fumo oscuro od ombra!
Io del piacer di quella prima vista
così presa restai, ch'avria precorso
il mio pronto voler tardo consiglio,
85 se non mi ritenea con duro freno
rimembranza, vergogna, ira e disdegno.
Ma poiché meco egli tentò parlando
d'amore il guado, e pur vendetta io chiesi:
chiesi vendetta, ed ebbi fede in pegno
90 di vendetta e d'amor; mi diedi in preda
al suo volere, al mio desir tiranno,
e prima quasi fui che sposa, amante;
e me n'avidi a pena. E come poscia
l'alto mio genitor con ricca dote
95 suo genero il facesse; e come in segno
di casto amor e di costante fede
la sua destra ei porgesse a la mia destra;
come pensasse di voler le nozze
celebrar in Arane, e corre i frutti
100 del matrimonio nel paterno regno,
e di sua gente e di sua madre i prieghi
mi fosser porti e loro usanza esposta,

I was told that from the famous kingdom
of the proud Goths he had come to our realm,
65   of Norway, and to my own father
to ask my hand in marriage: whence, I was so taken
with that generous countenance
and that virtue made illustrious by fame,
I almost forgot my vows and my shame.
70   For I had promised to my aged father
that I, if asked, would not desire, or take
if sought, a noble lover, knight or spouse
who would not swear to wreak revenge
for his dead son, my brother;
75   and this I confirmed on the same solemn, sacred day
when my brother was born and, by propitious fate,
my father took the crown and the royal mantle,
the day in which each year pomp and festivity is renewed,
though since the pomp has turned almost funereal.
80   How many promises and oaths you scatter
on the wind, O Love, like black smoke or black shadows!
I was so taken with the pleasure
of that first sight, that my quick will
would have run on ahead of tardy reason
85   if remembrance, shame, anger and disdain
had not restrained me with their steely bit.
But when he tried, by talking to me,
to cross the ford of love, I asked for vengeance.
Yes, revenge I craved, and was assured a pledge
90   of revenge and love; I surrendered, a prey
to his will, to my own tyrannous desire,
and was almost a lover before being a bride,
though almost unawares. And how, afterwards,
my noble father with a rich dowry
95   made him his son-in-law; and how as a sign
of pure love and firm loyalty
he stretched his right hand out to mine;
how he decided to celebrate the nuptials
in Arana, and reap the fruits
100   of marriage in his father's kingdom;
how his people's and his mother's prayers
were brought me and their rites explained

tutto è già noto a voi. Noto è pur anco
che pria ch'al porto di Talarma insieme
105   raccogliesse le navi, in riva al mare,
in erma riva e 'n solitaria arena,
come sposo non già, ma come amante,
ei fece le furtive occulte nozze,
che sotto l'ombre ricoprì la notte,
110   e ne l'alto silenzio; e fuor non corse
la fama e 'l suono del notturno amore,
ch' in lui tosto s'estinse; e nullo il seppe,
se non forse sol tu, che nel mio volto
de la vergogna conoscesti i segni.
115   Or poi che giunti siam ne l'alta reggia
de' magnanimi Goti, ov'è l'antica
suocera, che da me nipoti attende,
che s'aspetti non so, né che s'agogni;
ma si ritarda il desiato giorno.
120   Già venti volte è il sol tuffato in grembo,
da che giungemmo, a l'ocean profondo,
e pur anco s'indugia; ed io fratanto
(deggio 'l dire o tacer?), lassa, mi struggo
come tenera neve in colle aprico.

NUTRICE

125   Regina, come or vano il timor vostro
e 'l notturno spavento in voi mi sembra,
così giusta cagion mi par che v'arda
d'amoroso desio; né dee turbarvi
il vostro amor: ché giovanetta donna
130   che per giovane sposo in cor non senta
qualche flamma d'amore, è più gelata
che dura neve in orrida alpe il verno.
Ma la santa onestà temprar dovrebbe
e l'onesta vergogna ardor soverchio,
135   perch'ei s'asconda a' desiosi amanti.
Ma non sarà più lungo omai l'indugio,
ché già s'aspetta qui, se 'l vero intendo,
de la Suezia il re di giorno in giorno.

all this is already known to you. You also know
how he, before he gathered the ships
105   at Talarma's port, by the seashore
on a deserted beach, on lonely sand,
not as a husband yet, but as a lover,
he carried on the furtive secret nuptials
which the night covered in its shadows
110   and amid deep silence; and no word
nor rumor of our nocturnal bliss spread forth,
love that in him was soon to be extinguished
and no one knew of it, save you alone,
who read the signs of shame upon my face.
115   And now we have arrived in the high palace
of the great-hearted Goths, where dwells my aged
mother-in-law, who awaits grandchildren from me,
I do not know what we are waiting for, nor what we crave;
in the meantime the hoped-for day is still delayed.
120   The sun has plunged already twenty times,
since we arrived, in the deep ocean's lap,
and still we tarry. But I meanwhile
(should I speak or keep silent?) oh me, am wasting away
like freshly fallen snow on a sunny hill.

NURSE

125   Queen, just as your fear
and nocturnal torment now seem vain,
so it seems that a just cause, as I can see,
is burning you up with love's desire;
but do not let your love distress you: a young woman
130   who for her youthful bridegroom does not feel
some flame of love in her heart is colder
than hard-packed snow in winter on a horrid Alpine peak.
But blessed honesty, as well as honest modesty,
should temper excessive ardor,
135   so that it may be hidden from eager lovers.
But there will be no further long delay,
for, any day now, if what I hear is true,
the king of Sweden is expected here.

ALVIDA

Sollo, e più la tardanza ancor molesta
140   me per la sua cagion. Così vendetta
veggio del sangue mio? così del padre
consolar posso l'ostinato affanno
e placar del fratel l'ombra dolente?
Posso e voglio così? Non lece adunque
145   premere il letto marital se prima
a noi d'Olma non viene il re Germondo,
di tutta la mia stirpe aspro nemico?

NUTRICE

Amico è del tuo re; né dee la moglie
amare e disamar co 'l proprio affetto,
150   ma con le voglie sol del suo marito.

ALVIDA

Siasi come a voi pare; a voi concedo
questo assai volentier, ch'io voglio e deggio
d'ogni piacer di lui far mio diletto.
Così potessi pur qualche favilla
155   estinguer del mio foco e de la flamma,
o piacer tanto a lui, ch'ad altro intende,
ch'egli pur ne sentisse eguale ardore.
Lassa, ch'in van ciò bramo e 'n van l'attendo,
né mi bisogna ancor pungente ferro
160   che nel letto divida i nostri amori
e i soverchi diletti. Ei già mi sembra
schivo di me per disdegnoso gusto:
perché da quella notte a me dimostro
non ha segno di sposo o pur d'amante.
165   Madre, io pur ve 'l dirò, benché vergogna
affreni la mia lingua e risospinga
le mie parole indietro. A lui sovente
prendo la destra e m'avicino al fianco:
ei trema, e tinge di pallore il volto,
170   che sembra (onde mi turba e mi sgomenta)
pallidezza di morte e non d'amore;

ALVIDA

I know, and the delay distresses me
140   all the more for this reason. Is this how
I see my blood avenged? Is this how
I am to comfort my father's persistent grief,
and placate my brother's grieving shade?
Can I—do I—want this? Is it not licit, then,
145   to enter the nuptial bed unless
King Germondo first comes to us from Olma—
he, the arch-enemy of my whole race?

NURSE

He is a friend of your king; and a wife
must neither love nor cease to love as she pleases,
150   but only according as her spouse desires.

ALVIDA

Let it be as you say; this I grant you
most willingly—that I want and must
make his every delight my own pleasure.
If only that way I could quench but one spark
155   of my fire and my flame,
or so please him whose mind's on other things,
as to make him, in turn, feel an equal passion.
Oh me, in vain do I long for this and vainly I await it,
nor do I yet need the piercing iron
160   to keep our loves apart in bed
and the excessive pleasures. Already he seems
to avoid me in a disdainful manner
for since that night he has not shown me again
a sign of how a spouse or even a lover behaves.
165   Mother, I nonetheless will tell you, although shame
restrains my tongue and strives to hold
my words in thrall. Often I take
his hand in mine and move close to his side:
he trembles, and his face takes on a pallor
170   that seems (and this upsets and dismays me)
the pallor of death and not of love;

o 'n altra parte il volge, o 'l china a terra,
turbato e fosco; e se talor mi parla,
parla in voci tremanti, e co' sospiri
175   le parole interrompe.

NUTRICE

O figlia, i segni
narrate voi d'ardente intenso amore.
Tremare, impallidir, timidi sguardi,
timide voci e sospirar parlando
scopron talora un desioso amante.
180   E se non mostra ancor l'istesse voglie
che mostrò già ne le deserte arene,
sai che la solitudine e la notte
sono sproni d'amore ond'ei trascorra;
ma lo splendor del sole, il suon, la turba
185   del palagio real sovente apporta
lieta vergogna, in aspettando un giorno
che per gioia maggior tanto ritarda.
E s'egli era in quel lido amante ardito,
accusar non si dee perch'or si mostri
190   modesto sposo ne l'antica reggia.

REGINA*

Piaccia a Dio che sia vero. Io pur fra tanto,
poi ch'altro non mi lece, almen conforto
dal rimirarlo prendo. Or vengo in parte
ov'egli star sovente ha per costume,
195   in queste adorne logge o 'n questo campo
ov'altri i suoi destrier sospinge e frena,
altri gli muove a salti o volge in cerchio.

NUTRICE

Altra stanza, regina, a voi conviensi,
vergine ancor, non che fanciulla e donna.
200   Ben ha camere ornate il vostro albergo,

---

*Alvida

or he averts his glance elsewhere, or he looks down,
perturbed and dismal; and if at times he speaks to me,
he speaks with a trembling voice,
175   and interrupts his words with sighs.

NURSE

Dear daughter,
you describe the signs of a burning, intense love.
Trembling, growing pale, shy glances,
a timid voice and sighs while talking
reveal at times a lover full of desire.
180   And if he does not show the same desire
he once revealed to you on those deserted sands,
you know that solitude and night
are spurs of love that make one transgress;
whereas daylight, the bustle, and the throng
185   of the royal palace often bring
welcome shame as you await the day
so long delayed to make your bliss far greater.
And if he was a bold lover on that shore,
you must not blame him now if he appears
190   a modest husband in his ancient palace.

QUEEN [ALVIDA]

Please God that it be true! I still, meanwhile,
since I can do nothing else, find some solace
in looking at him. Now I come to the place
where customarily he often stays—
195   these pleasant loggias, or this field
where people spur and curb their steeds,
and others make them trot or circle around.

NURSE

Another place would be more suited to you, O queen,
a maiden still, a child still, yet a woman.
200   Your mansion has many pleasant rooms,

ove potrete, accompagnata o sola,
spesso mirarlo dal balcon soprano.

SCENA SECONDA

NUTRICE sola.

Non so ch'in terra sia tranquillo stato
o pacifico sì, che no 'l perturbi
205 o speranza o timore o gioia o doglia;
né grandezza sì ferma, o nel suo merto
fondata o nel favor d'alta fortuna,
che l'incostante non atterri o crolli
o non minacci. Ecco felice donna
210 pur dianzi, e tanto più quanto men seppe
di sua prosperità, che nata a pena
fu in alto seggio di fortuna assisa.
Ed or, quando parea che più benigno
le fosse il cielo e più le stelle amiche,
215 per l'alte nozze sue teme e paventa,
e s'adira in un tempo e si disdegna.
Ma dove amor comanda è l'odio estinto,
e cedon l'ire antiche al novo foco.
E s'al casto e soave e dolce ardore
220 si dilegua lo sdegno, ancor si sgombri
il sospetto e la tema; e poi ch'elegge
d'amar quel ch'ella deve, amor le giovi.
Ami felicemente; e 'l lieto corso
di questa vita, che trapassa e fugge,
225 non l'interrompa mai l'invida sorte,
che far subito suole il tempo rio.
Ma temo del contrario, e mi spaventa
del suo timor cagione antica occulta,
non sol novo timor, ch'è quasi un segno
230 di futura tempesta; e l'atre nubi
risolver si potranno al fin in pianto,

where you'll be able, in company or alone,
often to look at him from the balcony above.

SCENE TWO

NURSE (alone)

I wonder if on earth there is a tranquil
or a peaceful state that is not disturbed
205   by hope or fear or joy or pain;
or a greatness so solid, so well founded in its merits
or in the favor of good fortune,
that the inconstant goddess does not fell or quake
or threaten. Here is a woman
210   who until now was happy—and more so while she did not know
her happiness—and who, as soon as she was born,
was placed by fortune on a lofty throne.
And now just when it seemed that heaven
and the stars were still more friendly to her,
215   she fears for her own royal wedding, and trembles,
and grows angry and disdainful both at once.
But where love rules hate lives no more,
and ancient wrath surrenders to new fire.
And if before a chaste, sweet, gentle passion
220   hostility gives way, let suspicion
and fear also vanish; and since she chooses
to love the man she must, may love be kind to her.
May she love happily; and may the happy course
of this life, which passes and flees away,
225   never be interrupted by envious fate
that suddenly can turn joy into grief.
But I fear the opposite, and am afraid
of some old, hidden cause of her terror,
not only of her new fear, almost a sign
230   of an impending storm; and the gloomy clouds
may ultimately lead to tears

se legitimo amor non solve il nembo.
Ma ecco il re, cui la regina aspetta.

SCENA TERZA

TORRISMONDO RE, CONSIGLIERO.

[TORRISMONDO]

Ahi, quando mai la Tana o 'l Reno o l'Istro,
235   o l'inospite mare o 'l mar vermiglio,
o l'onde caspe o l'ocean profondo
potrian lavar occulta e 'ndegna colpa
che mi tinse e macchiò le membra e l'alma?
Vivo ancor dunque, e spiro e veggio il sole?
240   Ne la luce del mondo ancor dimoro?
e re son detto, e cavalier m'appello?
La spada al fianco io porto, in man lo scettro
ancor sostegno, e la corona in fronte?
E pur v'è chi m'inchina e chi m'assorge,
245   e forse ancor chi m'ama: ahi, quelli è certo
che del suo fido amor coglie tal frutto.
Ma che mi giova, oimè, s'al core infermo
spiace la vita, e se ben dritto estimo
ch'indegnamente a me questa aura spiri
250   e 'ndegnamente il sole a me risplenda;
se 'l titolo real, la pompa e l'ostro,
e 'l diadema gemmato e d'or lucente,
e la sonora fama e 'l nome illustre
di cavalier m'offende, e tutti insieme
255   pregi, onori, servigio io schivo e sdegno;
e se me stesso in guisa odio ed aborro
che ne l'essere amato offesa io sento?
Lasso, io ben me n'andrei per l'erme arene
solingo, errante; e ne l'Ercinia folta
260   e ne la negra selva, o 'n rupe o 'n antro
riposto e fosco d'iperborei monti,

unless legitimate love dispels the storm.
But here comes the king my queen is waiting for.

SCENE THREE

KING TORRISMONDO, COUNSELOR

[TORRISMONDO]

Oh, when will the Don or Rhine or Danube,
235   or the unfriendly sea or the Red Sea,
or the Caspian waves or the ocean deep
ever wash the hidden and unworthy guilt
that stained and soiled my limbs and soul?
Do I live still then, and breathe and see the sun?
240   In the light of the world do I live still?
Am I still known as king, still call myself a knight?
Do I carry the sword at my side still, hold the sceptre
in my hand, and wear the crown upon my head?
And are there still people who bow and rise to meet me,
245   and perhaps love me still: oh, he alone is sure
who of his faithful love gathers such fruit.
But what good is it to me, alas, if to this sickened heart
life is unwelcome, and if most rightly I believe
that this breeze wafts for me undeservedly,
250   and I am not worthy that the sun should shine
if the royal title, the pomp and purple cloak,
and the bejewelled tiara shining with gold,
and the resounding and illustrious title
of knight offend me; and praise,
255   honors, homage I altogether shun and abhor;
and if I hate and loathe myself in such a way
as to feel offended by my being loved?
Alas, readily would I go through lonely sands,
alone and wandering; and in thick Ercinia
260   and in the Black Forest, or over the rocks and caves,
hidden and gloomy, of the Hyperborean Mountains,

o di ladroni in orrida spelunca,
m'asconderei da gli altri, il dì fuggendo,
e da le stelle e dal seren notturno.
265   Ma che mi può giovar, s'io non m'ascondo
a me medesmo? Oimè, son io, son io,
quel che fuggito or sono e quel che fuggo:
di me stesso ho vergogna e scorno ed onta,
odioso a me fatto e grave pondo.
270   Che giova ch'io non oda e non paventi
i detti e 'l mormorar del folle volgo,
o l'accuse de' saggi, o i fieri morsi
di troppo acuto o velenoso dente,
se la mia propria conscienza immonda
275   altamente nel cor rimbomba e mugge;
s'ella a vespro mi sgrida ed a le squille;
se mi sveglia le notti e rompe il sonno
e mille miei confusi e tristi sogni?
Misero me, non Cerbero, non Scilla
280   così latrò come io ne l'alma or sento
il suo fiero latrar; non mostro od angue
ne l'Africa arenosa, od Idra in Lerna,
o di Furia in Cocito empia cerasta
morse giamai com'ella rode e morde.

CONSIGLIERO

285   Se la fede, o signor, mostrata in prima
ne le fortune liete e ne l'averse
porger può tanto ardire ad umil servo
ch'osi pregare il suo signor tal volta
perch'i pensieri occulti a lui riveli,
290   io prego voi che del turbato aspetto
scopriate la cagion, gli affanni interni,
e qual commesso abbiate errore o colpa
che tanto sdegno in voi raccolga e 'nfiammi
contra voi stesso, e sì v'aggravi e turbi:
295   ché di lungo silenzio è grave il peso
in sofferendo, e co 'l soffrir s'inaspra,
ma si consola in ragionando e molce;
ed uom ch'al fin deporre in fidi orecchi

or in the horrid dens of highwaymen
I would hide myself from others, shunning the daylight,
and from the stars and the clear nighttime skies.
265   But what use is it to me if I cannot hide
from myself? Oh me, it is I, it is I,
whom I have just now fled from and who flees:
shame, disgrace, and abomination
have made me hateful and a grievous burden to myself.
270   What does it avail me that I do not hear and fear
the rumors and the grumbling of the foolish crowd,
the charges of the wise, or the fierce bites
of very sharp or poisoned tooth,
if my own befouled conscience
275   resounds and bellows in the depths of my heart;
if it chides me in the evening and at the morning bells;
if it awakens me at night and interrupts my sleep
and my thousand confused, and joyless dreams?
Wretched me! Never did Cerberus nor Scylla
280   bark so much as this savage barking
I hear in my soul; neither monster nor snake
in sandy Africa, or in Lernaean Hydra,
or a Fury's horrid serpent in Cocytus
ever bit as my conscience now gnaws and bites.

COUNSELOR

285   My lord, if faith, already shown
in favorable as well as adverse fortune,
can lend such boldness to a humble servant
that from time to time, he dares to beg his master
to reveal his hidden thoughts to him,
290   I beg you to lay bare the reason
for your troubled look, for your inner anguish,
and whatever mistake or sin you might have committed,
capable of amassing and kindling such rage in you
against yourself, afflicting and troubling you so:
295   for heavy is the burden of long silence
in sorrow, and it worsens with new sorrow,
and is only consoled and assuaged by speech;
he who, confiding, finally dares

il noioso pensier parlando ardisca,
300   l'alma sua alleggia d'aspra e dura salma.

TORRISMONDO

O mio fedele, a cui l'alto governo
di mia tenera età conceder volle
il re mio padre e signor vostro antico,
ben mi ricordo i detti e i modi e l'opre
305   onde voi mi scorgeste; e quai sovente
mi proponeste ancor dinanzi a gli occhi
d'onestà, di virtù mirabil forme,
e quai di regi o di guerrieri essempi,
che ne l'arti di pace o di battaglia
310   furon lodati; e qual acuto sprone
di generosa invidia il cor mi punse,
e qual di vero onor dolce lusinga
invaghir mi solea. Ma troppo accresce
questa dolce memoria il duolo acerbo,
315   ché quanto io dal sentier che voi segnaste
mi veggio traviato esser più lunge,
tanto più contra me di sdegno avampo.
E s'ad alcun, fra quanti il sol rimira
o la terra sostiene o 'l mar circonda,
320   per vergogna celar dovessi il fallo,
esser voi quel devreste: alti consigli
da voi già presi, e poi gittai e sparsi.
Ma 'l vostro amor, la fede un tempo esperta,
l'etate e 'l senno e quella amica speme
325   che del vostro consiglio ancor m'avanza,
conforti al dir mi son, benché paventa
e 'norridisce a ricordarsi il core,
e per dolor rifugge, onde sdegnosa
s'induce a ragionar la tarda lingua:
330   però in disparte io v'ho chiamato e lunge.
Devete rammentar ch'uscito a pena
di fanciullezza, e di quel fren disciolto
che già teneste voi soave e dolce,
fui vago di mercar fama ed onore:
335   onde lasciai la patria e 'l nobil padre

entrust his troubled thoughts to faithful ears,
300   relieves his soul of a harsh, oppressive weight.

TORRISMONDO

My faithful servant, to whom
the king my father and your former lord
wished to entrust the lofty guidance of my tender age,
well I remember the words, the ways and deeds
305   with which you guided me, and how you often
displayed before my eyes
wondrous examples of honesty and virtue,
and what examples of regal and warlike virtue
praised for their arts of peace or for their skill
310   in battle; and like a sharp spur
they pierced my heart with warming emulation,
and, as a pleasant allurement of true honor,
they used to enamor me. But this sweet memory
too much augments the sharpness of my pain,
315   for the further I see myself astray
from the path you showed me
the more do I flare up in wrath against myself.
And if from any one the sun shines on
and the earth nourishes or the sea surrounds,
320   I ought to hide my fault in shame,
you should be that one: noble advice
I took from you, only to cast and strew it on the ground.
And yet your love, the trust I once enjoyed,
your age, your wisdom, and the friendly hope
325   of your counsel that is still left to me
are comfort to my words, though my heart
is frightened and shies with horror at the very thought,
and balks for grief; wherefore only reluctantly
my tardy tongue can be convinced to speak:
330   that's why I called you aside and out of hearing.
You must recall, as soon as I emerged
from childhood, and was freed of
that soft and gentle curb you held on me,
how eagerly I wished to seek out fame and honor:
335   therefore, I left my native land, my noble father,

e gli eccelsi palagi, e vidi errando
vari estrani costumi e genti strane;
e sconosciuto e solo io fui sovente
ove il ferro s'adopra e sparge il sangue.
340 In quelli errori miei, com'al Ciel piacque,
mi strinsi d'amicizia in dolce nodo
co 'l buon Germondo ch'a Suezia impera,
giovene anch'egli, e pur di gloria ardente
e pien d'alto desio d'eterna fama.
345 Seco i Tartari erranti e seco i Moschi,
cercando i paludosi e larghi campi,
seco i Sarmati i' vidi e i Rossi e gli Unni,
e de la gran Germania i lidi e i monti;
seco a l'estremo gli ultimi Biarmi
350 vidi tornando, e quel sì lungo giorno
a cui succede poi sì lunga notte;
ed altre parti de la terra algente
che ghiaccia a' sette gelidi Trioni,
tutta lontana dal camin del sole.
355 Seco de la milizia i gravi affanni
soffersi, e seco ebbi commune un tempo
non men gravi fatiche e gran perigli
che ricche prede e gloriose palme,
da nemici acquistate e da tiranni:
360 onde sovente in perigliosa guerra
egli scudo mi fé del proprio petto
e mi sottrasse a dispietata morte,
ed io talor, là dove amor n'aguaglia,
la vita mia per la sua vita esposi.
365 Ma, dapoi che moriro i padri nostri,
sendo al governo de' lasciati regni
richiamati ambodue, gli offici e l'opre
non cessar d'amicizia, anzi disgiunti
di loco, e più che mai di core uniti,
370 cogliemmo ancor di lei frutti soavi.
Misero, or vengo a quel che mi tormenta.
Questo mio caro e valoroso amico,
pria che facesse elezione e sorte
noi de l'arme compagni e de gli errori,
375 trasse in Norvegia a la famosa giostra,

and these lofty palaces, and, wandering, I saw
many strange customs and foreign people;
a stranger and alone, I often lived
where swords are wielded and where blood is shed.

340   In those travels of mine, as it pleased Heaven,
I formed a close and sweet friendship
with the good Germondo who rules over Sweden—
young like me and, like me, eager for glory
and nobly yearning for eternal fame.

345   Scouring the marshy and the open tracts,
with him I saw the nomad Tartars and the Muscovites,
with him I saw the Sarmatians, the Russians and the
    Huns,
and the shores and mountains of great Germany;
and as we returned together, in the far North

350   I saw the furthermost Biarmians, and that long day
followed by a no less lengthy night;
and other parts of the frigid earth
that lies frozen beneath the seven icy stars of the Great
    Bear,
far, far away from the course of the sun.

355   With him I bore the soldier's heavy lot,
with him I had in common once,
no less heavy travails and great perils
than copious spoils and glorious victories
earned in the fight with enemies and tyrants:

360   from whom often, in perilous battles,
he shielded me with his own chest
and rescued me from many a merciless death,
and often I, in turn, where love makes us equals,
I risked my life for his.

365   But, after our fathers died,
after each of us was called to rule
the kingdoms we inherited, the duties and deeds
of friendship did not die; on the contrary, though separated
by distance but more than ever united in spirit,

370   friendship's sweet fruits we reaped still.
Oh wretched me, now I have come to that which vexes me.
This dear and valiant friend of mine,
before election and chance made us
companions in arms and in our wanderings,

375   had come to Norway for the famous joust

ond'ebbe ei poscia fra mille altri il pregio.
Ivi in sì forte punto a gli occhi suoi
si dimostrò la fanciulletta Alvida,
ch'egli sentissi in su la prima vista
380   l'alma avampar d'inestinguibil fiamma.
E bench'ei far non possa, o non ardisca,
che fuor traluca del suo ardor favilla
che da gli occhi di lei sia vista e piaccia,
pur nudrì nel suo core ardente foco.
385   Né lunghezza di tempo o di camino,
né rischio, né disagio, né fatica,
né veder novi regni e nove genti,
selve, monti, campagne e fiumi e mari,
né di nova beltà novo diletto,
390   né s'altro è, che d'amor la face estingua,
intepediro i suoi amorosi incendi.
Ma, de' pensieri esca facendo al foco,
tutto quel tempo a gli altri il tenne occulto
ch'errò per varie parti; e del suo core
395   secretari sol fummo Amore ed io.
Ma poiché richiamato al nobil regno
egli s'assise ne l'antico seggio,
l'animo a le sue nozze anco rivolto,
mille strade tentando, usò mille arti,
400   mille mezzi adoprò, mille preghiere
or come re porgendo, or come amante,
liberal di promesse e largo d'oro,
sol per indur d'Alvida il vecchio padre
che la sua figlia al suo pregar conceda;
405   ma indurato il trovò di core e d'alma:
perché, d'ingegno, di costumi e d'opre
altero il re canuto, anzi superbo,
di natura implacabile, e tenace
d'ogni proposto, e di vendetta ingordo,
410   la pace ricusò con gente aversa
da cui tal volta depredato ed arso
vide il suo regno, e violati i tempi,
dispogliati gli altari, e tratti i figli
da le cune piangendo, e da' sepolcri
415   le ceneri de gli avi e sparse al vento.

in which he was victorious over thousands.
There, the young maiden Alvida appeared
with such intensity before his eyes
that he felt, at first sight,
380   his soul burn with an unquenchable flame.
And, though he could not or he did not dare
allow any spark of his flame to glimmer forth
when her eyes could have seen it and been pleased,
nonetheless, in his heart he nourished a burning fire.
385   And neither length of time or travel,
risk or hardship or toil,
nor the sight of new kingdoms and new peoples,
woods, mountains, fields, rivers and seas,
nor any new beauty's new delight,
390   or anything else designed to kill love's flame
could cool the raging fire in his breast.
But, with his thoughts as tinder to that fire,
all of the time he roamed in different lands,
he kept the secret; and of his heart,
395   the only confidants were love and I.
But when, recalled to his noble kingdom,
he sat upon the ancient throne,
and his thoughts turned to marriage once again,
trying a thousand paths, he used a thousand wiles,
400   a thousand ways, a thousand entreaties,
presented now as king and now as lover,
lavish with promises and generous with gold,
only to convince Alvida's aged father
that he should grant his daughter to his prayers;
405   but he found him inflexible in heart and soul:
for the gray-haired monarch, proud, utterly scornful
in mind and manners and deeds,
ever tenacious in every decision,
and implacable by nature, and thirsty for revenge,
410   refused peace with his enemies
by whose hand he had often seen his kingdom
plundered and burned, temples profaned,
altars stripped, and crying infants
snatched from their cradles, and ancestors' ashes
415   seized from their tombs and cast upon the wind;

Da cui, non ch'altri, un suo figliuol medesmo,
senza lagrime no, né senza lutto,
ma pur senza vendetta, anciso giacque
orribilmente; e l'uccisor Germondo
420   egli stimò ne la sanguigna mischia,
non l'essercito solo o solo il volgo.
E veramente ei fu ch'in aspra guerra
n'ebbe le spoglie, e pur non volle il vanto.
Poiché sprezzare ed aborrir si vide
425   de l'inclita Suezia il re possente,
par che dentro arda tutto, e fuori avampi
di giusto sdegno incontra il fiero veglio,
che di lui fatto avea l'aspro rifiuto.
Non però per divieto o per repulsa,
430   o per ira o per odio o per contrasto,
del primo amore intepidì pur dramma.
E ben è ver che ne gli umani ingegni,
e più ne' più magnanimi e più alteri,
per la difficoltà cresce il desio
435   in guisa d'acqua che rinchiusa ingorga,
o pur di fiamma in cavernoso monte,
ch'aperto non ritrova uscendo il varco
e di ruine il ciel tonando ingombra.
Dunque ei fermato è di voler, malgrado
440   del crudo padre, la pudica figlia,
e di piegar, comunque il ciel si volga
e sia fermo il destin, varia la sorte,
la donna; o di morir ne l'alta impresa.
D'acquistarla per furto o per rapina
445   dispose; e mille modi in sé volgendo
ora d'accorgimento ed or di forza,
al fin gli altri rifiuta, e questo elegge.
Per un secreto suo fido messaggio
e per lettere sue con forti prieghi
450   mi strinse a dimandar la figlia al padre,
e avutala poi con sì bella arte,
la concedessi a lui, che n'era amante,
né re saria di re genero indegno.
Io, se ben conoscea che questo inganno
455   irritati gli sdegni e forse l'arme

by whose hand, none other than his very son,
not without tears, not without mourning,
but still without revenge, lay robbed of life
most horribly; and he held Germondo
420   to be the killer in that bloody fight,
and not the army or the common troops alone.
And truly it was he who in bitter war
had had the trophies, though he refused the boast.
Seeing himself despised and loathed,
425   the mighty king of famous Sweden
seemed to be on fire within, but flared without,
filled with just wrath against the proud old man
who had rejected him so harshly.
But not for all the father's veto and rejection,
430   not for his wrath, his hatred, or his opposition,
did his first love abate in the least its heat.
And true it is that in the human mind,
and more in the most magnanimous and proud,
hardship makes desire grow,
435   like water that, when trapped, will form a whirlpool,
or, like fire inside a hollow mountain
that cannot find an exit,
and, thundering, engulfs the sky with debris.
Therefore he is determined, despite her cruel father,
440   to have the virtuous daughter,
and, however the sky may turn and fate be fixed
and fortune change, to bend his lady to him,
or die in the great attempt.
He decided to win her by deception
445   or by abduction; and pondering within himself
a thousand means, now of force, now of cleverness,
he finally rejected the others and chose this one.
By means of letters carried in secret
by a loyal messenger, he strongly urged me
450   to ask her father for his daughter's hand;
and having had her by such an ingenious deception,
that I then give her to him who was her lover,
nor would he, a king, be a son-in-law unworthy of a king.
Though well aware that this deception
455   would rouse the wrath, perhaps the arms

incontra me de la Norvegia avrebbe,
estimai ch'ove è scritto, ove s'intenda
d'onorata amicizia il caro nome,
quel che meno per sé parrebbe onesto
460   acquisti d'onestà quasi sembianti;
e se ragion mai violar si debbe,
sol per l'amico violar si debbe;
ne l'altre cose poi giustizia osserva.
E posposi al piacer del caro amico
465   l'altrui pace e la mia, tanto mi piacque
divenir disleal per troppa fede.
Questo fisso tra me, non per messaggi,
né con quell'arti che sovente usarsi
soglion tra gli alti regi in pace o 'n guerra,
470   del suocero tentai la stabil mente;
ma gli indugi troncai: rapido corsi
del mio voler messaggio e di me stesso.
Ei gradì la venuta e le proposte
e congiunse a la mia la real destra,
475   ed a me diede e ricevé la fede
ch'io di non osservar prefisso avea.
Ed io tolto congedo, e la mia donna
posta su l'alte navi, anzi mia preda,
spiegai le vele; e ne gli aperti campi
480   per l'ondoso ocean drizzando il corso,
lasciava di Norvegia i porti e i lidi.
Noi lieti solcavamo il mar sonante,
con cento acuti rostri il mar rompendo,
e la creduta sposa al fianco affissa
485   m'invitava ad amar pensosa amando.
Ben in me stesso io mi raccolsi e strinsi,
in guisa d'uomo a cui d'intorno accampa
dispietato nemico. Il tempo largo,
e l'ozio lungo e lento, e 'l loco angusto,
490   e gli inviti d'amor, lusinghe e sguardi,
rossor, pallore e parlar tronco e breve
solo inteso da noi, con mille assalti
vinsero al fin la combattuta fede.
Ahi ben è ver che risospinto Amore
495   più fiero e per repulsa e per incontro

of Norway against me,
I reflected, that, wherever the dear name
of honored friendship is set down or valued,
that which seems less than honest in itself
460   may almost take the appearance of honesty;
and, if right is ever to be violated,
only for a friend should it be violated,
while in all else justice must be observed.
Thus I preferred a dear friend's happiness
465   to others' peace and to my own, so glad was I
to become disloyal out of too great loyalty.
Having made up my mind, not through ambassadors,
nor by those means that are most often used
among exalted kings in peace and war,
470   I tried the firmness of my father-in-law's mind;
and to avoid delay, I swiftly ran myself—
the messenger of my own will, my own ambassador.
He welcomed my arrival and my proposals,
and joined his royal hand to mine,
475   and gave to me, and in his turn received, that pledge
I had decided never to observe.
And after I took leave and placed my lady
—rather, my prey—upon the mighty ships,
I set sail; and in the open main,
480   through the swelling ocean waves I set my course.
I left the ports and litorals of Norway.
Gaily we ploughed the sounding sea,
breaking it with a hundred pointed prows,
while my presumed bride clung to my side,
485   loving and pensive, urging me to return her love.
Of course I withdrew and massed my forces in myself
like a man on every side besieged
by his ruthless enemy. The time on hand,
the long slow idleness, closeness of space,
490   love's invitations, flatteries and glances,
blushing, blanching, and brief and broken words
that we alone could hear, with a thousand sorties
at last overcame my long-embattled faith.
Oh, how true it is! Love, if repelled,
495   returns to the attack more fierce

ad assalir sen torna, e legge antica
è che nessuno amato amar perdoni.
Ma sedea la ragion al suo governo
ancor frenando ogni desio rubbello,
500 quando il sereno cielo a noi refulse
e folgorar da quattro parti i lampi;
e la crudel fortuna e 'l cielo averso
con Amor congiurati, e l'empie stelle
mosser gran vento e procelloso a cerchio,
505 perturbator del cielo e de la terra
e del mar violento empio tiranno,
che quanto a caso incontra intorno avolge,
gira, contorce, svelle, inalza e porta,
e poi sommerge; e ci turbaro il corso
510 tutti gli altri fremendo, e Borea ad Austro
s'oppose irato, e muggiar quinci e quindi,
e Zefiro con Euro urtossi in giostra;
e diventò di nembi e di procelle
il mar turbato un periglioso campo;
515 cinta l'aria di nubi, intorno intorno
una improvisa nacque orribil notte,
che quasi parve un spaventoso inferno,
sol da' baleni avendo il lume incerto;
e s'inalzar al ciel bianchi e spumanti
520 mille gran monti di volubile onda,
ed altrettante in mezzo al mar profondo
voragini s'aprir, valli e caverne,
e tra l'acque apparir foreste e selve
orribilmente, e tenebrosi abissi;
525 ed apparver notando i fieri mostri
con varie forme, e 'l numeroso armento
terrore accrebbe; e 'n tempestosa pioggia
pur si disciolse al fin l'oscuro nembo;
e per l'ampio ocean portò disperse
530 le combattute navi il fiero turbo;
e parte ne percosse a' duri scogli,
parte a le travi smisurate, sovra
il mar sorgenti in più terribil forma,
talché schiere parean con arme ed aste;
535 e 'n minacciose rupi o 'n ciechi sassi,

for being fended off or parried, for it is an ancient law
that no one who is loved is absolved from not loving.
But reason was still sitting at the helm
curbing every rebellious desire,
500 when all at once the clear sky blazed above us
and lightning flashed from four sides;
and cruel fortune and the hostile sky
conspiring with Love, and the evil stars
aroused a mighty, furiously whirling wind,
505 to upset earth and sky,
and violently and wickedly tyrannize the sea,
for whatever it finds in its path, it wraps itself around,
spins, twists, uproots, bears up and carries off,
and then submerges; all the other winds, raging,
510 disturbed our path, and wrathful Boreas
turned against Auster, and both howled here and there,
and Zephyr clashed with Eurus in a joust,
and the sea, whipped up, became a perilous
battlefield of squalls and storms.
515 The air all surrounded with clouds,
a sudden dreaded night arose all about,
which seemed almost a frightening hell
dimly lit by lightning alone;
and a thousand tall mountains of curving waves
520 rose white and foaming toward the sky,
and as many chasms, in the midst of the deep sea,
and valleys and caverns opened up,
and in the water forests and woods appeared,
awful to look upon, and gloomy abysses;
525 and horrible monsters in a thousand forms
appeared swimming, and the numerous herd
increased our terror; and finally the darkness
of the firmament broke down into a stormy rain,
and over the vast ocean, the fierce whirlwind
530 carried and scattered the hard-tried ships,
some of which it dashed against the rugged cliffs,
others against immense tree trunks,
rising out of the sea in the most dreadful shapes,
like troops with arms and spears;
535 and in threatening reefs or hidden rocks,

che son de' vivi ancor fiero sepolcro;
parte a le basi di montagne alpestri
sempre canute, ove risona e mugge,
mentre combatte l'un con l'altro flutto,
540 e 'l frange e 'nbianca. e come il tuon rimbomba
e di spavento i naviganti ingombra;
parte inghiotinne ancor l'empia Caribdi,
che l'onde e i legni intieri absorbe e mesce:
son rari i notatori in vasto gorgo.
545 Ma co 'l flutto maggior nubilo spirto
il nostro batte e 'l risospinge a forza,
sì ch'a gran pena il buon nocchiero accorto
lui salvò, sé ritrasse e noi raccolse
d'uno altissimo monte a' curvi flanchi,
550 dove mastra natura in guisa d'elmo
forma scolpito a meraviglia un porto,
che tutti scaccia i venti e le tempeste,
ma pur di sangue è crudelmente asperso,
fiero principio e fin d'acerba guerra.
555 Qui ricovrammo sbigotiti e mesti,
ponendo il piè nel solitario lido.
Mentre l'umide vesti altri rasciuga
ed altri accende le fumanti selve,
con Alvida io restai de l'ampia tenda
560 ne la più interna parte. E già sorgea
la notte amica de' furtivi amori,
ed ella a me si ristringea tremante
ancor per la paura e per l'affanno.
Questo quel punto fu che sol mi vinse.
565 Allora amor, furore, impeto e forza
di piacere amoroso, al cieco furto
sforzar le membra oltra l'usanza ingorde.
Ahi lasso, allor per impensata colpa
ruppi la fede, e violai d'onore
570 e d'amicizia le severe leggi.
Contaminato di novello oltraggio,
traditor fatto di fedele amico,
anzi nemico divenuto amando,
da indi in qua sono agitato, ahi lasso,
575 da mille miei pensieri, anzi da mille

that are ever a cruel tomb to the living;
some at the base of Alplike mountains,
forever white, where the sea resounds and roars
while one wave fights with the other,
540   and breaks and whitens, and like thunder roars,
and weighs the sailors down with fright;
other ships were swallowed, still, by pitiless Charybdis
who absorbs and sucks down the waves and entire ships:
rare are the swimmers in the vast vortex.
545   But with the biggest wave a new wind
struck our ship and pushed it back by force,
so that with great difficulty the brave sagacious steersman
saved her, then withdrew himself and gathered us
within the curving shelter of a most lofty mountain's
    flanks,
550   where Mother Nature marvellously shaped
a port carved in the form of a helmet
which drives all winds and storms away,
but yet its walls are cruelly stained with blood—
the fierce beginning and end of a bitter war.
555   Here we found refuge, bewildered and subdued,
setting foot on the lonely shore.
While some dry their wet garments
and others kindle the smoky wood,
with Alvida I remained in the innermost part
560   of the spacious tent. And already the night,
friend to furtive loves, was climbing the sky
and, trembling with fear and exhaustion,
she was still clinging to me.
This was the one moment that won me over.
565   This was when love, passion, and the impetuous force
of love's pleasure forced my limbs,
greedy beyond their wont, to the blind theft.
Oh woe is me, it was then that with unpremeditated sin
I broke my promise, and violated the stern laws
570   of honor and friendship.
Contaminated by new outrage,
now a faithful friend no more, I was a traitor,
or, rather, an enemy because of love.
I have been troubled, ever since, alas,
575   by a thousand thoughts, or, worse, by a thousand

vermi di penitenza io son trafitto,
non sol roder mi sento il core e l'alma,
né mai da' miei furori o pace o tregua
ritrovar posso. O Furie, o dire, o mie
580   debite pene, e de' non giusti falli
giuste vendicatrici! Ove ch'io volga
gli occhi, o giri la mente e 'l mio pensiero,
l'atto che ricoprì l'oscura notte
mi s'appresenta, e parmi in chiara luce
585   a tutti gli occhi de' mortali esposto.
Ivi mi s'offre in spaventosa faccia
il mio tradito amico, odo l'accuse
e le giuste querele, odo i lamenti,
l'amor suo, la costanza, ad uno ad uno
590   tanti merti, tante opre e tante prove
che fatte egli ha d'inviolabil fede.
Misero me, tra i duri artigli e i morsi
d'impura conscienza e di dolore,
gli amorosi martiri han loco e parte;
595   e di lasciar la male amata donna,
che lasciar converria, così m'incresce,
che di lasciar la vita insieme io penso.
Questo il più facil modo, e questa sembra
la più spedita via d'uscir d'impaccio.
600   E poi che 'l duro, inestricabil nodo,
ond'amore e fortuna or m'hanno involto,
sciogliere più non si può, s'incida e spezzi.
Ch'avrei questo conforto almen partendo
da questa luce a me turbata e fosca,
605   ch'io medesmo la pena e la vendetta
farei del caro amico e di me stesso,
l'onta sua rimovendo e la mia colpa,
se rimover si può commesso fallo:
giusto in me, benché tardi, e per lui forte.

CONSIGLIERO

610   Signor, tanto ogni mal più grave è sempre
quanto è in più nobil parte, e dal soggetto
diversa qualità prende l'offesa.

worms of remorse I have been pierced,
and not only my heart and soul do I feel consumed,
but never can I find rest or peace
from my passions. O cruel Furies,
580 O my deserved pangs, rightful avengers
of my unjust faults! Wherever I turn
my eyes or my mind or my thoughts,
the deed which the dark night covered
appears before me, and seems displayed
585 in broad daylight to the eyes of all mortals.
There my betrayed friend appears
with a dreadful expression; I hear his charges
and his just complaints, I hear his laments,
his love, his constancy, and one by one
590 all of his many merits, the many deeds
and proofs of his inviolable loyalty.
Wretched me, between the cruel claws and gnawing
of a guilty conscience and of grief,
love's torture still endures;
595 and so deeply do I regret leaving the ill-loved woman,
whom I nonetheless ought to leave,
that I think I shall quit life at the same time.
This is the easiest way, and this seems
the fastest way out of this predicament.
600 And since the hard, inextricable knot,
in which love and fortune have now entangled me,
can be untied no more, let it be cut and severed.
This compensation at least I would have, leaving
the light, to me so dark and murky—
605 I myself would be responsible for my own punishment
and for avenging the wrong done to my dearest friend,
thus wiping out his shame and my guilt,
if a sin, once committed, can ever be erased:
and, however belatedly, I would prove just to myself,
and strong for his sake.

COUNSELOR

610 My Lord, the more grievous is the wrong,
the worthier the place in which it dwells; from its subject
the offense takes on a different quality.

E quinci avien che sembra un leggier colpo
ne le spalle sovente e ne le braccia
615   e ne l'altre robuste e forti membra
quel ch'a gli occhi saria gravoso, e certa
e dogliosa cagion d'acerba morte.
E però questo error, che posto in libra
per sé non fora di soverchio pondo,
620   e saria forse lieve in uom del volgo
ed in quelle amicizie al mondo usate
ov'è l'util misura angusta e scarsa,
od in quell'altre che 'l diletto accoppia,
molto (ch'io già negar no 'l voglio o posso)
625   in animo gentil grave diventa,
tra grandezza di scettri e di corone,
e tra 'l rigor di quelle sante leggi
che la vera amicizia altrui prescrisse.
Error di cavalier, di re, d'amico
630   contra sì nobil cavaliero e re,
contra amico sì caro e sì fedele
fu questo vostro; e dee chiamarsi errore,
o, se volete pur, peccato e colpa
o d'ardente desio, di cieco e folle
635   amor, si dica impetuoso affetto:
nome di scelaraggine ei non merta.
Lunge per Dio, signor, sia lunge, e sevro
da questa opra e da voi titolo indegno.
Non soggiacete a non dovuto incarco:
640   ché s'uom non dee di falsa laude ornarsi,
non dee gravarsi ancor di falso biasmo.
Non sete, no, la passion v'accieca,
o traditore o scelerato od empio.
Scelerato è colui, se dritto estimo,
645   che la nostra ragion, divina parte
e del Ciel prezioso e caro dono,
da la natura sua travolge e torce,
come si svolge il rio dal proprio corso,
e la piega nel male, onde trabocca,
650   ed incontra al voler di chi la diede
guida a l'opre la fa malvagie ed empie,
precipitando; e 'l precipizio è fraude.

And so it happens that what seems a harmless blow
on the shoulders or the arm
615   or on the other vigorous and strong limbs,
would be a serious impact to the eyes,
and a sure and painful cause of untimely death.
And so this wrong, which, if placed on a scale,
would not of itself carry excessive weight,
620   and would, perhaps, be slight in a common man
and in the kind of friendship normal in the world,
in which utility is the mean and petty measure,
or in that other kind that pleasure binds,
becomes (this I must not, cannot deny)
625   grave in a noble soul, who dwells
among the greatness of scepters and crowns,
in a world ruled by the rigor of those sacred laws
which true friendship prescribed to human kind.
Yours was the error of a knight, a king, a friend
630   against such a noble knight and king,
against a friend so dear and faithful;
and it must be called an error,
or, if you will, a sin and fault
of ardent desire, of blind and foolish love—
635   let's say impetuous affection:
but it does not deserve the name of wickedness.
Far be it, by my God, my lord, far be it,
to give this deed and you such an unworthy name.
Do not subject yourself to an unearned burden:
640   for if a man must not adorn himself with false praise,
so must he not burden himself with false blame.
Passion blinds you, but, no, you are not
treacherous or wicked or impious.
Wicked is he, if rightly I discern,
645   who distorts and turns away from its own nature
our human reason, the divine part of us,
the dear and precious gift of Heaven,
just as a stream is turned from its own course;
and who then bends it towards evil, so that it overflows its
    banks,
650   and, against the will of Him who gave it,
makes it a guide to wrong and evil deeds,
falling precipitously—and the precipice's name is fraud.

Ma chi senza fermar falso consiglio
di perversa ragion trascorra a forza
655 ove il rapisce il suo desio tiranno,
scelerato non è, per grave colpa
dove amore il trasporti o pur disdegno.
D'ira e d'amor, possenti e fieri affetti,
la nostra umanitade ivi più abonda
660 ov'è più di vigore; e rado aviene
che generoso cor guerriero ed alto
non sia spinto da loro e risospinto,
come da venti procelloso mare.
Però non ricusiate al dolor vostro
665 quel freno aver che la ragion vi porge.
Lascio tanti famosi e chiari essempi
e d'Alcide e d'Achille e d'Alessandro,
e lascio il vaneggiar de' più moderni
regi vinti d'amore, e prima invitti.
670 Vedeste bella e giovinetta donna,
e fu nel poter vostro, e non vi mosse
la bellezza ad amar: costretto o tardi
voi rispondeste a gli amorosi inviti,
dando ad amore e tre repulse e quattro:
675 raffrenaste il desio, gli sguardi e i detti.
Al fin amor, fortuna, il loco e 'l tempo
vinser tanta costanza e tanta fede.
Erraste, e fu d'Amore e vostro il fallo;
ma senza scusa almeno o senza essempio
680 egli non fu: però di morte è indegno.
Né morte, ch'uom di propria mano affretti,
scema commesso errore, anzi l'accresce.

TORRISMONDO

Se morte esser non può pena od emenda
giusta del fallo, almen del mio dolore
685 fia buon rimedio o fine.

CONSIGLIERO

Anzi principio
e cagion fora di maggior tormento.

But he who, without evil intent,
runs, swept by perverted reason
655   wherever his tyrannical desire leads him,
is not an evil man, however grave the fault
to which love may transport him or his rage.
Our human nature abounds with greater rage
and love—powerful and wicked feelings—
660   if greater is its vigor; and it seldom happens
that a generous, noble, and warrior soul
is not driven one way and the other by them
as a stormy sea is by the wind.
Therefore, do not refuse to give your grief
665   that curb which reason gives you.
I will pass over many famous and illustrious examples—
Hercules, Achilles, and Alexander;
nor will I mention the follies of more recent kings,
previously unvanquished and then won by love.
670   You saw a beautiful young woman,
and she was in your power, and you were not moved
to love by beauty: you responded to love's invitations
reluctantly and only when compelled;
you gave love any number of rebuffs,
675   curbed your desire, your glances and your words.
Finally love, fortune, the place and time
overwhelmed such constancy and such faith.
You sinned, and it was Love's sin and your own;
but the sin at least was not without excuse,
680   not without example: therefore it does not warrant death.
Nor does death, which man may hasten by his own hand,
diminish an error already committed—rather it makes it
    worse.

TORRISMONDO

If death cannot be punishment or a just
recompense for sin, it will be, at least, a good remedy,
685   if not the end of my sorrow.

COUNSELOR

Rather, it would be the start
and cause of a still greater torment.

TORRISMONDO

Come viver debb'io, sposo d'Alvida,
o pur di lei privarmi? Io ritenerla
non posso, che non scopra insieme aperta
690   la debil fede; e s'io da me la parto,
come l'anima mia restar può meco?
Il duol farà quel che non fece il ferro.
Non è questo, non è fuggir la morte,
ma scegliersi di lei più acerbo modo.

CONSIGLIERO

695   Non è duol così acerbo e così grave
che mitigato al fin non sia dal tempo,
confortator de gli animi dolenti,
medicina ed oblio di tutti i mali.
Ma d'aspettare a voi non si conviene
700   commun rimedio e 'l suo volgar conforto;
ma dal valore interno e da voi stesso
prenderlo, e prevenir l'altrui consiglio.

TORRISMONDO

Tarda incontra al dolor sarà l'aita,
se dee portarla il tempo; e debil fia
705   se da la debil mia virtù l'attendo.

CONSIGLIERO

Virtù non è mai vinta, e 'l tempo vola.

TORRISMONDO

Vola, quando egli è portator de' mali;
ma nel recare i beni è lento e zoppo.

CONSIGLIERO

Ei con giusta misura il volo spiega;
710   ma nel moto inegual de' nostri affetti
è quella dismisura e quel soverchio;
e noi pur la rechiam là suso al cielo.

TORRISMONDO

How should I live then—as Alvida's husband?
or should I renounce her? I cannot
keep her, without revealing, at the same time,
690 the weakness of my word: and if I dismiss her,
how can my soul remain within me?
Sorrow will do what the sword did not do.
This is no way of escaping death,
but of choosing a more painful way of dying.

COUNSELOR

695 There is no pain so sharp and grave
that it is not finally appeased by time,
comforter of afflicted hearts,
medicine and oblivion of all evils.
But it is not right for you
700 to wait for such a common remedy and its vulgar comfort;
rather you must draw your comfort from your inner worth
and from yourself, and thus forestall help from outside.

TORRISMONDO

Help for suffering arrives too late,
if time must bring it; it will be feeble help
705 if I expect it from my feeble virtue.

COUNSELOR

Virtue is never conquered, and time flies.

TORRISMONDO

It flies when it brings us evils;
but, when it brings good things, it is slow and halt.

COUNSELOR

Time with an equal measure spreads its wings;
710 but in the unequal motion of our affections
lies the excess and lack of measure
which we attribute to the heavens above.

TORRISMONDO

Ma s'egli avvien che la ragione e 'l tempo,
ragion, misero me, vinta ed inerme,
715   dal dolor mi ricopra e mi difenda,
fia questa moglie di Germondo, e mia?
Se la fede ch'io diedi, e potea darle,
fu stabilita pur (come al ciel piacque)
con l'atto sol del matrimonio occulto,
720   fatta è pur mia. S'io l'abbandono e cedo,
la cederò qual concubina a drudo.
A guisa dunque di lasciva amante
si giacerà nel letto altrui la sposa
del re de' Goti; ed ei soffrir potrallo?
725   Vergognosa union, crudel divorzio,
se da me la disgiungo, e 'n questa guisa
la congiungo al compagno, ond'ei schernito
non la si goda mai pura ed intatta.
Tale aver non la può, ché 'l furor mio
730   contaminolla e 'l primo fior ne colse.
Abbia l'avanzo almen de' miei furori,
ma com'è legge antica, e passi almeno
a le seconde nozze onesta sposa,
se non vergine donna. Ah non sia vero
735   che, per mia colpa, d'impudichi amori
illegitima prole al fido amico
nasca, e che porti la corona in fronte
de la Suezia il successor bastardo.
Questo, questo è quel nodo, oimè dolente,
740   che scioglier non si può, se non si tronca
il nodo ov'è la vita
a queste membra unita.

CONSIGLIERO

Signor, forte ragione e vera è questa
perché non sia, come rassembra, onesto
745   che, voi restando in vita, Alvida possa
unirsi in compagnia co 'l re Germondo;
ma non si reca già, né può recarsi,

TORRISMONDO

But if it should occur that time and reason—
reason, alas, now conquered and unarmed—
715   shelter and defend me against pain,
will she be Germondo's wife, as well as mine?
Though the oath I swore to her—the only oath I could
    swear—
was sanctioned (as it pleased Heaven)
only by the covert act of matrimony,
720   she still belongs to me. If I abandon and yield her,
I give her as a concubine to a lover.
Will, then, the bride of the king of the Goths
lie, like a lustful mistress, in someone else's bed?
And will he stand for such a thing?
725   A shameful union, a cruel divorce indeed,
if I separate her from myself; and is this how
I will join her to my friend, so that, mocked,
he may never enjoy her pure and undefiled?
Thus he can never have her, because my frenzy
730   contaminated her, plucking her first flower.
Let him have, at least, the remnant of my lust,
but in keeping with an ancient law, let her go (at least),
to her second nuptials as an honest bride,
if not a virgin. Oh, God forbid
735   that through my fault an illegitimate offspring
of shameless love should be born to my faithful
friend, and that a bastard successor
should wear the crown of Sweden on his brow.
This, this is that knot, alas so painful,
740   which cannot be undone except by severing
the knot whereby life
is joined to these limbs of mine.

COUNSELOR

Lord, this is a strong and veritable reason
why it's not honorable, as it may seem,
745   that, as long as you remain alive, Alvida should
be joined in marriage to King Germondo;
but this does not mean, nor can it imply,

che debbiate a voi stesso empio e spietato
armar la destra ingiuriosa, e l'alma
750 a forza discacciar dal nobil corpo,
ove quasi custode Iddio la pose,
onde partir non dee pria che, fornita
la sua custodia, ei la richiami al Cielo.
Nulla dritta ragion ch'a ciò vi spinga
755 ritrovar si potria, ch'in van si cerca
giusta in terra cagion d'ingiusto fatto.
Ma se voi senza vita, o senza donna
dee rimaner Germondo, or si rimanga
senza l'amata donna il re Germondo.

TORRISMONDO

760 Egli privo d'amante, ed io d'amico
e d'onor privo ancor nel tempo stesso,
come viver potremo? Ahi dura sorte!

CONSIGLIERO

Dura; ma sofferir conviene in terra
ciò che necessità comanda e sforza,
765 necessità regina, anzi tiranna,
se non quanto è il voler libero e sciolto:
ch'a lei soggetti son gli egri mortali
e tutte in ciel le stelle, erranti e fisse,
tutti i lor cerchi; e ne' lor corsi obliqui
770 servano eterni, e 'n variar costanti,
gli ordini suoi fatali e l'alte leggi.

TORRISMONDO

Faccia quanto è prefisso il mio destino.

CONSIGLIERO

Pur veggio di salvare alto consiglio
vostra fama e l'onor, che quasi affonda.
775 E s'egli è ver ch'abbia sì fermo amore
l'alte radici sue nel molle petto
d'Alvida, anzi nel core e ne le fibre,

that, impious and pitiless against yourself,
you should arm an injurious hand,
750 and forcibly drive your soul out of your noble body,
where, almost as a guardian, God placed it,
whence it must not leave until, having fulfilled
its guardianship, He recalls it to Heaven.
No just reason that might push you to this
755 could ever be found, for vainly on earth
do we seek a rightful reason for a wrongful deed.
But if you must remain without life or Germondo
without his lady, then let King Germondo
remain without the woman he loves.

TORRISMONDO

760 He without his beloved, and I without my friend
and at the same time without my honor,
how can we live? O cruel fate!

COUNSELOR

Cruel, yes: but on earth one must bear
what necessity commands and inflicts;
765 necessity is a queen, or better, a tyrant,
except in so far as our wills are true and unhampered;
for unhappy mortals are subject to her
as well as all the wandering and fixed stars in the sky
and all their spheres; and in their oblique courses
770 they eternally obey, though steady in their changes,
her fatal orders and her sovereign laws.

TORRISMONDO

Let my destiny do what is preordained.

COUNSELOR

Yet I see a noble course of action that may save
your fame and honor, which are nearly sinking.
775 And if it is true that such unchangeable love
has its deep roots in Alvida's soft breast—
indeed, in her heart and her very fibers,

consentir non vorrà ch'ignoto amante,
nemico amante ed odioso amante,
780   tinto del sangue suo, le giaccia appresso.
Ella d'amarlo e di voler negando,
e pertinace a' preghi o pur costante,
vi porgerà cagion quattro e sei volte
di ritenerla, e diece forse, e cento.
785   E direte: "Non lece e non conviensi
a cavaliero il far oltraggio a donna.
Pregherò teco amico; e teco insieme
ogni arte usar mi giova ed ogni ingegno;
ma sforzar non la voglio". Il buon Germondo,
790   s'egli è di cor magnanimo e gentile,
farà ch'amore a la ragion dia loco.
Così la sposa al fin, così l'amico,
così l'onor si salverà.

TORRISMONDO

L'onore
seguita il bene oprar, come ombra il corpo.

CONSIGLIERO

795   Questo, ch'onor sovente il mondo appella,
è ne l'opinioni e ne le lingue
esterno ben, ch'in noi deriva altronde;
né mai la colpa occulta infamia apporta,
né gloria accresce alcun bel fatto ascoso.
800   Ma perché viva con l'onor l'onesto
e con l'amico l'amicizia e 'l regno,
diasi d'Alvida in vece a lui Rosmonda,
sorella vostra; e se l'età canuta
può giudicar di feminil bellezza,
805   via più d'Alvida è bella.

TORRISMONDO

Amor non vuole
cambio, né trova ricompensa al mondo
donna cara perduta.

she will not allow an unknown lover—
an enemy and hateful lover,
780   stained with her blood—to lie down at her side.
By denying that she loves him—or that she ever will—
and tenacious and constant against all his insistence,
she will give you four and six and perhaps ten
and even a hundred reasons why you should keep her.
785   And you will say: "It is not right, and does not behoove
a knight to take a lady against her will.
With you, I will beg her as your friend; and with you
it is fitting that I use every skill and talent;
but I cannot force her." The good Germondo,
790   if he has a magnanimous and gentle heart,
will see to it that love will yield to reason.
In this way finally, your bride, your friend,
your honor will be saved.

TORRISMONDO

Honor
follows good deeds, as a shadow the body.

COUNSELOR

795   This thing which the world is wont to call honor,
is an external thing that lies in men's opinions
and in their words and comes to us from outside.
Nor does a hidden fault bring infamy,
nor does fame add to a hidden achievement.
800   But, so that honesty may survive along with honor,
and your friendship and your kingdom along with your
    friend,
let him have Rosmonda, your sister,
instead of Alvida; if my old age
can still judge a woman's beauty,
805   she is far more beautiful than Alvida.

TORRISMONDO

Love does not suffer
exchanges, nor can it find any reward in the world
for a dear lady lost.

CONSIGLIERO

Amor d'un core
per novello piacer così fia tratto
come d'asse si trae chiodo per chiodo.

TORRISMONDO

810   Lasso, la mia soror disprezza e sdegna
ed amori ed amanti e feste e pompe,
come già fece ne l'antiche selve
rigida ninfa, o ne' rinchiusi chiostri
vergine sacra.

CONSIGLIERO

È casta insieme e saggia,
815   e i soavi conforti e i saggi prieghi
e 'l buon consiglio e le preghiere oneste
soppor faranle al novo giogo il collo.

TORRISMONDO

O mio fedel, nel disperato caso
quel consiglio che sol m'avanza in terra
820   da voi m'è dato. Io seguirollo, e quando
vano ei pur sia, per l'ultimo refugio
ricovrerò ne l'ampio sen di morte,
porto de le miserie e fin del pianto,
ch'a nessuno è rinchiuso e tutti accoglie
825   i faticosi abitator del mondo,
e tutti acqueta in sempiterno sonno.

(IL FINE DEL PRIMO ATTO)

CORO

O Sapienza, o del gran Padre eterno
eterna figlia, o dea, di lui nascesti
anzi gli dei celesti,
830   a cui nulla altra fu nel Ciel seconda;
e da' stellanti chiostri al Lago Averno,

COUNSELOR

Love can be driven
out of a man's heart by new pleasure,
as a nail is driven out of a board by another nail.

TORRISMONDO

810   Alas, my sister scorns and disdains
loves and lovers and marriage feasts and pomp,
as the severe nymph used to do
in the ancient forests, or the sacred virgin
in a secluded cloister.

COUNSELOR

She is pure and obedient as well:
815   gentle urgings, prudent pressure,
good advice, and well-meant insistence
will persuade her to bow her neck to the new yoke.

TORRISMONDO

O my faithful friend, in this desperate situation
the only course left on earth to me
820   comes from you. I will follow it, and, should it
prove futile, as my last refuge
I will find shelter in death's ample bosom—
this haven from miseries and end to tears
is closed to no one, and welcomes all
825   the weary dwellers of the world,
appeasing all in everlasting sleep.

(END OF ACT ONE)

CHORUS

[Wisdom is invoked. Let her be propitious to the Nordic
peoples, accustomed to war, but nonetheless ready for the
arts of civilization and desirious of peace.]

O Wisdom, eternal daughter of our great
eternal Father, O goddess, born from Him
before the heavenly gods,
830   to whom no one else was second in Heaven:
and from the starlit cloisters to Lake Avernus,

e dovunque Acheronte oscuro inonda
o Stige atra circonda,
nulla s'aguaglia al tuo valor superno.
835   O dea possente e gloriosa in guerra,
ch'ami ed orni la pace e lei difendi,
se qui mai voli e scendi,
fai beata l'algente e fredda terra.
Mentre l'Impero ancor vaneggia ed erra
840   fuor d'alta sede, e 'l tuo favor sospendi,
non sdegnar questa parte,
perché nato vi sia l'orrido Marte.

E quando i suoi destrier percote e sferza
sovra l'adamantino e duro smalto
845   e porta fero assalto
e fa vermigli i monti e 'l giel sanguigno,
tu rendi lui, come sovente ei scherza,
più mansueto in fronte e più benigno,
d'irato e di maligno,
850   tu che sei prima e non seconda o terza.
Tu la discordia pazza e 'l furor empio,
tu lo spavento e tu l'orror discaccia,
e si disgombri e taccia
ogni atto iniquo, ogni spietato essempio.
855   Tu, peregrina diva, altari e tempio
avrai, pregata, ove ascoltar ti piaccia.
Deh, non voltarne il tergo,
ché peregrina avesti in Roma albergo;

ma inanzi al seggio ove d'eterne stelle
860   ne fa segno tuo padre, e tuoni e lampi
sparge in cerulei campi
e fulminando irato arde e flammeggia,
placalo, e queta i nembi e le procelle,
e seco aspira a questa invitta reggia
865   perch'onorar si deggia
ché non siamo a tua gloria alme rubbelle.
Noi siam la valorosa antica gente
onde orribil vestigio anco riserba
Roma, e quella superba

and wherever dark Acheron floods
or black Styx surrounds,
nothing can equal your supreme worth.
835   O goddess mighty and glorious in war,
you who love and adorn peace, and defend her,
if you ever descend and fly down to earth,
you make our cold and frozen earth blessed.
While the Empire is still wandering and astray
840   far from its high seat, and you suspend your favor,
do not disdain these reaches of the earth,
simply because horrid Mars was born here.

And when he lashes and whips his steeds
over the adamantine, frozen land,
845   and launches a fierce attack
and turns the mountains crimson and the ice bloody,
oh, make him, since he has often been known to dally,
meeker in countenance and more affable,
no longer wrathful and malevolent,
850   you who are first, not second or third.
Oh, drive out mad discord and impious fury,
oh, drive out fright and horror,
and let every iniquity and every ruthless example
vanish and be still.
855   You, heavenly goddess, shall have altars and temples;
you shall be prayed to, if it pleases you to heed our prayers.
Oh, do not turn your back on us,
for, though now a pilgrim, you once found shelter in
      Rome;

but, before the throne from where your father beckons to us
860   with his eternal stars, hurling his lightnings and
      thunderbolts
through the blue fields of the sky,
and flashing with rage, burns and blazes,
appease him, and silence the squalls and storms,
and with him look with favor upon this unvanquished
      royal palace
865   since it should be honored,
for we are not souls rebellious to your glory.
We are the valiant, ancient race
of whom Rome still preserves a terrible trace,
not to mention that proud one

870   che n'usurpa la sede alta e lucente.
        Quinci gran pregi ha l'Orto e l'Occidente,
        gli ha gloriosi più di fronda o d'erba,
        perché del nostro sangue
        ivi la fama e la virtù non langue.

875   E 'n questo clima ov'Aquilon rimbomba
        e con tre soli impallidisce il giorno,
        di fare oltraggio e scorno
        al ciel tentar poggiando altri giganti.
        E monte aggiunto a monte e tomba a tomba,
880   alte ruine e scogli in mar sonanti
        a folgori tonanti,
        son opre degne ancor di chiara tromba.
        D'altri divi altri figli i regni nostri
        reggeano un tempo, altre famose palme
885   ebber le nobili alme
        e que' che già domar serpenti e mostri.
        E là 've pria fendean con mille rostri
        le navi che portar cavalli e salme,
        poscia sostenne il pondo
890   de gli esserciti armati il mar profondo.

        Ed ora il re ch'il freno allenta e stringe,
        de l'auree spoglie d'occidente onusti
        cento avi suoi vetusti
        può numerare, e di gran padre è figlio.
895   A lui, che per onor la spada cinge.
        deh rivolgi dal Ciel pietosa il ciglio,
        s'è vicino il periglio,
        tu che sei pronta a' valorosi e giusti.
        E se l'alme, deposto il grave incarco,
900   a le sedi tornar del Ciel serene
        da le membra terrene,
        tardi ei sen rieda a te leggiero e scarco.
        Ed armato il paventi al suon de l'arco
        l'ultima Tile e le remote arene,
905   e la più rozza turba,
        e s'altri a noi contrasta o noi perturba.

870 who usurps Rome's high and shining seat.
From this region East and West have great examples of
    valor,
more glorious than any crown woven of leaves or grass,
because the fame and worth
of our blood is not languishing yet.
875 And in this clime where the north wind resounds,
where with three suns the day is dim,
other giants tried to climb to heaven
to work outrage and ignominy;
and mountains placed on top of mountains, tomb upon
    tomb,
880 great landslides and cliffs in the sounding sea
which echoes with thunderbolts
are works still worthy of a famous poet's trumpet.
Other children of other gods ruled our kingdoms
once; other famous rewards
885 were given to noble heroes
and to those who tamed monsters and serpents.
And there, where once with a thousand prows
the ships would cleave the sea,
carrying steeds and beasts of burden, there the deep sea
890 later bore the weight of armies in full war array.

And now the king who slackens and tightens our bridle
can number a hundred of his ancestors
laden with golden spoils from the West,
and is the son of a mighty father.
895 To him, who girds his sword for the sake of honor,
oh, mercifully turn your eyes from Heaven,
if danger is near,
you who are ever ready to help the strong and just.
And if souls, finally rid of their grievous burden,
900 return to Heaven's peaceful seats
from their earthly limbs,
let him return there, light and unburdened, as late as can
    be.

And in his armor may he be feared at the sound of his bow,
by utmost Thule and the most distant sands,
905 by the most barbaric horde
and any others who oppose or trouble us.

O diva, i rami sacri
tranquilla oliva a te non erge e spande,
né si tesson di lei varie ghirlande;
910   ma pur altra in sua vece il re consacri
alma e felice pianta:
tu sgombra i nostri errori, o saggia e santa.

O goddess, here no peaceful olive tree
spreads out or lifts its sacred boughs towards you,
nor are various garlands woven from its leaves;
910   but let the king, instead, consecrate another
sacred and happy plant;
you, erase our errors, you, O wise and holy.

ATTO SECONDO

MESSAGGERO, TORRISMONDO, CORO.

[MESSAGGERO]

Me di seguire il mio signore aggrada,
o calchi il ghiaccio de' canuti monti,
915   o le paludi pur ch'indura il verno.
Ed or quanto m'è caro e quanto dolce
l'esser venuto seco a l'alta pompa
ne la famosa Arana. Ei segue, e 'ntanto
al re de' Gotti messagiero io giungo
920   perch'io gli dia del suo arrivar novella.
Ma chieder voglio a que' ch'insieme veggio
ove sia del buon re, l'aurato albergo.
O cavalieri, io di Suezia or vegno
per ritrovare il re: dov'è la reggia?

CORO

925   È quella che t'addito, ed ei medesmo
quel che là vedi tacito e pensoso.

MESSAG[GERO]

O magnanimo re de' Goti illustri,
de l'inclita Suezia il re possente
a voi manda salute e questa carta.

ACT TWO

MESSENGER, TORRISMONDO, CHORUS

[MESSENGER]

I am content to follow my master,
whether he tread the ice of snow-white mountains,
915   or the swamps that winter hardens.
And now how dear and sweet it is to me
to have come here with him to the solemnities
in famed Arana. He follows after; meanwhile
I am here, messenger to the ruler of the Goths,
920   to bring the news of his imminent arrival.
But let me ask those people gathered there
where the gilded palace of the good king is.
O knights, I come from Sweden
to seek the king: where is the royal palace?

CHORUS

925   There the palace stands; and the king himself
is the man you see there, silent and wrapt in thought.

MESSENGER

O magnanimous King of the illustrious Goths,
glorious Sweden's mighty king
sends you his greetings and this letter.

TORRISMONDO

930 La lettra è di credenza. Espor vi piaccia
quel ch'ei v'impose.

MESSAG[GERO]

Il mio signor Germondo
dentro a' confin del vostro regno è giunto,
e già vicino; e pria che 'l sole arrivi
del lucido oriente a mezzo il corso,
935 sarà ne la famosa e nobil reggia;
ed ha voluto ch'io messaggio inanzi
porti insieme l'aviso e porga i prieghi
perché raccolto ei sia come conviensi
a l'amicizia, a cui sarian soverchi
940 tutti i segni d'onore e tutti i modi
che son fra gli altri usati. Ei si rammenta
del dolce tempo e de l'età più verde,
de l'error, de' viaggi e de le giostre,
de l'imprese, de' pregi e de le spoglie,
945 de la gloria commune e de la guerra;
ma più del vostro amor. Né d'uopo è forse
ch'io lo ricordi a chi 'l riserba in mente.

TORRISMONDO

Oh memoria, oh tempo, oh come allegro
de l'amico fedel novella ascolto!
950 Dunque sarà qui tosto. Oimè, sospiro
perch'a tanto piacer non basta il petto,
talch'una parte se 'n riversa e spande.

CORO

La soverchia allegrezza e 'l duol soverchio,
venti contrari a la serena vita,
955 sofflan quasi egualmente e fan sospiri;
e molti sono ancor gl'interni affetti
da cui distilla, anzi deriva il pianto,
quasi da fonti di ben larga vena:
la pietate, il piacer, il duol, lo sdegno:

TORRISMONDO

930 This letter is of credence. Please expound
 what he commanded you.

MESSENGER

 My master, King Germondo
 has arrived within the boundaries of your kingdom,
 and is already near; and before the sun reaches
 the midpoint of its course in the bright east,
935 he will be at your famous and noble Court;
 he wanted me to precede him as his messenger
 to bring you word of his arrival and express
 his wish that he be welcomed as befits
 your friendship, to which
940 all special signs of honor and all ceremony
 you use with other guests would be superfluous.
 He remembers the sweet time and your greener years,
 your wanderings, your travels and the jousts,
 the adventures, the prowess, and the spoils,
945 the glory and the battles that you shared,
 but, most of all, your love. Perhaps it is unnecessary
 that I remind one who has all this stored in memory.

TORRISMONDO

 O memories, O time, how I rejoice
 to hear news of my loyal friend!
950 So, he will soon be here. Oh, I sigh
 because my breast can hardly hold so much delight—
 so that a portion of it overflows and spills.

CHORUS

 Excessive joy and excessive pain,
 winds adverse to a tranquil life
955 blow almost equally and cause our sighing;
 and many are the inner feelings still
 which cause our tears to spring, or rather, pour,
 as from a truly copious fountainhead:
 pity, for instance, pleasure, grief, or anger:

960 tal ch'il segno di fuor non è mai certo
     di quella passion che dentro abonda.
     Ed or nel signor nostro effetti adopra
     l'infinita allegrezza, o così parmi,
     qual suole in altri adoperar la doglia.

                              MESSAG[GERO]

965 Signor, se con sì ardente e puro affetto
     amate il nostro re, giurar ben posso
     ch'è l'amor pari, e l'un risponde a l'altro;
     e non ha, quanto il sole illustra e scalda,
     di lui più fido amico.

                              TORRISMONDO

          Esperto il credo.
970 Anzi certo sono io che 'l ver si narra.

                              MESSAG[GERO]

     Ei de le vostre nozze è lieto in modo
     che 'l piacer vostro in lui trasfuso inonda
     a guisa di gran pioggia o di torrente.
     Gioisce al suon di vostre lodi eccelse
975 o per l'arti di pace o di battaglia;
     gioisce se i costumi alcuno essalta
     e racconta i viaggi, i lunghi errori,
     la beltà de la sposa, il merto e i pregi;
     e del padre e di voi sovente ei chiede.

                              TORRISMONDO

980 N'udrà liete novelle. E lieto ascolto
     le vostre anch'io; ma, del camin già lasso,
     deh non vi stanchi il ragionar più lungo.
     Sarà da me raccolto il re Germondo
     com'egli vuole. È suo de' Goti il regno
985 non men ch'egli sia mio: però'comandi.
     Voi prendete riposo. E tu 'l conduci
     a le sue stanze, e sia tua cura intanto

960 so that the outward signs are never a certain clue
 to the emotion that abounds within.
 And now limitless joy is eliciting
 the same effects in our lord (or so it seems to me)
 that grief is wont to stir in other men.

MESSENGER

965 Lord, if with such ardent and pure affection
 you love our king, I can swear
 that his love is just as great, the one matches the other;
 and the whole world which the sun illuminates and
  warms
 does not contain a truer friend than him.

TORRISMONDO

    I believe it from experience.
970 Indeed I am certain that you speak the truth.

MESSENGER

 He is so happy about your wedding
 that your joy, pouring into him, overflows
 like heavy rain or like a mountain torrent.
 He rejoices to hear your lofty praises,
975 either of your arts of peace or those of war;
 he rejoices if someone extols your character
 or narrates your travels, your lengthy wanderings,
 the beauty, worth and merits of your bride,
 and often he inquires of her father and of you.

TORRISMONDO

980 He will hear cheerful news. I, too, well-pleased,
 listen to yours; but, weary as you are of your journey,
 do not tire yourself with further talk.
 King Germondo will be welcomed by me
 as he desires. The kingdom of the Goths is his
985 no less than it is mine: therefore, he has only to ask.
 You, rest now. And you, take him
 to his chambers, and at the same time, make sure

ch'egli onorato sia: ché ben conviensi,
e 'l merta il suo valor, l'ufficio e 'l tempo,
990 e l'alta degnità di chi ce 'l manda.

SCENA SECONDA

TORRISMONDO solo.

Pur tacque al fine, e pur al fin dinanzi
mi si tolse costui, ch'a me parlando
quasi il cor trapassò d'acuti strali.
O maculata conscienza, or come
995 mi trafigge ogni detto! Oimè dolente,
che fia se di Germondo udrò le voci?
Non a Sisifo il rischio alto sovrasta
così terribil di pendente pietra,
come a me il suo venire. O Torrismondo,
1000 come potrai tu udirlo? o con qual fronte
sostener sua presenza? o con quali occhi
drizzar in lui gli sguardi? o cielo, o sole,
ché non t'involvi in una eterna notte?
o perché non rivolgi adietro il corso,
1005 perch'io visto non sia, perché non veggia?
Misero, allora avrei bramato a tempo
che gli occhi mi coprisse un fosco velo
d'orror caliginoso e di tenebra,
ch'io sì fissi li tenni al caro volto
1010 de la mia donna. Allor traean diletto
onde non conveniasi; or è ben dritto
che stian piangendo a la vergogna aperti,
e di là traggan noia onde conviensi,
perché la man costante il ferro adopre.
1015 Ma vien l'ora fatale e 'l forte punto
ch'io cerco di fuggire; e 'l cerco indarno,
se non costringe la canuta madre
la figlia sua, col suo materno impero,
sì come io l'ho pregata, ella promesso.
1020 E so ch'al mio pregar fia pronta Alvida.

that he is honored: for it is fitting, and well-deserved—
for his worth, the office and the occasion,
990   and the high dignity of the one who sends him.

SCENE TWO

TORRISMONDO (alone)

At last he is silent, and at last this fellow
is gone from my sight. His words
were like pointed darts piercing my heart.
O guilty conscience, how
995   each word transfixes me! Unhappy me!
How will I act when I hear Germondo's voice?
The peril of the rock hanging over Sisyphus
is much less grievous
than his coming is to me. O Torrismondo,
1000   how will you hear him out? With what face
stand in his presence? With what eyes will you
direct your gaze towards him? O Heaven, O Sun,
why do you not engulf yourself in an eternal night?
Why do you not turn back your course,
1005   so that I may neither be seen nor see?
Wretch that I am! That would have been the time
for a dark veil of murky horror
and gloom to cover my eyes, before I held them
riveted on the beloved face
1010   of my lady. Then they drew delight
from where they should not have; now it is only just
they should stay open, weeping, before their shame
and draw discomfort from where they should,
so that the firm hand can resort to the sword.
1015   Now comes the fatal hour and the moment
I try to flee; but vainly do I seek it,
unless my aged mother is able to prevail
upon her daughter with her maternal power,
as I have begged her to do and she has promised.
1020   And I know that Alvida will be willing to do what I ask.

Ma chi m'affida, oimè, che di Germondo
l'alma piegar si possa a novo amore?
E se fia vano il più fedel consiglio,
non ha rimedio il male altro che morte.

SCENA TERZA

ROSMONDA

1025   O felice colei, sia donna o serva,
        che la vita mortal trapassa in guisa
        che tra via non si macchi, e non s'asperga
        nel suo negro e terren limo palustre.
        Ma chi non se n'asperge? Ahi non sono altro
1030   serve ricchezze al mondo e servi onori
        ch'atro fango tenace intorno a l'alma,
        per cui sovente in suo camin s'arresta.
        Io, che d'alta fortuna aura seconda
        portando alzò ne la sublime altezza
1035   e mi ripose nel più degno albergo,
        de' regi invitti e gloriosi in grembo,
        e son detta di re figlia e sorella,
        dal piacer, da l'onore e da le pompe
        e da questa real superba vita
1040   fuggirei, come augel libero e sciolto,
        a l'umil povertà di verde chiostro.
        Or tra vari conviti e vari balli
        pur mal mio grado io spendo i giorni integri
        e de le notti a' dì gran parte aggiungo:
1045   onde talor vergogna ho di me stessa,
        s'a vergine sacrata a Dio nascendo
        è vergogna l'amar cosa terrena;
        ma chi d'amor si guarda e si difende?
        o non si scalda a la vicina fiamma?
1050   Misera, io non volendo amo ed avampo
        appresso il mio, signor, ch'io fuggo, e cerco
        dapoi che l'ho fuggito; indi mi pento,
        del mio voler non che del suo dubbiosa.

But who assures me, alas, that Germondo's heart
can be persuaded to turn towards a new love?
And if the most reliable counsel proves futile,
evil has no remedy other than death.

SCENE THREE

ROSMONDA

1025 Oh, happy is she—mistress or servant—
who lives her mortal life in such a manner
as not to soil herself along the way, and is not besmirched
with its black and marshy, slimy mire!
But who is not besmirched with it? Ah, on this earth
1030 enslaving riches and enslaving honors are nothing
but black tenacious ooze around the soul,
a slough which often stops it on its way.
I whom the favorable wind of fortune
raised to sublime heights,
1035 and placed in the worthiest of abodes,
among unvanquished, glorious kings;
I, who am called the daughter and the sister of a king,
would gladly flee like a bird, uncaged and free,
to the humble poverty of a green cloister,
1040 away from pleasure, away from pomp and honor,
and from this proud, royal existence.
Yet here I am among banquets and balls,
against my will, spending my entire days,
and even adding a good portion of the night to the day,
1045 and for this reason I am at times ashamed of myself,
since a virgin consecrated at birth to God
cannot without shame ever love an earthly thing;
but who can be guarded or protected against love?
who is not warmed if the flame of love is near?
1050 Woe is me, I love and burn against my will
next to my lord, whom I both shun and seek
after I've fled him; afterwards, I repent,
doubtful of my own will, not just of his.

E non so quel ch'io cerchi o quel ch'io brami,
1055   e se più si disdica e men convenga
come sorella amarlo o come serva.
Ma s'ei pur di sorella ardente amore
prendesse a sdegno, esser mi giovi ancilla,
ed ancilla chiamarmi e serva umile.

SCENA QUARTA

REGINA MADRE, ROSMONDA.

[REGINA]

1060   A te sol forse ancora è, figlia, occulto
ch'oggi arrivar qui deve il re Germondo.

ROSMONDA

Anzi è ben noto.

REGINA

Non ben si pare.

ROSMONDA

Che deggio far? Non so ch'a me s'aspetti
1065   alcuna cura.

REGINA

O figlia,
con la regina sposa insieme accorlo
ancor tu dei. S'è quel signor cortese,
quel re, quel cavalier che suona il grido,
ei tosto sen verrà per farvi onore.

ROSMONDA

1070   Io così credo.

1055 I know not what I seek or what I long for,
whether it's more unbecoming and less befitting
to love him as a sister or a servant.
But, if he should scorn a sister's ardent love,
let being a servant be of some avail,
calling myself his handmaid and his humble slave.

SCENE FOUR

QUEEN MOTHER, ROSMONDA

[QUEEN]

1060 Daughter, to you alone perhaps it is still a secret
that King Germondo is to arrive today.

ROSMONDA

On the contrary, it is well known.

QUEEN

One would not think so.

ROSMONDA

What should I do? I am not aware
1065 that anything is expected of me.

QUEEN

O daughter,
together with the queen-bride, you too
must welcome him. If he is that gentle lord,
that king, that knight that everyone proclaims him,
shortly he will be coming here to honor you.

ROSMONDA

1070 So I believe.

REGINA

Or come dunque
sì gran re ne l'altero e festo giorno
così negletta di raccor tu pensi?
Perché non orni tue leggiadre membra
1075   di preziosa vesta? e non accresci
con abito gentil quella bellezza
ch'il cielo a te donò cortese e largo,
prendendo, come è pur la nostra usanza,
l'aurea corona, o figlia, o l'aureo cinto?
1080   Bellezza inculta e chiusa in umil gonna
è quasi rozza e mal polita gemma
ch'in piombo vile ancor poco riluce.

ROSMONDA

Questa nostra bellezza, onde cotanto
se'n va femineo stuol lieto e superbo,
1085   di natura stimo io dannoso dono,
che nuoce a chi 'l possede ed a chi 'l mira.
Lo qual vergine saggia anzi devrebbe
celar ch'in lieta danza od in teatro
spesso mostrarla altrui.

REGINA

Questa bellezza
1090   proprio ben, propria dote e proprio dono
è de le donne, o figlia, e propria laude,
come è proprio de l'uom valore e forza.
Questa in vece d'ardire e d'eloquenza
né diè natura, o pur d'accorto ingegno;
1095   e fu più liberale in un sol dono
ch'in mille altri ch'altrui dispensa e parte;
ed agguagliamo, anzi vinciam, con questa
ricchi, saggi, facondi, industri e forti.
E vittorie e trionfi e spoglie e palme
1100   le nostre sono, e son più care e belle
e maggiori di quelle onde si vanta

QUEEN

How is it, then,
you think of welcoming so informally
such a great king, on this great and festive day?
Why do you not adorn your fair limbs
1075 with some rich garment? and increase
with elegant clothes that beauty
which kind and generous Heaven bestowed on you,
wearing, dear daughter, as our custom demands,
the golden crown, O daughter, or the golden sash?
1080 Beauty, if neglected and hidden in a humble dress,
is like a rough, ill-polished gem
that shines but feebly in a worthless setting.

ROSMONDA

This beauty of ours, which makes
the female sex so satisfied and proud,
1085 I deem a harmful gift of nature,
which damages its possessor as well as its admirer.
A prudent maid should hide it
rather than flaunt it constantly to others
in carefree dance or in a public theater.

QUEEN

This beauty
1090 is woman's own prerogative and dowry
and gift, dear daughter, and her proper praise,
just as courage and strength are virtues proper to a man.
This, rather than enterprise and eloquence
or a cunning mind, nature has given us;
1095 and in this one gift she was more lavish
than in the thousand gifts she bestows and grants to men:
with this we equal or, better yet, surpass
the rich, the wise, the eloquent, the industrious, the
  strong.
And ours are victories, triumphs, spoils
1100 and laurels dearer and more coveted
and greater than those a man can boast of,

l'uom, che di sangue è tinto e d'ira colmo:
perch'i vinti da loro aspri nemici
odiano la vittoria e i vincitori;
1105 ma da noi vinti sono i nostri amanti,
ch'aman le vincitrici, e la vittoria
che gli fece soggetti. Or s'uomo è folle,
s'egli ricusa di fortezza il pregio,
non dei già tu stimare accorta donna
1110 quella che sprezzi il titol d'esser bella.

ROSMONDA

Io più tosto credea che doti nostre
fossero la modestia e la vergogna,
la pudicizia, la pietà, la fede,
e mi credea ch'un bel silenzio in donna
1115 di felice eloquenza il merto aguagli.
Ma pur s'è così cara altrui bellezza
come voi dite, tanto è cara, o parmi,
quanto ella è di virtù fregio e corona.

REGINA

Se fregio è, dunque esser non dee negletto.

ROSMONDA

1120 S'è fregio altrui, è di se stessa adorna.
E bench'io bella a mio parer non sia
sì come pare a voi, ch'in me volgete
dolce sguardo di madre, ornar mi deggio,
ché sarò, se non bella, almeno ornata.
1125 Non per vaghezza nova o per diletto,
ma per piacere a voi, del voler vostro
è ragion ch'a me stessa io faccia legge.

REGINA

Ver dici e dritto estimi, e meglio pensi.
E vo' sperar ch'al peregrino invitto
1130 parrai quale a me sembri, onde ei sovente
dirà fra se medesmo sospirando:

a man stained with blood and full of wrath:
for the fierce enemies that they defeat
abhor such victories and those who win them;
1105   whereas those vanquished by us are our lovers,
and they love the victors as well as the victory
that made them subjects. Now, if a man is foolish
to refuse the ornament of fortitude,
you must not call a woman wise
1110   if she scorns the attribute of being beautiful.

ROSMONDA

On the contrary, I thought that
modesty and shyness were our virtues—
chastity, piety, purity, and faith;
and I thought that a woman's golden silence
1115   equalled the merits of felicitous eloquence.
But, if a woman's beauty is, as you say,
so dear, it is so dear—or so it seems to me—
insofar as it is the ornament and crown of virtue.

QUEEN

If it's an ornament, it should not be neglected.

ROSMONDA

1120   If it's an ornament, it needs no cultivation.
And though, in my opinion, I am not as beautiful
as I may seem to you, who look at me
with sweet maternal eyes, I must adorn myself,
so as to be, if not beautiful, at least adorned.
1125   Not because of any new desire or delight of mine,
but only to please you, it is most fitting
that I should make your will my only law.

QUEEN

You speak the truth, judge rightly, and think best.
I dare to hope that our unvanquished guest
1130   will see you as I do, so that he often
will murmur to himself, with a sigh:

"Già sì belle non son, né sì leggiadre
le figliuole de' principi sueci".

ROSMONDA

Tolga Iddio che per me sospiri o pianga
1135   od ami alcuno, o mostri amare.

REGINA

Adunque
a te non saria caro, o cara figlia,
che re sì degno e sì possente in guerra
sospirasse per te di casto amore,
in guisa tal ch'incoronar le chiome
1140   a te bramasse e la serena fronte
d'altra maggior corona e d'aureo manto,
e farti (ascolti il Cielo i nostri preghi)
di magnanime genti alta reina?

ROSMONDA

Madre, io no 'l vo' negar, ne l'alta mente
1145   questo pensiero è già riposto e fisso,
di viver vita solitaria e sciolta
in casta libertade; e 'l caro pregio
di mia virginità serbarmi integro
più stimo ch'acquistar corone e scettri.

REGINA

1150   Ei ben si par che, giovenetta donna,
quanto sia grave e faticoso il pondo
de la vita mortal, a pena intendi.
La nostra umanitade è quasi un giogo
gravoso, che natura e 'l Cielo impone,
1155   a cui la donna o l'uom disgiunto e sevro
per sostegno non basta, e l'un s'appoggia
ne l'altro, ove distringa insieme amore
marito e moglie di voler concorde,
compartendo fra lor gli offici e l'opre.
1160   E l'un vita da l'altro allor riceve

"The daughters of Swedish princes were never
so lovely or so fair."

ROSMONDA

1135
God forbid that anyone should sigh or weep
for me or love me, or display his love.

QUEEN

.   Then
it would not be welcome to you, dear daughter,
that such a worthy king, so powerful in war,
should sigh with such pure love for you
as would make him long to crown
1140
your tresses and your carefree brow
with another greater crown and golden mantle,
and make you (may the heavens hear our prayers)
the noble queen of a magnanimous people?

ROSMONDA

Mother, I will not deny it: deep within my mind
1145
this purpose is already fixed and sealed:
to live an unattached and solitary life
in honest freedom; for I would rather keep
the precious prize of my virginity intact
than conquer crowns and sceptres.

QUEEN

1150
Young woman that you are, it is clear
you hardly understand how wearisome
and grievous is the burden of this mortal life.
Our humanity is like a heavy yoke,
which nature and Heaven impose,
1155
and no woman or man single and alone
is equal to it; that is why one leans
upon the other, whenever love conjoins
husband and wife with a concordant will,
dividing tasks and toils between them.
1160
Then, one of them receives life from the other

quasi egualmente, e fan leggiero il peso,
cara la salma e dilettoso il giogo.
Deh, chi mai vide scompagnato bue
solo traendo il già comune incarco
1165 stanco segnar gemendo i lunghi solchi?
Cosa più strana a rimirar mi sembra
che donna scompagnata or segni indarno
de la felice vita i dolci campi;
e ben l'insegna, a chi riguarda il vero,
1170 l'esperienza, al bene oprar maestra.
Perché l'alto signore a cui mi scelse
compagna il Cielo, e 'l suo co 'l mio volere,
in guisa m'aiutò, mentre egli visse,
a sopportar ciò che natura o 'l caso
1175 suole apportar di grave e di molesto,
ch'alleggiata ne fui; né sentì poscia
cosa, onde soffra l'alma il duol soverchio.
Ma poiché morte ci disgiunse, ahi morte
per me sempre onorata e sempre acerba,
1180 sola rimasa e sotto iniqua salma,
di cadendo mancar tra via pavento,
ed a gran pena, da gli affanni oppressa,
per l'estreme giornate di mia vita
trar posso questo vecchio e debil fianco.
1185 Lassa, né torno a ricalcar giamai,
lo sconsolato mio vedovo letto,
ch'io no 'l bagni di lagrime notturne,
rimembrando fra me ch'un tempo impressi
io solea rimirar cari vestigi
1190 del mio signore, e ch'ei porgea ricetto
a' piaceri, a' riposi, al dolce sonno,
a' soavi susurri, a' baci, a' detti,
secretario fedel di fido amore,
di secreti pensier, d'alti consigli.
1195 Ma dove mi transporti a viva forza,
memoria innamorata?
Sostien ch'io torni ove il dover mi spinge.

almost with equal share, whereby they make their fardel
    light,
their burden pleasant, and their yoke delightful.
Pray tell me, whoever saw an unmatched ox
pulling the once-shared load alone,
1165   and wearily, with mournful lowing, plough the long-drawn
    furrows?
But a stranger thing seems to me the sight
of an unmarried woman treading
happy life's sweet fields in vain;
and experience, the teacher of good deeds,
1170   teaches it well to one who heeds the truth.
For the noble lord, for whom Heaven
chose me as his companion—and Heaven's will was also
    mine—
helped me, while he was alive,
to bear whatever hardship and travail
1175   nature and chance are wont to bring; in such a way
I felt relieved of them; nor did my soul, after our marriage,
suffer anything that seemed excessive grief.
But since death separated us—ah, death,
forever honored and forever bitter—
1180   having been left alone and sorely burdened,
I fear that I may fall along the way,
and with much anguish and oppressed by worries,
through the last days of my life,
I drag this old, weak frame of mine in pain.
1185   Alas, nor do I ever press again
my disconsolate, widowed bed,
without I bathe it with nocturnal tears,
remembering it was there I used to see
imprinted the dear shape of my beloved lord,
1190   and that this marriage bed received and welcomed
our pleasures, rest, sweet sleep,
soft whispers, kisses, words,
the faithful confidant of faithful love,
of secret thoughts, of solemn purposes.
1195   But where are you leading me against my will,
my still-enamored mind?
Let me return to where my duty guides me.

S'a me diede allegrezza e fece onore
il bene amato mio signor diletto,
1200   io spesso ancor gli agevolai gli affanni;
e quanto in me adoprava il buon consiglio,
tanto in lui (s'io non erro) il mio conforto,
e 'l vestir seco d'un color conforme
tutti i pensieri, ed il portare insieme
1205   tutto quel ch'è più grave e più noioso
nel corso de la vita. E mentre intento
era a stringere il freno, a rallentarlo
a' Goti vincitori, a mover l'arme,
ad inflammare, ad ammorzar gl'incendi
1210   di civil Marte o pur d'estrania guerra,
sovra me tutto riposar gli piacque
il domestico peso. E seco un tempo
questa vita mortal, se non felice
(ché felice non è stato mortale),
1215   pur lieta almeno e fortunata i' vissi;
e sventurata sol perché quel giorno
a me non fu l'estremo, e non rinchiuse
queste mie stanche membra in quella tomba
ov'egli i nostri amori e 'l mio diletto
1220   se 'n portò seco, e se gli tien sepulti.
Oh pur simil compagno e vita eguale
a te sia destinato; e tal sarebbe,
per quel che di lui stimi, il re Germondo.
Tu, s'avvien ch'egli a te s'inchini e pieghi,
1225   schifa non ti mostrar di tale amante.

ROSMONDA

Se ben di noi che siamo in verde etate
quella è più saggia che saper men crede,
e de la madre sua canuta il senno
molto prepone al giovenil consiglio
1230   nel misurar le cose, io pur fra tanto
oserò dir quel ch'ascoltai parlando.
La compagnia de l'uom più lieve alquanto
può far la noia, e può temprar l'affanno
onde la vita feminile è grave.

And if my dear beloved lord
gave me joy and honored me,
1200   often I, too, made his anxieties easier;
and just as his good counsel worked in me,
in the same measure (unless I am mistaken) my comfort
worked in him, and my putting on thoughts
of the same hue as his, and our shared bearing
1205   of all that is most grievous and most noxious
in the course of life. And while he was intent
on tightening or slackening his rule
over the victorious Goths, taking up arms,
or stirring or extinguishing the fires
1210   of civil strife or else of foreign war,
it pleased him to entrust the whole domestic
burden to me. And for a while with him I spent
this mortal life, if not in carefreeness
(for without care our mortal state can never be),
1215   at least in gladness and favored by fortune;
unfortunate only because that fatal day
was not my last as well, and did not shut
these tired limbs of mine in that same tomb
to which he took our love and my delight
1220   with him, and keeps them ever buried.
Oh, a like companion and a life like mine
be destined for you; and such,
if I have judged him well, would Germondo be.
You, should he kneel and bow before you,
1225   do not appear loath to welcome such a lover.

ROSMONDA

Though, among those of us still young in years,
the wisest is the one who thinks she knows the least,
and values her experienced mother's wisdom
over the unripe judgment of the young
1230   in weighing matters, still I will presume
to repeat what I have heard in conversation.
The company of a man can mitigate
vexations somewhat, ease the suffering
that makes a woman's life so wearisome.

1235 Ma s'in alcune cose ella n'alleggia,
 più ne preme ne l'altre, e quasi atterra,
 e maggior peso a la consorte aggiunge
 che non le toglie in sofferendo. Ed anco
 molto stimar si può diffìcil soma
1240 il voler del marito, anzi l'impero,
 qualunque egli pur sia, severo o dolce.
 Or non è ella assai gravosa cura
 quella de' figli? A l'infelice madre
 non paion gravi a la più algente bruma
1245 lor notturni viaggi e i passi sparsi,
 ed ogni error ch'i peregrini intrica,
 la povertà, l'essiglio e gli altri risci,
 e le pallide morti e i lunghi morbi,
 fianchi, stomachi, febri? E s'odo il vero,
1250 la gravidanza ancora è grave pondo,
 e lungo pondo, e doloroso il parto.
 Sì ch'il figliuol, ch'è de le nozze il frutto,
 è frutto al padre, ed a la madre è peso:
 peso anzi il nascer grave, e poi nascendo,
1255 né poi nato è leggiero. E pur di questo,
 di cui la vita virginale è scarca,
 il matrimonio più n'aggrava e 'ngombra.
 Che dirò, s'egli avien che sian discordi
 il marito e la moglie, o se la donna
1260 s'incontra in uom superbo e crudo e stolto?
 Infelice servaggio ed aspro giogo
 puote allor dirsi il suo. Ma sian concordi
 d'animi, di volere e di consiglio,
 e viva l'un ne l'altro: or che ne segue?
1265 Forse questa non è pensosa vita?
 Allor quanto ama più, quanto conosce
 d'essere amata più la nobil donna,
 tanto a mille pensieri è più soggetta,
 ed a gli affetti suoi gli affetti ascosi
1270 del suo fedel, come sian propi, aggiunge.
 Teme co 'l suo timor, duolsi co 'l duolo,
 con le lagrime sue lagrima e piange,
 e co 'l suo sospirar sospira e geme.

1235 But if in certain things it brings relief,
it burdens and almost crushes us in others,
and adds more to the weight a woman has to bear
than it takes from her ills. And furthermore
a husband's will—or, better still, his rule—
1240 whichever it may be, severe or sweet,
might still be thought an onerous imposition.
Now, is not the care of children
a most oppressive care? To an unhappy mother
do not her children's nighttime journeys,
1245 their wanderings in the coldest weather,
and every risk that lies in wait for pilgrims—
poverty, exile, every kind of danger,
and pallid deaths and lingering illnesses,
pains, aches and fevers—seem hard enough to bear?
1250 And if I must believe what I am told, childbearing also
is a heavy burden, and a long one, and bitter pain is
childbirth.
So that a child, the so-called fruit of marriage,
is fruit for his father only, a burden to his mother—
a heavy weight before and during birth,
1255 nor is it lighter afterwards. Yet with
this weight of which the unmarried life is free,
marriage encumbers and further oppresses us.
What will I say, if it should come about
that husband and wife disagree, or if a woman
1260 should choose a proud, a cruel, and a foolish man?
Unhappy slavery and a harsh yoke indeed
hers must be called. But even if they are in harmony
in soul, in will, and in opinions
and one lives for the other: what's the result?
1265 Perhaps this too is not a life of care?
In such a case, the more she loves, the more she knows
that she is loved, the more a noble woman
is subject to countless apprehensions,
adding to her own fears the hidden cares
1270 of her faithful spouse, as if they were her own.
She fears with his fear, suffers with his grief,
grieves and weeps with his tears,
and with his sighs she sighs and moans.

E benché sia sicura in chiusa stanza
1275   o 'n alto monte o 'n forte eccelsa torre,
è pur sovente esposta a' casi aversi
ed a' perigli di battaglia incerta.
Di ciò non cerco io già stranieri essempi,
perché de' nostri oltra misura abondo.
1280   E da voi gli prendo io, ch'a me tal volta
contra la ragion vostra in vece d'arme
altre varie ragioni a me porgete.
Ma se 'l marito a la gran madre antica
dopo l'estremo passo al fin ritorna,
1285   ella sente il dolor d'acerba morte;
e seco muore in un medesmo tempo
a' piaceri, a le gioie, e vive al lutto.
Onde conchiuderei con certe prove
che sia noioso il matrimonio e grave.
1290   Ch'in lui sterile vita o pur feconda,
l'esser amata od odiosa, apporta
solleciti pensier, fastidi e pene
quasi egualmente. Ed io no 'l fuggo e sprezzo
solo per ischivar gli affanni umani;
1295   ma più nobil desio, più casto zelo
me de la vita virginale invoglia.
Ed a me gioveria lanciare i dardi
tal volta in caccia e saettar con l 'arco,
e premer co' miei gridi i passi e 'l corso
1300   di spumante cinghiale, e, tronco il capo,
portarlo in vece di famosa palma:
poiché non posso il crin d'elmo lucente
coprirmi in guerra, e sostener lo scudo
che luna somigliò di puro argento,
1305   con una man frenando alto destriero
e con l'altra vibrar la spada e l'asta,
come un tempo solean feroci donne
che da questa famosa e fredda terra
già mosser guerra a' più lontani regni.
1310   Ma se tanto sperare a me non lece,
almen somiglierò, sciolta vivendo,

And though she may be safe in a locked room,
1275   atop a mountain or in a high and sturdy tower,
still she is often prey to adverse fortunes
and to the dangers of uncertain battle.
I need not look for foreign illustrations:
our own experience supplies more than I need.
1280   And I take them from you yourself, who at times
provide me with a host of other reasons
as arms against your arguments.
But if, after his final exit, a husband
returns at last to the mighty Ancient Mother,
1285   his consort feels the grief of bitter death,
and dies at once along with him
to pleasure and delight, and lives in mourning.
Thus, I conclude with unanswerable proofs:
marriage is a bitter state and burdensome.
1290   For in it, a barren or a bearing life,
whether she be loved or hated, brings on
gnawing apprehensions, pains and sorrows
almost in equal measure.
And I do not shun and scorn it
solely to avoid human suffering;
1295   but a more noble desire, a more chaste zeal
makes me embrace a virginal life.
It would please me more at times to cast the spear
in the hunt, and draw the bow,
and press with shouts on the heels
1300   of a foaming wild boar, and, severing its head,
bear it aloft as a victorious trophy:
since in battle I cannot hide my hair
beneath a shining helmet, nor bear the shield
shaped like a moon of pure silver,
1305   while curbing with one hand a noble steed
and with the other brandishing a sword and spear,
just as, in ancient days, those fearsome women did
who from this famous frigid land
waged war against the farthest realms.
1310   But if I am not free to hope so much,
at least in living free I shall resemble

libera cerva in solitaria chiostra,
non bue disgiunto in male arato campo.

REGINA

Non è stato mortal così tranquillo,
1315   quale ei si sia, del quale accorta lingua
molte miserie annoverar non possa:
però lasciando i paragoni e i tempi
de le vite diverse, io certo affermo
che tu sol non sei nata a te medesma.
1320   A me che ti produssi, a tuo fratello
ch'uscì del ventre istesso, a questa invitta
gloriosa cittate ancor nascesti.
Or perché dunque (ah cessi il vano affetto)
in guisa vuoi di solitaria fera
1325   viver selvaggia e rigida e solinga?
Chiede l'utilità del nostro regno
e del caro fratel che pieghi il collo
in così lieto giorno al dolce giogo.
A la patria, al germano, a vecchia madre
1330   fia 'l tuo voler preposto? Ahi non ti stringe
la materna pietà? Non vedi ch'io
del mio corso mortal tocco la meta?
Perché dunque s'invidia il mio diletto?
Non vuoi ch'io veggia, anzi ch'a morte aggiunga,
1335   rinovellar questa mia stanca vita
ne l'imagine mia, ne' miei nepoti,
nati da l'uno e l'altro amato figlio?

ROSMONDA

Già non resti per me che bella prole
te felice non faccia. Egli è ben dritto
1340   ch'obbedisca la figlia a saggia madre.

REGINA

Degna è di te la tua risposta, e cara.
Or va, t'adorna, o figlia, e t'incorona.

a doe still wild in the untrod thicket,
and not an unyoked ox in an ill-tilled field.

QUEEN

There is no mortal state so tranquil—
1315   whatever it be—as to prevent a cunning tongue
listing a thousand miseries against it.
However, setting comparisons aside
and life's different ages, I say for sure
that you were not born solely for yourself.
1320   For me, who gave you life, for your brother
who was born from the same womb, for this
    unvanquished,
glorious city, you were also born.
So why, then (let these pointless longings cease!)
do you wish to live as wild and cold
1325   and lonesome as a solitary wild beast?
The good of our kingdom
and of your dear brother demands that you bow your neck
to the sweet yoke on such a happy day.
Will you place your will before your country, your brother
1330   and your aging mother? Oh, does not love of your mother
compel you? Can you not see that I
am reaching the end of my mortal course?
Why then is all that delights me refused?
Do you not want me to see, before I reach my end,
1335   my weary life renewed
in my own image, in my grandchildren,
born from both my beloved children?

ROSMONDA

Let me not rob you of the happiness
of having heirs. For it is only right
1340   a daughter should obey her wise mother.

QUEEN

Your answer suits your worth and is most welcome.
Now go, and dress yourself, put on your crown, my
    daughter.

SCENA QUINTA

REGINA MADRE sola.

Infelice non è dolente donna,
se ne' suoi figli il suo dolor consola
1345 e 'n lor s'appoggia, e quasi in lor s'avanza,
e de la vita allunga il dubbio corso;
e depone i fastidi e i gravi affanni
a guisa di soverchio inutil fascio
ch'impedisce il viaggio, anzi il perturba.
1350 Non si vede per lor, né si conosce,
né sprezzata, né sola, né deserta,
né odiosa od aborrita vecchia.
E 'l numero de' figli è caro, e basta,
se l'un maschio è di lor, femina è l'altra.
1355 In tal numero a pieno oggi s'adempie
la mia felicitade, o si rintegra
se desiosa fu già. Felice madre
di prole fortunata, e lieto giorno!
[Certo del sommo Dio son dono i figli;
1360 ed egli che donolli ancor gli serva,
gli guarda, gli difende, anzi gli accresce.]
[Come ora io veggio i miei cresciuti al colmo
di valor, di fortuna e di bellezza.]
Ma ecco il re se 'n viene: un lume io veggio
1365 de gli occhi miei che d'ostro e d'or risplende,
mentre l'altro s'adorna in altra pompa.

SCENA SESTA

REGINA MADRE, TORRISMONDO.

[REGINA]

Dopo molte ragioni e molti preghi
si rende al voler nostro al fin Rosmonda,

SCENE FIVE

QUEEN MOTHER (alone)

A grieving woman is not unhappy
if she can find comfort for grief in her children,
1345   and lean on them: and live on as it were in them,
prolonging the doubtful course of this her life;
lay down her troubles, and her grievous burdens
like an excessive, useless load
that hinders or, rather, disrupts her journey.
1350   Because of them she does not feel
that she is scorned, deserted or abandoned,
a hated and despised old woman.
Their number is both welcome and sufficient
if one of them is male, the other female.
1355   This number brings my happiness today
complete fulfillment, it is made whole again
if ever it was lacking. Happy mother
of fortunate offspring and happy day!
[Certainly children are the great God's gift;
1360   and He who granted them to us still preserves them,
watches over them, defends them, indeed he makes them
    greater.]
[As I today see mine, grown to the peak
of valor, fortune, beauty.]
But here comes the king: I see one light
1365   of my eyes shine with gold and purple,
while the other decks herself in other splendor.

SCENE SIX

QUEEN MOTHER, TORRISMONDO

[QUEEN]

After much argument and many prayers
Rosmonda at last surrenders to our will,

ma non in guisa che piacer dimostri.
1370 Anzi io la vidi tra dolente e lieta
sospirando partirsi. Oh pur congiunte
sian nozze a nozze, ond'il piacer s'accresca,
e si doppin le feste e i giuochi e i balli.
Fia contenta (o ch'io spero) a vecchia madre
1375 d'aver creduto, ed al fratello insieme.

TORRISMONDO

Non è saggio colui ch'insieme accoppia
vergine sì ritrosa e re possente
contra 'l piacer di lei; ma, s'io non erro,
fora simil pazzia condurre in caccia
1380 sforzati i cani. Or sia che può: se l'abbia,
s'ei la vorrà

REGINA

Ma con felice sorte.

TORRISMONDO

Sia felice, se può. Ma nulla manchi
a la nostra grandezza, al nostro merto:
abito signoril, ricchezza e pompa.
1385 S'ornin cento con lei vergini illustri
d'aurea corona ancora e d'aureo cinto,
ed altrettante ancora illustri donne,
pur con aurea corona ed aureo cinto,
seguano Alvida. Ella di gemme e d'auro,
1390 come sparso di stelle il ciel sereno,
fra le seguaci sue lieta risplenda.
Abbia scettro, monil, corona e manto,
e s'altro novo fregio, altro lavoro
d'abito antico in lei vaghezza accresce.
1395 Ma questa è vostra cura e vostra laude,
e, in aspettando il re, l'ore notturne
tolte per sì bell'opre avete al sonno.
Ora a voi, cavalieri, a voi mi volgo,
giovani arditi. Altri sublime ed alto

though without showing any sign of pleasure.

1370   Rather, I saw her sighing, as she left,
half sad, half cheerful. Oh, let nuptials
be added to nuptials, whence pleasure may grow,
let feasting, games and dances multiply!
Let her be happy (so I hope) for heeding

1375   her aged mother's urging and her brother's.

TORRISMONDO

He is not wise who matches
so reticent a maid and such a mighty king
against her will; but, if I'm not mistaken,
it would be just as mad to force unwilling dogs

1380   to hunt. But come what may: let him have her
if he will take her.

QUEEN

And with a happy outcome.

TORRISMONDO

Let her be happy, if she can. But nothing
that our greatness and our rank entails be lacking:
noble garments, wealth and pomp.

1385   Let a hundred high-born maidens deck themselves
with golden crowns and golden sashes,
and let the same number of noble matrons,
they, too, wearing gold crowns and golden sashes,
attend Alvida. Let her shine with gems and gold,

1390   like the clear sky strewn with stars,
happy among her maids in waiting.
Let her have sceptre, necklace, crown and mantle,
whatever new ornament, whatever handiwork
of ancient finery enhance her beauty.

1395   But this is your care, the praise of this is yours,
for, awaiting the king, you stole nocturnal hours
from sleep for such fair works as these.
Now to you, O knights, to you I turn,
bold youths. Let some of you construct a castle

1400 drizzi un castel di fredda neve e salda,
   e 'l coroni di mura intorno intorno;
   faccian le sue difese, e faccian quattro
   ne' quattro lati suoi torri superbe;
   e da candida mole insegna negra,
1405 dispiegandosi a l'aure, al ciel s'inalzi;
   e vi sia chi 'l difenda e chi l'assalga.
   Altri nel corso, altri mostrar nel salto
   il valor si prepari, altri lanciando
   le palle di gravoso e duro marmo,
1410 altri di ferro, il qual sospinge e caccia
   la polve e 'l foco, il magistero e l'arte,
   Altri si veggia in saettar maestro
   ne la meta sublime; e 'n alto segno,
   d'una girevole asta in cima afflsso
1415 quasi volante augel, balestri e scocchi
   rintuzzate quadrella, in sin ch'a terra
   caggia disciolto. Altri in veloce schermo
   percota o schivi, e 'n su l'adversa fronte
   faccia piaga il colpir, vergogna il cenno
1420 de le palpebre a chi riceve il colpo.
   Altri di grave piombo armi la destra
   e d'aspro cuoio e dur l'intorni e cinga,
   perché gema il nemico al duro pondo.
   Altri sovra le funi i passi estenda,
1425 e sospeso nel ciel si volga e libri.
   Altri di rota in guisa in aria spinto
   si giri a torno; altri di cerchio in cerchio
   passi guizzando, e sembri in acqua il pesce;
   altri fra spade acute ignudo scherzi.
1430 Altri in forma di rota o di grande arco
   conduca e riconduca un lieto ballo,
   d'antichi eroi cantando i fatti eccelsi
   a la voce del re, ch'indrizza e regge
   co 'l suon la danza; e i timpani sonanti
1435 e con lieti sonori altri metalli
   sotto il destro ginocchio avinte squille
   confondan l'alte voci e 'l chiaro canto.
   Ed altri salti armato al suon di tromba

1400   towering and tall from cold and solid snow,
    and crown it all around with battlements;
    let them prepare defenses, and reinforce it
    with four proud towers at its four corners;
    from the white structure, let a black ensign
1405   rise to the sky and flutter in the wind;
    let some defend it while others attack.
    Let others show their valor in the race,
    others in jumping, putting shot
    made out of ponderous and solid marble
1410   while others still display their skill
    at firing iron balls with fire and powder.
    Let others be seen, masters of archery,
    to fire at a lofty target, a high mark
    fixed on the top of a revolving pole
1415   like a flying bird; let them aim and shoot
    blunt arrows until it falls dislodged
    down to the ground. Let others, in deft
    skirmish, deal or avoid the blows, and on
    their adversary's forehead inflict a wound;
    and let it be deemed a shame if he
1420   who receives the hit so much as blinks an eyelid.
    Let others wrap their fists in heavy lead
    bound round with rough, hard leather; let them make
    their opponents groan at the heavy weight.
    Another on the tightrope try his steps
1425   and spin and turn suspended in the sky.
    Let others be sent whirling through the air
    like cartwheels, others thread hoop after hoop
    wriggling like fish in water;
    others dance, naked, among pointed swords.
1430   Let others, forming a wheel or a great bow,
    lead back and forth a lively dance,
    chanting the great deeds of our ancient heroes
    at the king's bidding; he will call the figures
    and lead the dance; and beating kettledrums
1435   with other cheerful-sounding metal instruments,
    with tinkling bells attached to their right knees,
    mingle their ringing notes with the clear song.
    Let another caper, armed from top to toe,

o di piva canora, or presto or tardi,
1440 facendo risonar nel vario salto
le spade insieme e sfavillar percosse.
Altri, dove in gran freddo il foco accenso
de gli abeti riluce e stride e scoppia,
con lungo giro intorno a lui si volga:
1445 sì che l'estremo caggia in viva flamma,
rotta quella catena, e poi risorto
da' compagni s'inalzi in alto seggio.
Altri là dove il giel s'indura e stringe,
condurrà i suoi destrier quasi volanti.
1450 Ed altri a prova su 'l nevoso ghiaccio
spinga or domite fere, e già salvagge,
c'hanno sì lunghe e sì ramose corna
e vincer ponno al corso i venti e l'aura.
Ed altri armato di lorica e d'elmo
1455 percoteransi urtando il petto e 'l dorso,
di trapassar cercando il duro usbergo
e penetrare il ferro e romper l'aste.
Ed io (ch'è già vicino il re Germondo
a la sede real) li movo incontra
1460 con mille e mille cavalieri adorni,
vestiti al mio color purpureo e bianco,
che già fra tutti gli altri a prova ho scelti.
L'altre diverse mie lucenti squadre
a cavallo ed a piè fratanto accolga
1465 il mio buon duce intorno a l'alta reggia,
e i destrier di metallo, onde rimbomba
la flamma ne l'uscir d'ardente bocca
con negro fumo. e i miei veloci carri;
e lungo spazio di campagna ingombri,
1470 sotto vittoriosa e grande insegna.

(IL FINE DEL SECONDO ATTO)

1440

to the shrill trumpet's sound or wailing bagpipe,
the varied rhythm of his dance, now fast, now slow,
causing the swords to clash and give off sparks.
Others, where in the bitter cold a bonfire
of firwood blazes, crackles and hisses,
go spinning round it in a drawn-out ring,

1445

so that the last falls in the scorching fire
when the chain is broken, and jumping back out
is borne aloft by his companions.
Let others, where the ice is hard and thick,
whip on their horses so they seem to fly.

1450

Let others, racing on the snowy ice,
drive the once wild but now domesticated beasts,
which have such long and branching horns
and can outrun the wind, outstrip the air.
Others, protected by breastplate and helmet,

1455

will joust together, striking chest and back,
trying to pierce the solid coat of mail
and penetrate the steel and break the lance.
And I (since King Germondo is already near
the royal seat), I'll ride to meet him

1460

with two thousand knights in full array,
all wearing my colors, crimson and white,
handpicked by me, the flower of all the rest.
Meanwhile my other several glittering squadrons
on horseback or on foot will be drawn up

1465

by my good general round the lofty palace,
my steeds of bronze, whose burning mouths
roar forth flames and black smoke,
and my speedy chariots;
and let them occupy vast tracts of fields,

1470

beneath my great all-conquering oriflamme.

(END OF ACT TWO)

CORO

Non sono estinte ancor l'eccelse leggi,
generate là sù ne l'alto Cielo,
de l'opre saggie e caste
e del parlar che l'onestà conservi:
1475   perch'ella qui ritrova alberghi e seggi
tra l'altissime nevi e 'l duro gelo,
e tra gli scudi e l'aste
vive secura, e tra ministri e servi.
Pensier vani e protervi
1480   sempre nido non fanno in nobil core;
né, perché la ragion il fren si toglia
ch'in altri regge amore,
del suo gentile ardir l'alma dispoglia,
ma de gli antichi essempi ancor l'invoglia.

1485   E potrebbe costei gravar la fronte
di lucido elmo, e seguitar nel corso
cervo non solo o damma,
ma de l'estranie genti ostile schiera,
come Ippolita in riva al Termodonte,
1490   d'un gran destrier premendo armato il dorso
con la sinistra mamma,
altra regina, e di sua gloria altera.
Ma se questa è guerrera,
chi farà di sue spoglie unqua trofeo?
1495   o chi potrà condurla avinta o presa?
quale Ercole o Teseo
avrà l'eterno onor di bella impresa,
s'in lei non è d'amor favilla accesa?

O de l'aurea speranza antica figlia,
1500   fama immortal, che gli anni avanzi e i lustri,
e dal sepolcro oscuro
l'uom talvolta fuor traggi e 'l togli a morte,
narra a costei, che tanto a lor somiglia,

CHORUS

[The chaste and virtuous maiden is praised and recommended to Fame.]

Even now the sovereign laws are not extinct,
inspired by Heaven above,
of good and chaste works
and words that heed decorum:
1475   for here, among deep snows and solid ice,
mid shields and lances,
virtue has its home and seat,
and lives securely among its ministers and servants.
Vain and arrogant thoughts
1480   never nest in a noble soul;
nor, though reason may grasp the reins
that love is wont to hold in others,
does it strip the soul of its noble daring,
but still inspires it to follow ancient examples of virtue.

1485   And she [Rosmonda] could press a shiny helmet
upon her forehead, and pursue in the hunt
not only a stag or fallow-deer,
but the hostile throngs of a foreign nation,
like Hippolyta by Thermodon's banks,
1490   pressing the armed back of a great steed
with her left breast—
a noble queen, proud of her glory.
But if she is a warrior,
who will ever have her spoils as a trophy?
1495   or who will lead her bound and captive?
Who, like Hercules or Theseus,
will have the undying honor of this noble feat,
if not a spark of love is lit in her?

Oh, may golden hope's ancient daughter,
1500   immortal fame, who prolongs time and lustra,
and often from the dark tomb
draws a man forth and snatches him from death,
tell to this maid, who so resembles them,

l'antiche donne e le moderne illustri,
1505   che sotto il pigro Arturo
ebbero insieme il cor pudico e forte.
Se per le vie distorte
da questa reggia invitta il sol disgiunge
correndo intorno i suoi destrieri aversi,
1510   non è turbato o lunge
tanto giamai, ch'i raggi in noi conversi
non miri di valor pregi diversi.

Vincan di casta madre
la sua vergine figlia i casti preghi,
1515   e l'arco rea fortuna altrove or tenda.
E più si stringa e leghi
l'una coppia con l'altra, e più s'accenda,
e più nel dubbio alta virtù risplenda.

tales of the ancient women and the modern heroines
1505   who, under slow Arcturus,
had purity of heart as well as strength.
Though over ways that lead away
from this unvanquished seat the sun
in his wheeling drives his recalcitrant steeds,
1510   still, he is never so clouded over or so distant
that, turning his rays upon us,
he may not gaze upon countless examples of virtue.

May a chaste mother's innocent prayers
win back her virgin daughter,
1515   and may evil fortune now aim her bow elsewhere.
And may both couples be ever more bound
to one another, and may high virtue blaze
and shine brighter still in these our doubtful days.

ATTO TERZO

CONSIGLIERO

A molti egri mortali (or mi sovviene
1520   di quel che spesso ho già pensato e letto)
fedel non fu de l'amicizia il porto,
che sovente il turbò, qual nembo oscuro,
il desio d'usurpar cittati e regni,
o gran brama d'onore, o d'alto orgoglio
1525   rapido vento, o pur disdegno ed ira
che mormorando mova atra tempesta.
Ma questo, ove il mio re nel mar solcando
de la vita mortal legò la nave
tutta d'arme e d'onore adorna e carca,
1530   e l'ancore il fermar co 'l duro morso,
s'àncora fu la fede e quinci e quindi:
questo, dico, sì lieto e sì tranquillo
seno de l'amicizia, ardente spirto
d'amor sossopra volse, e non turbolla,
1535   né turbar la poteva altra procella
prima né dopo. E 'l risospinse in alto
pur il medesmo amor tra duri scogli,
talch'è vicino ad affondar tra l'onde.
Io canuto nocchier siedo al governo,
1540   presto di navigare a ciascun vento
sì come piace al re. Parlare io debbo
con duci di Suezia e con Germondo,
perch'ei rivolga il cor dal primo oggetto;
e parlerò. Ma, sinché il re s'attende,
1545   lascerò gli altri riposar. Fra tanto

ACT THREE

COUNSELOR

	To many unhappy mortals (I now recall
1520	what I have often thought and read)
	friendship was not a trusted anchorage,
	for often, like a dark cloud,
	the desire to usurp cities and kingdoms troubled it,
	or excessive thirst for honor, or the swift wind
1525	of overweening pride, or else disdain and wrath
	that, brooding, summon up a pitch-black storm.
	But this harbor, where, as he ploughed the sea
	of mortal life, my master moored his ship
	all adorned and laden with arms and honors,
1530	and anchors held it with their solid grip,
	if mutual loyalty can be called an anchor—
	this mooring, I say, such a happy and calm
	haven of friendship, an ardent spirit
	of love turned upside down, but still could not dislodge it,
1535	nor could any other storm disturb it
	before or since. And he was driven back on the high seas
	among jagged rocks by the selfsame love,
	so that he's close to foundering amid the waves.
	And I, old steersman, sit at the helm,
1540	ready to sail to any compass point
	as it may please the king. I am supposed to speak
	with the leaders of Sweden and with Germondo,
	to get him to turn his affection away from its first object;
	and I will speak to him. But, while we await the king,
1545	I'll let the others rest. In the meantime

molte cose fra me volgo e rivolgo.
Dura condizione e dura legge
di tutti noi che siam ministri e servi!
A noi quanto è di grave qua giù e d'aspro
1550 tutto far si conviene, e diam sovente
noi severe sentenze e pene acerbe.
Il diletto e 'l piacer serbano i regi
a se medesmi, e 'l far le grazie e i doni.
Né già tentar m'incresce il dubbio guado,
1555 che men torbido sembra e men sonante
a chi men vi rimira e men v'attende:
ché leve ogni fatica ed ogni rischio
mi farà del mio re l'amore e 'l merto.
Ma spesso temo di tentarlo indarno,
1560 s'egli medesmo o prima o poi no 'l varca.
Favorisca fortuna il mio consiglio;
ceda il re di Suezia al re de' Goti
questo amor, questo giorno e queste nozze:
ché de gli antichi Goti è 'l primo onore;
1565 e pur cede a l'onore il grave e 'l forte
e 'l fortissimo ancora. E bench'agguagli
l'uno de l'altro re la gloria e l'opre,
questo è maggior per dignitate eccelsa
di tanti regi e cavalieri invitti
1570 che già l'imperio soggiogar del mondo.
Cedagli dunque l'altro. Ed è ben dritto.
Com'a l'alma stagion ch'i frutti apporta
partendo cede il pigro e 'l freddo verno;
o come de la notte il nero cerchio
1575 concede al sole, ove un bel giorno accenda
sovra i lucenti e candidi cavalli;
o come la fatica al dolce sonno;
o come spesso cede, in mar che frange,
quel che perturba a chi racqueta il flutto;
1580 dal sole impari e da le stelle erranti,
da le sublimi cose e da l'eterne
a ceder l'uomo a l'uom terreno e frale.
Forse altre volte, e già preveggio il tempo,
al mio signor non cederà Germondo;

I turn many things over and over in my mind.
A bitter condition and a bitter law—
the task of us ministers and servants!
All that is grievous and harsh here below
1550   falls to our lot, for often we must mete out
severe judgments and stern punishments.
Pleasure and delight kings keep for themselves,
and the distributing of gifts and graces.
Not that I'm loath to try to cross this unsure ford
1555   which looks less turbulent and less resounding
to one who looks less close and weighs it less:
for every risk and labor
will be made light by my king's love and merits.
But often I am afraid to try to cross in vain,
1560   if he himself does not, sooner or later, cross it.
Let fortune favor my counsel;
Let the king of Sweden yield to the king of the Goths
this love, this day and this marriage:
for the first honor belongs to the ancient Goths;
1565   and the grave and strong, even the strongest,
still yield to honor. And though the glory
and deeds of the one king equal the other's,
this king is greater for the lofty dignity
of so many victorious kings and knights
1570   who entertained command of all the world.
Let the other, then, yield to him. And rightly so.
Just as the sluggish and cold winter, moving on,
yields to the glorious season that prepares the fruits,
or just as the black circle of the night
1575   yields to the sun when the fair day lights up
over its bright and shining horses;
as toil gives way to pleasant sleep, or, on a raging sea,
the wind that stirs it up yields to the wind that calms the
        waves;
1580   so from the sun and from the wandering stars,
from sublime, that is, and from eternal things
let earthly, frail man learn to yield to man.
Perhaps some other time—and I already foresee the day—
Germondo will not bow before my master;

1585 ma ceduto gli fla. Così mantiensi
      ogni amicizia de' mortali in terra.

SCENA SECONDA

ROSMONDA sola.

      O possente Fortuna, a me pur anco,
      che fui dal tuo favor portata in alto,
      con sembiante fallace or tu lusinghi,
1590 e di altezza in altezza, ov'io paventi
      la caduta maggior, portarmi accenni,
      quasi di monte in monte. E veggio omai,
      o di veder pens'io, sembianze e forme
      d'inganni, di timori e di perigli.
1595 Oh quanti precipizi! Appressa il tempo
      da riflutar le tue fallaci pompe
      e i tuoi doni bugiardi. A che più tardo?
      a che non lascio le mentite spoglie
      e la falsa persona e 'l vero nome,
1600 se 'l mio valor non m'assicura ed arma?
      Bastava che di re sorella e figlia
      fossi creduta. Usurparò le nozze
      ancor d'alta regina, audace sposa
      e finta moglie e non verace amante?
1605 Potrò l'alma piegar d'un re feroce
      ch'altrove forse è volta, e voti i voti
      de la mia vera madre al fin saranno,
      a la cui tomba lagrimai sovente
      cercando di pietà lodi non false?
1610 Ahi, non sia vero. Io rendo al fine, io rendo
      quel ch'al fin mi prestò la sorte e 'l fato.
      L'ho goduto gran tempo. Altera vissi
      vergine e fortunata, ed or vivrommi
      di mia sorte contenta in verde chiostro.
1615 Altri, se più convienle, altri si prenda
      questo tuo don, Fortuna, e tu 'l dispensa
      altrui, come ti piace, o com'è giusto.

1585   but will be yielded to. Thus all friendship
among mortals is preserved on earth.

SCENE TWO

ROSMONDA (alone)

O mighty Fortune, with a deceitful mien
you flatter me again,
who by your favor was brought high,
1590   and now from height to height you seem to lead me,
as it were from mountaintop to mountaintop,
whence I fear the greatest fall. And now I see,
or seem to see, appearances and forms
of deceits, fears and perils.
1595   Oh, how many precipices! The time is approaching
when I must renounce your deceiving pomp
and your false gifts. Why do I tarry?
Why don't I leave the false pretenses
and the false person and the true name behind
1600   if my valor fails to give me safety and protection?
It was enough for me to be called a king's sister
and a king's daughter. Must I even usurp
the marriage of a queen—presumptuous bride,
dissembling wife, and untrue lover?
1605   Could I bend a fierce king's soul
that perhaps is turned elsewhere, and thus
in the end annul my real mother's vows
at whose tomb I often wept,
seeking earned praises for filial piety?
1610   Oh, let it not be so. I give back, I finally give back
that which fortune and fate lent me.
I have enjoyed it for a long time. I lived a proud
and fortunate maiden, and now, happy with my lot,
I will live in a verdant cloister.
1615   Let another, if it suits her more, let another take
this gift of yours, Fortune! To someone else
as you wish, or as is just, dispense it!

SCENA TERZA

TORRISMONDO, GERMONDO.

[TORRISMONDO]

Le nemicizie de' mortali in terra
esser devrian mortali ed aver fine;
1620   ma l'amicizie, eterne. Or siano estinte,
co' valorosi che morendo in guerra
tinsero già la terra e tinser l'onda
tre volte e quattro di sanguigno smalto,
l'ire e gli sdegni tutti. E qui cominci
1625   o pur si stabilisca e si rintegri
la pace e l'union di questi regni.

GERMONDO

Già voi foste di me la miglior parte,
or nulla parte è mia, ma tutto è vostro,
o tutto fia: se pur non prende a scherno
1630   vera amicizia quanto amore agogna,
ch'è d'altrui vincitor, da lei sol vinto.
Voi mi date ad Alvida. E 'nsieme Alvida
a me date voi solo. È vostro dono
il mio sì lieto amore e la mia vita.
1635   Ch'io per voi sono or vivo, e sono amante,
e sarò sposo. E s'ella ancor diviene
per voi mia donna, e sposa a' vostri preghi,
raccolto amore ov'accogliea disdegno,
qual fia dono maggior? Corone e scettri
1640   assai men pregio o pur trionfi e palme.

TORRISMONDO

Anzi io pur vostro sono. E me donando,
e lei che mia si crede, in parte adempio
il mio dever; ma non fornisco il dono
che me d'obligo tragga e voi d'impaccio.

SCENE THREE

TORRISMONDO, GERMONDO

[TORRISMONDO]

On earth, the hostilities of mortals
should be equally mortal and should end;
1620   but friendships should be eternal.
Now let all wrath and rancor be extinct,
as are the heroes who, dying in war,
once stained the earth and dyed the waves
three and four times with blood. And here,
1625   let the peace and union of our realms begin,
be re-established, knit again together.

GERMONDO

Time was, you were the better part of me;
now none of me is mine, but all is yours,
or will be: unless true friendship
1630   scorns all that love desires,
for love, which conquers all, yields but to friendship.
You give me to Alvida. And at the same time
you alone give Alvida to me. My blissful love,
my very life are thus your gift.
1635   For now I live because of you, and love,
and will be married. And if, thanks to your prayers,
she should become my lady and my wife,
gathering love where once there was disdain,
what present could be greater? Sceptres and crowns,
1640   triumphs and victories I value less.

TORRISMONDO

But I am also yours. Giving myself
and her who thinks she's mine, in part I pay
my debt; but my gift is not sufficient
to free me from my obligation, and you from your
    embarrassment.

1645 Sì darvi potessi io di nobil donna
il disdegnoso cor, ch'a me riserba,
come farò ch'il mio veggiate aperto.
Perché vane non sian tante promesse,
per me la bella Alvida ami Germondo,
1650 ami Germondo me. S'aspetta indarno
da me vendetta pur d'oltraggio e d'onta.
Vendicatela voi, ch'ardire e forza
ben avete per farlo.

GERMONDO

I vostri oltraggi
son pronto a vendicar. Dal freddo Carro
1655 mover prima vedrem Vulturno ed Austro,
e spirar Borea da l'ardenti arene,
e 'l sol farà l'occaso in oriente,
e sorgerà da la famosa Calpe
e da l'altra sublime alta colonna,
1660 ed illustrar d'Atlante il primo raggio
vedrassi il crine e la superba fronte,
e l'ocean nel salso ed ampio grembo
darà l'albergo oltre il costume a l'orse,
e torneranno i fiumi a' larghi fonti,
1665 e i gran mostri del mare in cima a' faggi
si vedran gir volando o sopra a gli olmi,
e co' pesci albergar ne l'acqua i cervi,
pria che tanta amicizia io tuffi in Lete
per novo amore. A' merti, al nome, a l'opra,
1670 debita è quasi la memoria eterna,
ed io questa rimembro e l'altre insieme:
però che grazia ognor grazia produce.

1645 Could I but offer you this noble woman's
 proud heart, which she reserves for me,
 as I will try to make mine open to you.
 So that these promises may not prove vain
 let Alvida love Germondo for my sake,
1650 and let Germondo love me. In vain she expects
 revenge of outrage and shame on my part.
 You must avenge her, for you have the boldness
 and the strength to do it.

GERMONDO

   The offenses done you
 I'm ready to avenge. But first we will see Vulturnus
1655 and Auster blowing from the frigid Wain
 and Boreas blowing from the blazing deserts;
 the sun will go down in the Orient
 and rise above Gibraltar in the West
 and over Hercules' other great column,
1660 and the first ray will be seen to light up
 Atlas' proud forehead and his hoary locks,
 and the ocean in its salty, ample bosom
 welcome the Bears, contrary to its custom;
 rivers will flow backwards to their springs
1665 and the great monsters of the sea will fly
 to the tops of beech-trees or the tops of elms,
 along with fishes deer will live in water,
 before I plunge such friendship into Lethe
 for a new love. Your merits, name and deeds
1670 deserve well nigh eternal memory,
 and I recall this deed as well as others:
 for grace invariably engenders grace.

SCENA QUARTA

TORRISMONDO, ALVIDA.

[TORRISMONDO]

Regina, ad onorar le vostre nozze
venuto è di Suezia il re Germondo,
1675   invitto cavaliero e d'alta fama,
e, quel che tutto avanza, è nostro amico;
né men vostro che mio; né tante offese
fece a' Norvegi mai la nobil destra
quanti farvi servigi ei brama e spera.
1680   Porger dunque la vostra a lui vi piaccia,
pegno di fede a di perpetua pace.
Fatelo perch'è mio, e perch'è vostro,
e perché tanto ei v'ama, e perch'il merta.

ALVIDA

Basti ch'è vostro amico: altro non chiedo.
1685   Perché sol dee stimar la donna amici
quei che 'l marito estima. E 'l merto e 'l pregio
e 'l valor e l'amor, per me soverchio,
m'è sol caro per voi. Ché vostra io sono,
e sol quanto a voi piace a me conviensi.

TORRISMONDO

1690   Questa del vostro amor, del vostro senno,
ho fede e speme. Oggi memoria acerba
non perturbi l'altero e lieto giorno
e la sembianza vostra e 'l vostro petto.

ALVIDA

Nel mio petto giammai piacere o noia
1695   non entrerà, che non sia vostro insieme.
Ché vostro è 'l mio volere, ed io ve 'l diedi
quando vi die' me stessa; e vostra è l'alma.

SCENE FOUR

TORRISMONDO, ALVIDA

[TORRISMONDO]

Good Queen, in honor of your nuptials
Sweden's King Germondo has come,
1675   a never vanquished knight of high renown,
and, more important still, he is our friend,
no less yours than mine; nor did his noble
right hand cause the Norwegians so much harm
as he now hopes and longs to serve you.
1680   May it please you, then, to offer him your right hand
as a token of faith and lasting peace.
Do it because he is mine and he is yours,
because he loves you dearly, and for his merits.

ALVIDA

It is enough to know he is your friend: I ask no more.
1685   For a woman must consider friends
only those her husband values. His merits and worth,
valor and love, too great for me,
are dear to me only because of you. For I am yours,
and I must do only what pleases you.

TORRISMONDO

1690   Such are the faith and hope I entertain
in your love and judgment. Let now no bitter memory
trouble so great and glad a day,
or your demeanor or your heart.

ALVIDA

Never will pleasure enter my heart,
1695   nor displeasure, that is not also yours.
For now my will is yours, I gave it to you
when I gave me to you; yours is my soul.

Posso io, s'a voi dispiaccio, odiar me stessa,
posso, se voi l'amate, amar Germondo.

TORRISMONDO

1700 Estingua tutti gli odii il nostro amore,
e nessuno odio il nostro amore estingua.

SCENA QUINTA

CAMERIERA, ALVIDA.

[CAMERIERA]

Questi doni a voi manda, alta regina,
il buon re mio signore e vostro servo:
ch'al servir non estima eguale il regno,
1705 né stimeria bench'il superbo scettro
i Garamanti e gli Etiopi e gli Indi
tremar facesse, e 'nsieme Eufrate e Tigre,
Acheloo, Nilo, Oronte, Idaspe e Gange,
Ato, Parnaso, Tauro, Atlante, Olimpo,
1710 e s'altro sorge tanto o tanto inaspra
lunge da noi famoso orribil monte.

REGINA

Di valoroso re leggiadri e ricchi
doni son questi, e portator cortese.

CAMERIERA

Non aguaglia alcun dono il vostro merto;
1715 ma non aggiate il donatore a sdegno,
ch'or vi presenta e la corona e 'l manto
e questa imago in preziosa gemma
scolpita.

I can, if I displease you, hate myself,
I can, if you too love him, love Germondo.

TORRISMONDO

1700　Let our love put away all hate,
and let no hate ever put out our love.

SCENE FIVE

MAID, ALVIDA

[MAID]

The good king, my master and your servant,
sends you these gifts, O noble Queen:
he would not put his kingdom on a par
1705　with serving you, even if his proud sceptre
caused Garamant to tremble, and Ethiop and Ind;
even if he ruled the Tigris and Euphrates,
Achelous, Nile, Orontes, Hydaspes, Ganges,
Athos, Parnassus, Taurus, Atlas, Olympus,
1710　or any other famous awful mountain
that towers so high and rocky far from us.

QUEEN [ALVIDA]

These are the exquisite and precious gifts
of a valiant king, and the bearer gracious.

MAID

No gift can match your worth;
1715　but do not spurn the donor
who now presents you with the crown and cloak,
this image graven on a precious stone.

ALVIDA

A prova la ricchezza e l'arte
contende, o l'opra la materia avanza;
1720   e la sua cortesia sì tosto aguaglia
del suo chiaro valor la fama illustre;
né mi stimò di tanto onore indegna.
Ma quai lodi o quai grazie al signor vostro
rendere io posso? o chi per me le rende?

CAMERIERA

1725   È grazia l'accettarli; e 'l don gradito
il donator d'obligo eterno astringe.

SCENA SESTA

ALVIDA, NUTRICE.

[ALVIDA]

Quai doni io veggio? e quai parole ascolto?
quale imagine è questa? a chi somiglia?
a me. Son io, mi raffiguro al viso,
1730   a l'abito non già. Norvegio o goto
a me non sembra. E perch'a' piedi impresse
calcata la corona e 'l lucido elmo,
e di strale pungente armò la destra?
e 'l leon coronato al ricco giogo,
1735   qual segno è d'altra parte, e 'l fregio intorno
ch'è di mirto e di palma insieme avvinto?
Questi nel manto seminati e sparsi
sono strali e facelle e nodi involti,
mirabile opra; e di mirabil mastro
1740   maraviglioso onor d'alta corona
come riluce di vermiglio smalto!
Sono stille di sangue. Il don conosco.
De la dolce vendetta il caro pregio

ALVIDA

Richness and art contend with one another,
indeed, the work surpasses the material;
1720   and so his courtesy is equal
to the illustrious renown of his bright worth;
nor was I deemed unfit for such an honor.
But with what praise or thanks can I repay
your master? Or who will give them for me?

MAID

1725   Your thanks is your acceptance; and the welcomed gift
binds the bestower with eternal bond.

SCENE SIX

ALVIDA, NURSE

[ALVIDA]

What gifts are these I see? What words I hear?
Whose image is this? Whom does it resemble?
Me. It is I, I recognize my face,
1730   but not my dress. It does not seem
Norwegian or Gothic. And why did he have
the crown and the gleaming helmet engraved at my feet,
why is the right hand armed with a piercing arrow?
Why is the crowned lion submitted to the yoke—
1735   what sign is on the other side, and the border round it
made of myrtle and of palm woven together?
These, sewn and scattered on the mantle,
are arrows and torches and inextricable knots—
a wondrous piece of work; and by a wondrous hand
1740   this marvelous honor of a lofty crown—
see how it shines there with its crimson glaze!
These drops are drops of blood. I know the gift.
The precious token of my sweet revenge,

e del mio lacrimare insieme i segni
1745   rimiro, e mi rammento il tempo e 'l loco.
E tu conosci di famosa giostra,
nutrice, il dono? È questo il prezzo, è questo,
e questa è la corona in premio offerta
al vincitor del periglioso gioco,
1750   ch'era poscia invitato ad altra pugna.
Ed io la diedi, e così volle il padre
mio sfortunato e del fratello anciso.

NUTRICE

La corona io conosco, e 'l dì rimembro
de le famose prove, e 'l dubbio arringo
1755   ch'al suon già rimbombò di trombe e d'armi;
ma l'altre cose, che 'l parlare accenna,
parte mi son palesi e parte occulte.
Perch'ancor non passava il primo lustro
vostra tenera età, che 'l vecchio padre,
1760   accioch'io vi nutrissi, a me vi diede,
dicendo: "Nudrirai nel casto seno
la mia vendetta e del mio regno antico,
de' tributi e de l'onte e de gl'inganni
e de l'insidie. È destinata in sorte".
1765   Egli più non mi disse, io più non chiesi.
Seppi dapoi ch'i più famosi magi
predicevano al re l'alta vendetta.

ALVIDA

Ma prima nuova ingiuria il duolo accrebbe,
e fé maggior ne l'orbo padre il danno.
1770   Perché a' Dani mandando aiuto in guerra
co 'l suo figliuol, che di lucenti squadre
troppo inesperto duce allor divenne,
contra i forti Sueci, a cui Germondo,
già ne l'arme famoso, ardire accrebbe,
1775   vi cadde il mio fratello al primo assalto,
dal feroce nemico oppresso e stanco.
Ei di seriche adorno e d'auree spoglie,

as well as the signs of my own tears
1745 once more I see, and I recall the time and place.
Do you, dear nurse, not recognize the trophy
of that famous joust? This is the prize!
This! This! And this the crown awarded
to the victor in that dangerous contest,
1750 later enjoined to fight another fight.
And I bestowed it; for such was the will
of my unhappy father, the father of my murdered brother.

NURSE

I recognize the crown, and I recall the day
of the great contest, and the field of dubious battle
1755 ringing with the sound of arms and trumpets;
but, of the other things that you have named,
certain are manifest, others are hidden.
Your tender years had not yet reached the age of five
when your aged father confided you
1760 into my care, for me to be your nurse,
declaring: "You will nurse in your chaste bosom
my own revenge and that of my ancient kingdom,
the tributes, the dishonors, the deceits,
the treachery I suffered. Fate decrees it."
1765 He said no more, I asked no more.
I later learned that the most famous wizards
had foretold great vendetta to the king.

ALVIDA

But first a new affront was added to his grief
and multiplied my bereaved father's loss.
1770 For, sending help to the warring Danes,
under his son's command, who in spite of his
    inexperience,
was made the leader of glittering squadrons
against the strong Swedes, in whom Germondo,
already famous in war, inculcated more courage,
1775 my brother fell at the first assault,
overcome and wearied by the ferocious enemy.
Yes, he, adorned in silk and golden spoils,

ch'io di mia propria mano avea conteste,
tutto splendea, sovra un destrier correndo,
1780 lo qual nato parea di flamma e d'aura;
e la corona ancor portava in fronte,
che 'l possente guerrier gli ruppe e trasse;
e gli uccise il cavallo e sparse l'armi,
e fé caderlo in un sanguigno monte,
1785 dove, ahi lassa, morì nel flor de gli anni.
E de le spoglie il vincitor superbo
indi partissi; e 'l suon dolente e mesto
si sparse intorno e 'l lagrimoso grido.
Altri danni, altre guerre, altre battaglie,
1790 altre morti seguiro in picciol tempo;
né poi successe certa e fida pace,
né fur mai queti i cori, o l'ira estinta.
Ecco a la giostra i cavalieri accoglie
il re mio padre, e com'altrui divolga
1795 publico bando in questa parte e 'n quella,
al vincitor promesso è 'l ricco pregio.
Vengon da' regni estrani al nostro regno
e da lontane rive a' lidi nostri
famosi cavalieri, a prova adorni
1800 di fino argento e d'or, di gemme e d'ostro,
d'altri colori e di leggiadre imprese.
Tutto d'arme e d'armati il suol risplende
de l'ampia Nicosia. Risuona intorno
di varii gridi e varii suoni il campo.
1805 Fuor de l'alta cittade il re n'alberga,
co' suoi giudici assiso in alto seggio;
io, fra nobili donne, in parte opposta.
Si rompon mille lance in mille incontri,
e mille spade fanno uscir faville
1810 da gli elmi e da gli usberghi: il pian s'ingombra
di caduti guerrieri e di cadenti:
è dubbia la vittoria, e 'l pregio incerto.
E mentre era sospesa ancor la palma,
apparve un cavalier con arme negre,
1815 ch'estranio mi parea, con bigie penne
diffuse a l'aura ventillando e sparse,
che parve al primo corso orribil lampo

which I had woven with my very hand,
all gleaming, as he rode upon a steed
1780 that seemed the offspring of the fire and wind;
and on his brow he wore the crown
the mighty warrior clove and seized,
and felled his horse, scattering abroad his arms,
and made him fall upon a bloody mound
1785 of corpses, where, alas, he died a flower
in bloom. And the proud winner of his spoils
went from there; and the sad and sorry
sound and tearful cry rang out all round.
Other losses, other wars, and other battles,
1790 other deaths followed in little time;
nor did a true and lasting peace ever ensue,
nor were hearts ever still, or wrath extinct.
So, at the joust, the king my father
assembles his nights, and as the herald
1795 proclaims in one place and another,
a precious prize is promised to the winner.
Famous knights from strange kingdoms
come to our own, they come from far-off climes
to our shores, each more tricked out than the next
1800 with gold and fine silver, jewels and purple,
with other colors and with curious emblems.
The ample land of Nicosia is all agleam
with arms and soldiers. The jousting field
rings round with various shouts and various echoes.
1805 The king is there outside of the high city,
sitting with his counselors on his high throne;
I, among noble women, on the far side.
A thousand lances are broken in a thousand clashes,
and a thousand swords make the sparks fly
1810 from helmets and coats of mail: the ground is littered
with fallen warriors and with warriors falling;
doubtful is the victory, and the prize uncertain.
And while the palm was undecided still,
there appeared a knight in sable armor,
1815 who seemed a foreigner, with ash-gray feathers
scattered to the wind and swaying in the breeze,
who sped like dreadful lightning in his first charge,

a cui repente segua atra tempesta.
Rotte già nove lance, il re m'accenna
1820   che mandi in dono al cavaliero un'asta.
Con questa di feroce e duro colpo
quel che gli altri vincea gittò per terra.
Né men possente poi vibrando apparse
la fera spada in varii assalti. Ei vinse,
1825   e poi fu coronato al suon di trombe.
Io volea porli in testa aurea corona,
ma non la volle a noi mostrare inerme:
ond'io la posi, ei la pigliò su l'elmo.
Cortesia ritrovò che 'l volto e 'l nome
1830   poté celarne, e si partì repente.
Né fu veduto più. Ma fur discordi
ragionando di lui guerrieri e donne.
Io seppi sol, ben mi rimembra il modo,
che si partiva il cavalier dolente
1835   mio servo, e di fortuna aspro nemico.
Or riconosco la corona e 'l pregio.
Era dunque Germondo? osò Germondo
contra i Norvegi in perigliosa giostra
dentro Norveggia istessa esporsi a morte?
1840   Tanto ardir, tanto core in vana impresa?
Poi tanta secretezza e tanto amore?
e sì picciola fede in vero amante?
E s'ei non era, onde, in qual tempo e quando
ebbe poi la corona? a chi la tolse?
1845   Chi gliela diede? ed or perché la manda?
Che segna il manto e la scolpita gemma?
o quai pensier son questi, e quai parole?

NUTRICE

Non so; ma varie cose asconde il tempo,
altre rivela, e muta in parte e cangia:
1850   muta il cor, il pensier, l'usanze e l'opre.

ALVIDA

Di mutato voler conosci i segni?
Son d'amante o d'amico i cari doni?

which is fast followed by a lowering tempest.
When he had broken nine lances, the king suggested
1820   I send a new lance as a gift to the knight.
With this, dealing a fierce and cruel blow,
he cast to the ground the victor of the rest.
Then, no less powerful in its many assaults,
did the cruel sword appear in its whirling. He won,
1825   and then was crowned to the sound of trumpets.
I desired to place a golden crown on his head
but he refused to show us his head uncovered:
so, I placed it and he received it on his helmet.
He found a courteous stratagem to conceal
1830   his face and his name, and speedily departed.
Nor was he ever seen again. But in talking about him,
warriors and women could not agree.
I only learned—well I remember how—
that the afflicted knight was leaving
1835   my servant, and the bitter enemy of fortune.
And now I recognize the crown and prize.
Was it Germondo, then? Did Germondo dare
against the Norwegians in dangerous joust,
inside Norway itself, to run the risk of death?
1840   Such boldness, such courage in a useless deed?
And then such secrecy and so much love?
And then so little faith in a true lover?
And if he was not the one, whence, how and when
did he obtain the crown? Whom did he take it from?
1845   Who gave it to him? Why does he send it now?
What does the cloak mean, and the sculptured jewel?
What is he thinking of, what did he say?

NURSE

I do not know; but time hides many things,
others it reveals, changes in part and alters:
1850   it alters hearts, thoughts, customs, and deeds.

ALVIDA

Do you recognize the signs of an altered will?
Are the dear gifts those of a lover or a friend?

Chi mi tenta, Germondo o 'l suo fedele?
Tenta moglie, od amica; amante, o sposa?
1855   Tenerli io deggio, o rimandarli indietro?
E s'io gli tengo pur, terrogli ascosi?
o gli paleserò? Scoperti o chiusi
al mio caro signor faranno offesa?
Il parlar gli fia grave, o 'l mio silenzio?
1860   Il timore, o l'ardir gli fia molesto?
Gli piacerà la stima, o 'l mio disprezzo?
Forse deggio io fallir perch'ei non erri?
o deggio forse amar perch'ei non ami?
o più tosto odiar perch'ei non odi?

NUTRICE

1865   Quai disprezzi, quali odii e quali amori
ragioni, o figlia, e qual timor t'ingombra?

ALVIDA

Temo l'altrui timor, non solo il mio;
e d'altrui gelosia mi fa gelosa
solo il sospetto: anzi il presagio, ahi lassa!
1870   Se troppa fede il mio signore inganna,
in lui manchi la fede, o in me s'accresca,
o pur creda a me sola: a me la serbi,
perch'è mia la sua fede, a me fu data.
A me chi la ritoglie, o chi l'usurpa?
1875   o chi la fa commune o la comparte?
O come la sua fede alcun m'aguaglia?
Ma forse ella non è soverchia fede.
È forse gelosia, che si ricopre
sotto false sembianze. Oimè dolente,
1880   deh, qual altra cagione ha 'l mio dolore
se non è il suo timor? S'egli non teme,
perché mi fugge?

NUTRICE

Il timor vostro il suo timor v'adombra,
anzi ve 'l finge; e se 'l timor lasciate,

Who tempts me—Germondo or his loyal friend?
Does he tempt a wife or a friend; a lover or a bride?
1855 Should I keep them, or send them back?
And, if I keep them, shall I keep them hidden?
Or shall I show them? Displayed or hidden,
will they offend my dear master?
Will my speech or my silence offend him?
1860 Will fear or boldness on my part distress him?
Will he be pleased by my appreciation or my contempt?
Must I do wrong so that he does not err?
Or should I love so that he does not love?
Or rather hate so that he does not hate?

NURSE

1865 Oh, what contempt is this, what hate, what love
you speak, my child? What fear encumbers you?

ALVIDA

I fear another's fear, not mine alone;
the mere suspicion—or rather, alas, the premonition—
of his jealousy makes me jealous;
1870 If too much faith deceives my master,
let him lose faith, or let it grow in me;
let him believe me only, keep his faith for me,
because his faith is mine, was pledged to me.
Who takes it from me, or who usurped it?
1875 Who makes it common property, who shares it?
Or how can anyone equal me in his trust?
But perhaps it is not excessive trust.
Perhaps it is jealousy, which hides itself
under false semblances. Oh, woe is me,
1880 what other reason is there for my grief
if not his fear? If he is not afraid,
why does he shun me?

NURSE

It's your own fear makes you see fear in him,
or better still, makes you imagine it. If you give up your
fear,

1885   non temerà, non crederò che tema.

ALVIDA

Quale amante non teme un altro amante?
quale amor non molesta un altro amore?

NUTRICE

L'amor fedele, io credo, e 'l fido amante.

ALVIDA

Ma fede si turbò talor per fede,
1890   non ch'amor per amor. S'amò primiero
Germondo re possente e re famoso,
cavalier di gran pregio e di gran fama,
e, come pare altrui, bello e leggiadro;
s'amò nemico, o pur nemica amando
1895   tenne occulto l'amor al proprio amico,
non è lieve cagion d'alto sospetto.

NUTRICE

Rara beltà, valore e chiara fama
del cavalier che fece i ricchi doni
se far non ponno or voi, regina, amante,
1900   già far non denno il vostro re geloso.
Deh, sgombrate del cor l'affanno e l'ombra
ch'ogni vostro diletto or quasi adugge.
Dianzi vi perturbava il sonno il sogno
fallace, che giamai non serva intere
1905   le sue vane promesse o le minacce,
e spavento vi diè notturno orrore
di simolacri erranti o di fantasmi;
or desta, nove larve a voi fingete,
e gli amici temete e 'l signor vostro;
1910   e paventate i doni, e chi gli porta
e chi gli manda, e le figure e i segni,
voi sola a voi cagion di tema indarno.

1885   he will not fear—I cannot believe he will fear.

ALVIDA

What lover does not fear another lover?
What love does not distress another love?

NURSE

A faithful love, I think, and a faithful lover.

ALVIDA

But faith has been upset at times by faith,
1890   and love by love. If Germondo was
the first to love, a great and mighty king,
a knight of great distinction and renown
and, as others see him, handsome and graceful;
and if he loved me, though an enemy, he kept
1895   his love a secret from his closest friend;
this is no small reason for grave suspicion.

MAID

If the rare beauty, valor and bright fame
of the knight who gave you these precious gifts
cannot, O Queen, bring you to love him,
1900   neither should they make your own king jealous.
For pity's sake, banish from your heart the anxiety and
    doubt
that now almost overshadow your delight.
Not long ago, your sleep was perturbed
by a deceptive dream which never entirely keeps
1905   its empty promises or threats,
and the nocturnal vision frightened you
of wandering ghosts and phantoms;
and now you are awake, you see new ghosts,
and suspect friends and even your master;
1910   you fear the gifts, the one who brings them to you,
the one who sends them, the figures and the signs;
you alone are the cause of your groundless fears.

ALVIDA

A qual vendetta adunque ancor mi serba
il temuto destino? e quale inganno
1915   o quali insidie vendicare io deggio?
ov'è l'ingannatore? ov'è la fraude?
Chi la ricopre, ahi lassa, o chi l'asconde?
O tosto si discopra, o stia nascosta
eternamente. Io temo, io temo, ahi lassa!
1920   E se del mio timor io son cagione,
par che me stessa io tema. E sol m'affida
del mio caro signore il dolce sguardo
e la sembianza lieta e 'l vago aspetto.
Egli mi raconsoli e m'assicuri.
1925   Egli sgombri il timor, disperda il ghiaccio.
Egli cari mi faccia i doni e i modi
e i donatori e i messi e i detti e l'opre;
e se vuole, odiosi. A lui m'adorno.

SCENA SETTIMA

ALVIDA, REGINA MADRE

[ALVIDA]

Son doni di Suezia. Il re Germondo
1930   me gli ha mandati, al figliuol vostro amico,
ed a me, quanto ei vuole. Ed io gradisco
ciò ch'al re mio signor diletta e piace.

REGINA

Ne 'l donare un gentile alto costume
serba l'amico re; ma i ricchi doni
1935   son belli oltre il costume, oltre l'usanza,
e convengon, regina, al vostro merto.
E noi corone avremo e care gemme
per donare a l'incontra. Onore è il dono;

ALVIDA

For what revenge, then, does fell destiny
preserve me? What deceitfulness,
1915   what stratagem must I avenge?
Where is the deceiver? Where the deceit?
Alas, who covers it, or who conceals it?
Let it be soon disclosed, or let it hide
eternally. I fear, I fear, alas!
1920   And if I am the cause of my own fear,
it seems I fear myself. I find trust only
in the sweet glance of my dear master
and in his happy face and handsome looks.
Oh, let him comfort and encourage me.
1925   Let him drive out the fear, scatter the ice.
Let him make dear the gifts and circumstances,
givers and messengers and words and deeds;
or, if he wishes, hateful. I put them on for him.

SCENE SEVEN

ALVIDA, QUEEN MOTHER

[ALVIDA]

These are the gifts from Sweden. King Germondo
1930   sent them to me, who is your son's best friend,
and mine, if your son so wills it. And I welcome
whatever delights and pleases the king my master.

QUEEN

In giving gifts, the king our friend respects
a noble and gentle custom; but such precious gifts
1935   are extraordinarily beautiful,
O Queen, and quite become your merit.
And we shall have crowns and precious jewels
to give him in exchange. Gifts are an honor;

      onorato esser dee com'egli onora:
1940   perch'è ferma amicizia e stabil fede
      se da l'onor comincia; ogni altra, incerta.

ALVIDA

      Certo è l'amor, certo è l'onor ch'io deggio
      a l'alto mio signor, certa è la fede,
      ch'i suoi più cari ad onorar m'astringe.

REGINA

1945   S'onora ne gli amici il re sovente,
      e ne' più fidi. Oggi è solenne giorno,
      giorno festo ed altero, e l'alta reggia
      adorna già risplende e 'l sacro templo.
      Venuto è 'l re Germondo e i duci illustri
1950   del nostro regno e i cavalieri egregi,
      d'Eruli un messo, un messaggier de gli Unni;
      mandati ha 'l re di Dacia i messi e i doni.

(IL FINE DEL TERZO ATTO)

CORO

      Amore, hai l'odio incontra e seco giostri.
      seco guerreggi, Amore,
1955   e con un giro alterno
      questo distruggi, e nasce il mondo eterno.
      Altro è, che non riluce a gli occhi nostri,
      più sereno splendore,
      altre forme più belle
1960   di sol lucente e di serene stelle.
      Altre vittorie in regno alto e superno,
      altre palme tu pregi,
      che spoglie sanguinose o vinti regi,

he should be honored as he is honoring:
1940   for friendship is firm and faith durable
          if they are based on honor; all else is unsure.

ALVIDA

Sure is the love, sure is the honor I owe
to my high master; sure is the faith
that bids me honor those who are dearest to him.

QUEEN

1945   Often we honor the king in honoring his friends
          and those who are most faithful. Today is a solemn day,
          a festive, auspicious day; the royal palace
          already shines adorned, as does the sacred temple.
          King Germondo has come with the illustrious leaders
1950   of our kingdom and the foremost knights,
          emissaries from the Heruli and the Huns;
          the king of Dacia too has sent envoys and gifts.

(END OF ACT THREE)

CHORUS

[Love is invoked, vanquisher of hate and lord of fortune,
and is besought not to take up arms against Friendship,
because they are the same thing.]

Love, you have hate against you and with him you joust,
with him you battle, Love,
1955   and, with a turn of Fortune's wheel,
          you destroy him, and the eternal world is born.
          There is another, brighter, splendor
          that does not shine before our mortal eyes;
          other and fairer forms
1960   of shining sun and limpid stars appear.
          New victories in a higher kingdom up above,
          on other palms you set more store
          than bloodied spoils or vanquished kings,

altra gloria, senza ira e senza scherno.
1965 Amore invitto in guerra,
perché non vinci e non trionfi in terra?

Perché non orni, o vincitor possente,
de' felici trofei
questa chiostra terrena
1970 con lieta pompa, ov'è tormento e pena?
Perch'il superbo sdegno e l'ira ardente
qua giuso e fra gli dei
non si dilegua e strugge,
se divo od uom non ti precorre e fugge?
1975 Ciò che l'ira ne turba or tu serena:
spengi le sue faville,
accendi le tue flamme e fa tranquille.
Stringi d'antica i nodi, Amor, catena
ond'anco è 'l mondo avinto,
1980 catenato il furore e quasi estinto.

Deh, non s'aguagli a te nemico indegno,
perché volga e rivolga
queste cose la sorte,
co 'l tornar dolce vita od atra morte.
1985 Diagli pur l'incostante instabil regno,
annodi i lacci o sciolga,
in alte parti o 'n ime
già non adegua il tuo valor sublime.
Tu, nel diletto e nel dolor più forte,
1990 miglior fortuna adduci,
e queste sfere o quelle orni e produci.
Tale, apra o serri in ciel lucenti porte,
o vada il sole o torni,
han possanza inegual le notti e i giorni.

1995 Contra fera discordia. Amor, contendi,
come luce con l'ombra.
Ma come l'arme hai prese
contra amicizia? ahi, chi primier l'intese?
S'offendi lei, pur te medesmo offendi;
2000 s'il tuo valor la sgombra
te scacci, e sechi in parti

another glory, free of anger and contempt.
1965 Love, undefeated in war,
why do you not conquer and triumph on earth?
Why do you not deck, O mighty conqueror,
with happy trophies
this earthly cloister,
1970 with happy pomp, where now are torment and pain?
Why do proud disdain and burning wrath
here below and among the gods
not vanish and melt away,
since neither god nor man can outrun or escape you?
1975 Whatever wrath disturbs us, you now assuage:
you extinguish its sparks,
you light your flames and keep them tranquil.
Love, tighten the knots of your ancient chain
with which the world is still bound,
1980 having bound fury in chains and almost slain him.
Oh, let not your unworthy enemy be your equal,
though fortune turn
and turn these things again
by alternating sweet life or black death.
1985 Whether, inconstant, it gives him his unsteady kingdom,
whether it binds or loosens the bonds
in high or in low places,
hate will never equal your sublime worth.
You, stronger both in pleasure and in pain,
1990 bring better fortune,
and the higher and the lower spheres you adorn and
frame.
Whether heaven's bright gates open or close,
whether the sun goes down or returns,
the power of night and day is not the same.

1995 Against fierce discord, Love, you should strive,
as light against darkness.
But how could you ever take up arms
against friendship? Ah, whoever heard of such a thing?
If friendship you offend, you offend yourself;
2000 if your valor puts friendship to flight,
you rout yourself, you tear yourself apart

s'amicizia da te dividi e parti.
Stendi l'arco per lei, signor cortese:
ella per te s'accinga
2005   e la spada per te raggiri e stringa.
Non cominci nova ira e nove offese,
né l'uno e l'altro affetto
turbi a duo regi il valoroso petto.

Deh, rendi, Amore, ogni pensiero amico.
2010   Amor, fa teco pace,
perch'è vera amicizia amor verace.

if friendship you divide and send away from you.
Bend not your bow, kind Lord, at friendship:
let friendship gird itself for you
2005 and grasp and wield the sword for you.
Let no new wrath or new offence begin.
Let neither passion
unsettle the brave breasts of the two kings.

Ah, Love, make every thought a friendly thought.
2010 Love, make peace with yourself,
for true love is true friendship.

ATTO QUARTO

SCENA PRIMA

CONSIGLIERO, GERMONDO.

[CONSIGLIERO]

Il venir vostro al re de' Goti, al regno,
a la reggia, signor, la festa accresce,
aggiunge l'allegrezza, i giochi addoppia,
2015 pace conferma in lei; spietata guerra,
il furore, il terror rispinge e caccia
oltre gli estremi e più gelati monti
e 'l più compresso e più stagnante ghiaccio
e i più deserti e più solinghi campi.
2020 Oggi Goti e Sueci, amiche genti,
non sol Norvegi e Goti, aggiunte insieme
ponno pur stabilir la pace eterna.
Oggi la fama vostra al ciel s'inalza
e quasi da l'un polo a l'altro aggiunge.
2025 Oggi par che paventi al suon de l'arco
l'Europa tutta e l'Occidente estremo,
e contra Tile ancor l'ultima Battro.
Perché non fan sì forti i nostri regni
stagni, paludi, monti e rupi alpestri
2030 e città d'alte mura intorno cinte
e moli e porti e l'ocean profondo,
come il vostro valor, ch'in voi s'aguaglia
a la vostra grandezza, e 'l nome vostro;
e i cavalieri egregi e i duci illustri.
2035 Lascio tanti ministri e tanti servi,

ACT FOUR

SCENE ONE

COUNSELOR, GERMONDO

[COUNSELOR]

Your coming to Gothland's king, and to his kingdom,
and to his royal palace, Sire, gives greater cause for
   celebration,
multiplies the joy, doubles the games,
2015   strengthens peace in the court; wards off and keeps at bay
pitiless war, its fury and its terror,
beyond the farthest and most frigid mountains
and the most firm-packed and most stagnant ice
and the most desolate and deserted steppes.
2020   Today, the Goths and Swedes are friendly peoples,
not just Goths and Norwegians, and united
we can establish everlasting peace together.
Today your renown rises to the sky
and almost reaches from one pole to the other.
2025   Today, at the sound of the bow, all of Europe
and the farthest West and, opposite to Thule,
even the furthermost Bactrus seems to tremble.
For lakes, swamps, mountains, rocky cliffs,
and cities girded round with massive walls,
2030   and breakwaters and ports and the deep ocean
make not our realms so strong
as does your valor, which equals
your greatness and your name,
your noble knights and famous generals.
2035   I leave aside your countless ministers and servants,

tante vostre ricchezze antiche e nove.
Ben senza voi sì grandi e sì possenti
l'umil plebe saria difesa inferma
di fragil torre, e voi le torri eccelse
2040   sete di guerra e i torreggianti scogli.
Chi voi dunque congiunge, a queste sponde
nova difesa fa e novo sostegno
del vostro onore, e l'assicura ed arma
contra l'insidie e i più feroci assalti.
2045   Non temerem che da remota parte
venga solcando il mar rapace turba
per depredarne, o ch'alto incendio inflammi
le già mature spiche o i tetti accenda.
Perché vostra virtù represse e lunge
2050   poté scacciar da noi gli oltraggi e l'onte.
Voi minacciando usciste, o regi invitti,
e l'un corse a l'occaso e l'altro a l'orto,
prima diviso e poi congiunto in guerra,
come duo gran torrenti a mezzo il verno,
2055   o duo fulmini alati appresso a' lampi,
quando flammeggia il cielo e poi rimbomba.
Ma del raro valor vestigia sparse
altamente lasciaste, offesi, estinti,
domi, vinti, feriti, oppressi e stanchi,
2060   duci, guerrieri, regi, eroi famosi.
Ed in mille alme ancor lo sdegno avampa,
e 'l desio d'alto imperio e di vendetta,
lo qual tosto s'accende e tardi estingue
e si nasconde a' più sereni tempi,
2065   ne' turbati si scopre, e fuor si mostra
tanto maggior quanto più giacque occulto.
Or che pensa il Germano o pensa il Greco?
o qual nutre sdegnando orribil parto
gravida d'ira la Panonia e d'arme?
2070   Queste cose tra me sovente io volgo.
E già non veggio più sicuro scampo
o più saggio consiglio, inanzi al rischio,
ch'unire insieme i tre famosi regni

your ancient wealth and all your new-won riches.
Without your greatness and your might,
the humble populace would be a weak defense
offered by a fragile tower, whereas you are
2040   the lofty towers of war, war's beetling cliffs.
He who makes, then, alliance with you, provides these
        shores
with new defenses, and a new support
for your honor, assuring and arming it
against perils and the cruellest assaults.
2045   We will not fear that from a remote shore
a greedy throng may come, plowing the sea,
to plunder us, or a raging fire may burn down
the already ripened ears of wheat or set our homes aflame.
For your valor has repressed and driven
2050   outrage and shame far from us.
Threatening, you went out, O unconquered kings,
and one coursed towards the sunset, the other towards the
        dawn,
divided at first, but joined in war thereafter,
like two torrents in mid-winter,
2055   or two winged thunderbolts following the lightning,
when the sky is set ablaze and resounds soon after.
But nobly you left evidence of your uncommon valor
scattered around, whether injured or dead,
broken, defeated, wounded, overcome, exhausted—
2060   leaders, soldiers, kings and famous heroes.
And in a thousand souls resentment still flares up,
and the desire for high empire and revenge,
swift to be enkindled, slow to die,
lying concealed during more peaceful times,
2065   only to reveal itself in time of trouble
far greater for having lain hidden so long.
And now what have the Germans or the Greeks in mind?
Or what terrible plan of vengeance does Pannonia,
swollen with arms and anger, nourish in disdain?
2070   On these things often within myself I muse,
and do not see a surer remedy,
or course of action, given the threat,
than to unite the three great kingdoms

che 'l gran padre Ocean quasi circonda
2075   e da gli altri scompagna e 'n un congiunge.
Perch'ogni stato per concordia avanza,
e per discordia al fin vacilla e cade.
Duo già ne sono uniti; e questo giorno
ch'Alvida e Torrismondo annoda e stringe,
2080   stringer potriasi ancor a voi Rosmonda,
ch'aguaglia a mio parer. Ma fia gran merto
non lasciar parte in tanta gloria al senso.
Molti sono tra voi legami e nodi
d'amicizia, d'amor, di stabil fede;
2085   e nessun dee mancarne. Aggiunto a' primi
sia questo novo e caro. E nulla or manchi
a lieta pace, or che dal Ciel discende
a tre popoli arcieri e 'n guerra esperti.
Fra' quai nessuno in amar voi precorse
2090   me d'anni grave. E questo ancor m'affida,
e la vostra bontà, la grazia e 'l senno:
talché primiero a ragionarne ardisco.
Ma non prego solo io. Congiunta or prega
questa, canuta e venerabil madre,
2095   antica terra, e di trionfi adorna.
E son queste sue voci e sue preghiere:
"O miei figli, o mia gloria, o mia possanza,
per le mie spoglie e per l'antiche palme,
per le vittorie mie famose al mondo,
2100   per l'alte imprese ond'è la gloria eterna,
per le corone de gli antichi vostri,
che fur miei figli e non venuti altronde,
questa grazia vi chiedo io vecchia e stanca;
e grazia a giusta età concessa è giusta".

GERMONDO

2105   Pensier canuto e di canuta etade
è quel ch'in voi si volge, e i detti lodo,
e gradisco il voler, gli affetti e l'opre.
Ma sì vera, sì ferma e sì costante
è la nostra amicizia, e strinse in guisa

which great Father Ocean surrounds almost entirely,
2075 separating them from the rest and joining them into one.
For every nation prospers through harmony,
but through discord totters and ultimately falls.
Two kingdoms are already united; and this day,
which ties in one bond Alvida and Torrismondo,
2080 could also unite to you Rosmonda, who is Alvida's match
in beauty, to my mind. Though in such a glorious union
it would be nobler not to allow the senses to have any part.
Between your kingdoms are many bonds and many ties
of friendship, love, and persevering faith;
2085 and no bond must be lacking. But let this new, dear knot
be added to these former bonds. And let nothing now
be lacking for a happy peace, now that it descends from
    Heaven
to three nations of archers expert in war.
No one amongst them has loved you more than I,
2090 though advanced in years. And this also gives me courage,
together with your goodness, grace and wisdom:
so that I dare be first to speak about it.
But I am not alone in begging you. Along with me now
this white-haired, venerable mother prays you—
2095 this ancient land, adorned with triumphs.
These are her words and these her prayers:
"O my children, my glory, and my might,
for all my spoils and ancient palms of victory,
for all my victories famed throughout the world,
2100 for all the high deeds whose glory is eternal,
for all the crowns of your great ancestors,
who were my own children and not from foreign climes,
I, old and weary, this grace now implore of you;
and grace is righteous granted to righteous age."

GERMONDO

2105 The wise thought of wise old age
is that which you now ponder, and I praise your words,
I welcome your wishes, loyalty and deeds.
And yet so true, so firm, so constant
is our friendship, and so insolubly

2110 amor, fede, valor duo regi errando,
che non si stringeria per nove nozze
con più tenace nodo o con più saldo.

CONSIGLIERO

Se nodo mai non s'allentò per nodo,
ma s'un simil per l'altro abonda e cresce,
2115 per legitimo amor non fia disciolta
vera amicizia, anzi sarà più salda.

GERMONDO

Amor, che fare il pò, confermi e stringa
amicizia fedel.

CONSIGLIERO

Migliori estimo
le nozze assai che l'amicizia ha fatte:
2120 l'altre pericolose.

GERMONDO

Ivi sovente
si ritrova gran lode ov'è gran rischio.

CONSIGLIERO

Lodato spesso è lo schifar periglio,
quando si schifa altrui.

GERMONDO

L'ardir più stimo,
se pò far gli altri arditi un solo ardito.

CONSIGLIERO

2125 Or de l'ardire è tempo, or del consiglio,
e s'ardire e consiglio in un s'accoppia,
fortuna ingiuriosa in van contrasta
a magnanima impresa, o lei seconda.

2110   did love, trust, valor bind two wandering kings,
that no new nuptials could ever bind them
with a stronger or a firmer knot.

COUNSELOR

If a knot was never loosened by another knot,
but if, being similar, they grasp and strengthen each other,
2115   true friendship will not be undone
by legitimate love: it will rather be made more firm.

GERMONDO

Let love, which can do this, confirm and strengthen
faithful friendship.

COUNSELOR

I value much more
a marriage based on friendship:
2120   others are dangerous.

GERMONDO

Great praise is often
found there where the risk is great.

COUNSELOR

Avoiding danger, too, is often praised,
when it is avoided for the sake of others.

GERMONDO

Boldness I esteem more,
if a single daring man can make others dare.

COUNSELOR

2125   Now it is time for boldness, now for counsel,
and, if audacity and counsel are joined together,
injurious fortune will oppose in vain
or favor in vain a noble enterprise.

Ma questo ancor sereno e chiaro tempo
2130   providenza veloce in voi richiede.
Congiunta ha 'l re norvegio al re de' Goti
la figlia. Ed oggi è lieto e sacro giorno,
ch'apre di stabil pace a gli altri il varco,
già aperto a voi. Nozze giungete a nozze,
2135   né siate voi fra tanto amor l'estremo.

GERMONDO

Primo sono in amare. Amai l'amico
di valor primo e 'n riamar secondo,
ed amerò finché 'l guerrero spirto
reggerà queste pronte o tarde membra.
2140   E mi rammento ancor ch'a lui giurando
la fede i' diedi, ed egli a me la strinse,
che l'un de l'altro a vendicar gli oltraggi
pronto sarebbe. Or non perturbi o rompa
novo patto per me gli antichi patti.
2145   E s'ei per liete nozze è pur contento
di pacifico stato e di tranquillo,
io ne godo per lui. Per lui ricovro
ne la pace e nel porto, e lascio il campo
e l'orrida tempesta e i venti aversi.
2150   Vera amicizia dunque il mar sonante
mi faccia, o queto; il ciel sereno, o fosco;
e di ferro m'avolga e mi circondi.
e mi tinga in sanguigno i monti e l'onde,
se così vuole, o 'l sangue asciughi e terga,
2155   e mi scinga la spada al fianco inerme.
Vera amicizia ancor mi faccia amante,
e, se le par, marito, e tutte estingua
d'Amore e d'Imeneo le faci ardenti,
o di Marte le flamme e 'l foco accresca.
2160   Così direte al re: lodo e confermo
che 'l vero amico mi discioglia o leghi.

But, however bright and favorable the circumstance,
2130   it yet requires swift foresight on your part.
The king of Norway has conjoined his daughter
to the king of the Goths. And today is the happy, holy day
that opens the way to lasting peace to them,
as it was opened once to you. Add one marriage to another;
2135   be not the last to share in so much love.

GERMONDO

I am the first in loving. I loved my friend,
worthier in deeds than me, second in love,
and I shall love him as long as my fighting spirit
sustains these vigorous or exhausted limbs.
2140   And I still remember that with an oath
I gave him my faith, and he joined his to mine:
each would be ready to avenge the harm
done to the other. Now, let no new pact
infringe or violate the old one.
2145   And if, through his joyful marriage, he is made content
to live in peace and in tranquillity,
I am happy for him. For his sake, I take shelter
in peace's haven, and quit the battlefield,
its fearful storms and adverse winds.
2150   Let true friendship, then, make the sea calm
or turbulent; the sky serene or sullen;
or let it encase and compass me in armor,
and stain the mountains and the waves with blood,
or, if it so wishes, let it staunch and purge the blood,
2155   and remove the sword from my defenseless side.
Let true friendship make me also a lover,
and, if it will, a husband; or let it douse
the burning torches of Love and Hymen,
and stir the fires and flames of Mars.
2160   Say this to the king: I approve and confirm
that my true friend may release or bind me.

SCENA SECONDA

GERMONDO solo.

Giusto non è che sia stimato indarno
malvagio il buono, o pur il buon malvagio,
perché perdita far di buono amico
2165   e de la cara vita è danno eguale;
ma tai cose co 'l tempo altri conosce,
ché sol pò il tempo dimostrar l'uom giusto.
Però se i giorni e l'ore e gli anni e i lustri
Torrismondo mostrar verace amico,
2170   parer non muto e di mutar non bramo,
anzi le vie del core io chiudo e serro
quanto m'è dato; e le ragioni incontra
al sospettar, ch'è sì leggiero e pronto
per sì varia cagion, raccolgo a' passi.
2175   Oh pur questa mia vera e stabil fede
non solo questo dì, ma un lungo corso
più mi confermi ancor d'anni volanti,
perché sian d'amicizia eterno essempio
l'invitto re de' Goti e 'l suo Germondo.
2180   Pur l'accoglienza e 'l modo ancor mi turba
assai diverso, e men sereno aspetto
che non soleva, e de la fé promessa
e di nostra amicizia e de gli errori
e de l'amata donna e del suo sdegno,
2185   dopo breve parlar lungo silenzio,
e breve vista dopo lunghi affanni.
Così peso di scettro e di corona
fa l'uom più grave, e con turbata fronte
spesso l'inchina, e di pensier l'ingombra.
2190   Solo amor non invecchia, o tardi invecchia.
A me sperato o posseduto regno,
o fatto danno o minacciata guerra,
tanto da sospirar giamai non porge,
ch'amor non tragga al tormentaso fianco
2195   altri mille sospiri. O liete giostre,
o cari pregi miei, corone ed arme,

SCENE TWO

GERMONDO (alone)

It is not just that without proof a good man
be judged evil, or a bad man good,
for to suffer the loss of a good friend
2165   or one's own precious life is just as harmful;
but it is time that makes such matters known,
for only time can prove a man is just.
Therefore if days, hours, years and decades,
show Torrismondo to be a true friend,
2170   I shall not change my mind—and do not wish to—
rather, my heart's inroads I close off and seal
as best I can; and I post sentinels at the passes of the mind
to bar suspicion's path, so quick and prompt,
and on such various grounds, to insinuate itself.
2175   Oh, not this day alone—may a long course
of flying years confirm still more my true
and steady faith and make the unvanquished
king of the Goths and his Germondo
an eternal paragon of friendship.
2180   Yet the strange manner of his welcome
perturbs me still, as does his mien, less calm
than it was wont to be, and, after a few words
upon his promised trust, our friendship, and our
    wanderings,
and the beloved lady and her disdain,
2185   long silence; likewise his brief appearance
after so many pains.
Thus the weight of a sceptre and a crown
bears a man down, and often bends him over
with troubled forehead, heaping him with worries.
2190   Only love is ever young, or grows old late.
Neither a kingdom, hoped-for or attained,
nor harm inflicted nor the threat of war
ever caused me to breathe so many sighs
as love draws by the thousandfold
2195   from my tormented breast. O happy jousts,
O cherished trophies, crowns and arms,

o vittorie, o fatiche, o passi sparsi,
al pensier non portate ora tranquilla
senza la donna mia. Saggi consigli,
2200 altre paci, altre nozze, ed altri modi
di vero amore, e d'amicizia aggiunte
lodo ben io. Ma per unirci insieme
sorella a me non manca, o stato od auro.
Ma faccia Torrismondo. A lui commesso
2205 ho 'l governo de l'alma, ed egli il regga.

SCENA TERZA

ROSMONDA, TORRISMONDO.

[ROSMONDA]

È semplice parlar quel che discopre
la verità. Però narrando il vero
con lungo giro di parole adorne
or non m'avolgo. O re, son vostra serva;
2210 e vostra serva nacqui e vissi in fasce.

TORRISMONDO

Non sei dunque Rosmonda?

ROSMONDA

Io son Rosmonda.

TORRISMONDO

Non sei sorella mia?

ROSMONDA

Né d'esser niego,
alto signor.

O victories, O toils, O wandering steps,
you do not bring my thoughts one tranquil hour
without my lady. Wise counsels,
2200   fresh alliances, another wedding, and other ways
of true love, and new signs of friendship
I praise. But, to bind us together,
I do not lack a sister or a kingdom or the wealth.
But let Torrismondo decide. To him I have entrusted
2205   the government of my soul: so let him rule it.

SCENE THREE

ROSMONDA, TORRISMONDO

[ROSMONDA]

The words that speak the truth are simple words.
Therefore, to speak the truth,
I will not wrap myself in lengthy coils
of ornate words. O king, I am your servant;
2210   I was born your servant and have been so since I was an
          infant.

TORRISMONDO

Are you not Rosmonda, then?

ROSMONDA

I am Rosmonda.

TORRISMONDO

Are you not my sister?

ROSMONDA

I cannot deny it,
noble master.

TORRISMONDO

Troppo vaneggi, ah folle!
Qual timor, quale error così t'ingombra
2215   che di stato servil tanto paventi?
Da tal principio a ricusar cominci?

ROSMONDA

Se femina ci nasce, or serva nasce
per natura, per legge e per usanza,
del voler di suo padre e del fratello.
2220   Ma fra tutte altre in terra o prima o sola
è dolce servitù servire al padre
ed a la madre, a cui partir l'impero
de' figli si devria. Né gli anni o 'l senno
fanno ogni imperio del fratel superbo.

TORRISMONDO

2225   Obbedisci a tua madre, ove ti piaccia.

ROSMONDA

Io non ho madre, ma regina e donna.

TORRISMONDO

Non sei tu di Rusilla unica figlia?

ROSMONDA

Né unica, né figlia esser mi vanto
de la regina de' feroci Goti.

TORRISMONDO

2230   E pur sei tu Rosmonda, e mia sorella?

ROSMONDA

Io sono altra Rosmonda, altra sorella.

TORRISMONDO

You rave too much, foolish girl!
What fear, what error burdens you so
2215   that you dread so much to be a servant?
Is this the way you prepare your refusal?

ROSMONDA

If one is born a woman, one is born a servant,
by nature, law and custom—a servant
of her father's and her brother's will.
2220   But among all servitudes on earth the first and only
the sweetest servitude is to serve one's father
and mother, who should share authority
over their children. And when he is of age
and reasonable, a brother's rule is never irksome.

TORRISMONDO

2225   Obey your mother, if you prefer.

ROSMONDA

I have no mother, only my queen and lady.

TORRISMONDO

Are you not Rusilla's only daughter?

ROSMONDA

I do not claim to be unique or be the daughter
of the queen of the fierce Goths.

TORRISMONDO

2230   And yet you are Rosmonda, and my sister?

ROSMONDA

I am a different Rosmonda, a different sister.

TORRISMONDO

Distingui omai questo parlar, distingui
questi confusi affanni.

ROSMONDA

A me fu madre
la tua nutrice, e poi nutrì Rosmonda.

TORRISMONDO

2235   Nova cosa mi narri, e cosa occulta,
e cosa che mi spiace e mi molesta.
Ma pur vizio è 'l mentir d'alma servile,
talché serva non sei, se tu non menti.

ROSMONDA

Serva far mi poté fortuna aversa
2240   de l'uno e l'altro mio parente antico.

TORRISMONDO

La tua propria fortuna il fallo emenda
de la sorte del padre, anzi il tuo merto.

ROSMONDA

Il merto è nel dir vero, il premio attendo
di libertà, se libertà conviensi.

TORRISMONDO

2245   S'è ciò pur vero, è con modestia il vero,
e men si crederia superbo vanto,
se dee credere il mal l'accorto e 'l saggio,
ove il non creder giovi.

ROSMONDA

È picciol danno
perder l'opinion, ch'è quasi un'ombra,

TORRISMONDO

It's time to explain your words, explain
these confused apprehensions.

ROSMONDA

My mother
was your nurse, who also nursed Rosmonda.

TORRISMONDO

2235   What you are telling me is strange and secret
and something that displeases and dismays me.
But lying is the vice of a servile soul:
so you are not a servant, if you are not lying.

ROSMONDA

It was my aged parents' adverse fortune
2240   that made me a servant.

TORRISMONDO

Then let your own good fortune, or your merit,
amend the failing of your father's luck.

ROSMONDA

My merit is to tell the truth: the prize of freedom
I await, if freedom is a fitting prize.

TORRISMONDO

2245   If this is true, it is a modest truth
and a proud boast would be less credible;
if wise and prudent, a man must believe the worst,
though not believing it would serve him better.

ROSMONDA

It is not much to lose
the world's opinion, which is like a shadow,

2250   e di finta sorella un falso inganno:
         anzi gran pro mi pare, ed util certo.

TORRISMONDO

         Quasi povero sia de' Goti il regno,
         cui può sì ricco far guerrera stirpe,
         le magnanime donne e i duci illustri.
2255   Ma deh, come sei tu vera Rosmonda,
         e finta mia sorella, e falsa figlia
         de la regina de gli antichi Goti?
         Chi fece il grande inganno o 'l tenne ascosto
         tanti e tanti anni? e qual destino o forza
2260   la fraude e l'arte a palesar t'astringe?

ROSMONDA

         Per mia madre e per me breve io rispondo.
         Fé l'inganno gentil pietà, non fraude,
         e 'l discopre pietà.

TORRISMONDO

             Tu parli oscuro,
         perché stringi gran cose in picciol fascio.

ROSMONDA

2265   Da qual parte io comincio a fare illustre
         quel ch'oscura il silenzio e 'l tempo involve?

TORRISMONDO

         Quel che ricopre, al fin discopre il tempo.
         Ma de le prime tu primier comincia.

ROSMONDA

         Sappi che grave già per gli anni, e stanca
2270   dopo la morte d'uno e d'altro figlio,
         dopo la servitù che d'ostro e d'oro
         ne l'alta reggia altrui sovente adorna,

2250   and the semblance of a pretended sister:
        instead, it seems a great advantage and a certain gain.

TORRISMONDO

As if the kingdom of the Goths were without consequence,
which is made so mighty by its race of warriors,
its noble women and illustrious leaders.
2255   But tell me, how can you be the real Rosmonda,
and my feigned sister, and the false daughter
of the queen of the ancient Goths?
Who planned so great a deception, and kept it hidden
for so many, many years? And what destiny or what force
2260   compels you now to reveal such fraud and conniving?

ROSMONDA

Briefly I will answer for my mother and for myself.
The deceit was brought about by gentle compassion, not
        by fraud,
and compassion leads me to disclose it.

TORRISMONDO

Obscure are your words,
for you bind many things in a small bundle.

ROSMONDA

2265   Where shall I begin to bring to light
what silence overshadows and time hides?

TORRISMONDO

That which is hidden, time finally uncovers.
But start from the very beginning.

ROSMONDA

You should know that, already well advanced in years,
2270   and weary following the death of both her sons,
after the years of servitude which, in lofty courts,
earns the reward of gold and purple robes,

la madre mia di me portava il pondo,
con suo non leggier duolo e gran periglio.
2275   Onde quel che nascesse a Dio fu sacro
da lei nel voto; ed egli accolse i preghi.
Talch'il descender mio nel basso mondo
non fu cagione a lei d'aspra partenza,
né 'l chiaro dì ch'io nacqui a lei funebre.

TORRISMONDO

2280   Dunque i materni, e non i propi voti
tu cerchi d'adempir, vergine bella?

ROSMONDA

Son miei voti i suoi voti, e poi s'aggiunse
al suo volere il mio volere istesso
quel sempre acerbo ed onorato giorno
2285   che giacque essangue e rendé l'alma al Cielo;
mentre io sedea dogliosa in su la sponda
del suo vedovo letto, e lagrimando
prendea la sua gelata e cara destra
con la mia destra. E le sue voci estreme,
2290   ben mi rammento, e rammentar me 'n deggio,
tra freddi baci e lagrime dolenti
fur proprio queste: "È pietà vera, o figlia,
non ricusar la tua verace madre,
che madre ti sarà per picciol tempo.
2295   Io ti portai nel ventre, e caro parto
ti diedi al mondo, anzi a quel Dio t'offersi
che regge il mondo e mi salvò nel rischio.
Tu, se puoi, de la madre i voti adempi,
e disciogliendo lei sciogli te stessa".

TORRISMONDO

2300   La tua vera pietà conosco e lodo.
Ma qual pietoso o qual lodato inganno
te mi diè per sorella, e l'altra ascose

my mother was carrying me in her womb
with no slight suffering and mortal danger.
2275   Therefore, with a vow she consecrated to God
the one who was to be born; and He listened to her
    prayers.
Because of this my descent into this low world
was not the cause of her harsh quitting of it,
nor the bright day when I was born a mournful one for
    her.

TORRISMONDO

2280   Then your mother's vows, and not your own,
you wish to fulfill, beautiful virgin?

ROSMONDA

Her vows are my vows, and, soon after,
my own will was added to her will:
on that ever bitter and honored day
2285   when she lay lifeless and rendered her soul to Heaven,
while mourning I sat upon the edge
of her widowed bed, and in tears
I held her icy, precious hand
in mine. And her final words,
2290   well I recall (and recollect I must)
among cold kisses and tears of grief
were these and no others: "True piety, my daughter,
consists in not denying your true mother,
who only for a brief time now will be your mother.
2295   I carried you in my womb, and as my dear offspring
I gave you to the world—rather, I offered you
to that God who rules the world and saved me in my peril.
Fulfill, if you can, your mother's vows,
and by releasing her, release yourself."

TORRISMONDO

2300   I know and praise your filial piety.
But what merciful, what praiseworthy deception
gave you to me as my sister, and hid the other

che fu vera sorella, e vera figlia
di magnanimo re, d'alta regina?

ROSMONDA

2305   Fé mia madre l'inganno, anzi tuo padre;
e pietà fu de l'una, e fu de l'altro
o consiglio, o fortuna, o fato, o forza.

TORRISMONDO

A chi si fece la mirabil fraude?

ROSMONDA

A la regina tua pudica madre,
2310   la qual mi stima ancor diletta figlia.

TORRISMONDO

In tanti anni del ver delusa vecchia
non s'accorge, non l'ode, e non conosce
la sua madre la figlia, o pur s'infinge?

ROSMONDA

Non s'infinse d'amar, né d'esser madre,
2315   se fa madre l'amor, che spesso adegua
le forze di natura, e quasi avanza.
Né di scoprire osai l'arte pietosa
che le schifò già noia e diè diletto,
ed or porge diletto e schiva affanno.

TORRISMONDO

2320   Ma come ella primiera al novo inganno
diè così stabil fede, e non s'accorse
de la perduta figlia, e poi del cambio?

ROSMONDA

La natura e l'età, che non distinse
me da la tua sorella, e 'l tempo e 'l luogo

who was my real sister, and the true daughter
of a generous king and a noble queen?

ROSMONDA

2305 My mother wrought the deceit—your father, rather;
and it was piety on her part, and counsel,
fortune, fate, or force on the other's part.

TORRISMONDO

Whom was this amazing fraud addressed to?

ROSMONDA

To your chaste mother the queen,
2310 who still believes me her beloved daughter.

TORRISMONDO

And in all these years has the aged victim
not realized, not heard the truth; and does the mother
not know her daughter, or is she pretending?

ROSMONDA

She did not pretend to love, nor to be a mother,
2315 if it is love, which often equals natural forces
and even surpasses them, that makes a mother.
Nor did I dare to uncover the piteous art
that spared her weariness and gave her joy,
and now gives her delight and spares her grief.

TORRISMONDO

2320 But what made her so ready to believe
in the novel deception, and not become aware
of her daughter's loss, and of the subsequent exchange?

ROSMONDA

Our natures and ages, which did not distinguish
me from your sister, and the time and place

2325   dove in disparte ambe nutriva e lunge
         la vera madre mia da l'alta reggia,
         tanto ingannar la tua; ma più la fede
         ch'ebbe ne la nutrice e nel marito.

                    TORRISMONDO

         Se la fede inganno, l'inganno è giusto.
2330   Ma dove ella nutrivvi?

                    ROSMONDA

                    Appresso un antro
         che molte sedi ha di polito sasso
         e di pumice rara oscure celle
         dentro non sol, ma bel teatro e tempio
         e tra pendenti rupi alte colonne,
2335   ombroso, venerabile, secreto.
         Ma lieto il fanno l'erbe e lieto i fonti,
         e l'edere seguaci e i pini e i faggi,
         tessendo i rami e le perpetue fronde,
         sì ch'entrar non vi possa il caldo raggio.
2340   Ne le parti medesme entro la selva
         sorge un palagio al re tra i verdi chiostri.
         Ivi tua suora ed io giacemmo in culla.

                    TORRISMONDO

         La cagion di quel cambio ancor m'ascondi.

                    ROSMONDA

         La cagion fu del padre alto consiglio,
2345   o profondo timor che l'alma ingombra.

                    TORRISMONDO

         Qual timore, e di che?

                    ROSMONDA

                    D'aspra ventura,
         che 'l suo regno passasse ad altri regi.

2325   where my real mother nursed both of us,
out of the way and far from the royal palace,
deceived your mother so; but, even more, the trust
she placed in the nurse and her own husband.

TORRISMONDO

If faith deceived her, then deceit is just.
2330   But where did she nurse you?

ROSMONDA

Next to a cave
that houses many seats of polished marble,
and has within not only gloomy cells
carved of rare pumice, but a spacious theater
and temple, and columns tall mid hanging rocks—
2335   a shadowed, venerable, secret place.
But cheered by grass, gladdened by springs,
and climbing ivy, pine and beech-trees,
weaving their branches and perennial leaves,
so that the sun's hot rays can never penetrate.
2340   In the same place, deep in the forest,
stands a royal palace among green glades.
There your sister and I lay in the cradle.

TORRISMONDO

You still have not revealed the cause of that exchange.

ROSMONDA

The reason was your father's hidden counsel
2345   or some deep fear encumbering his soul.

TORRISMONDO

What fear, of what?

ROSMONDA

Fear of a harsh eventuality—
that his kingdom might pass to other kings.

TORRISMONDO

E come nacque in lui questa temenza
di sì lontano male? o chi destolla?

ROSMONDA

2350   Il parlar la destò d'accorte ninfe,
ch'altrui soglion predir gli eterni fati.

TORRISMONDO

Dunque ei diede credenza al vano incanto,
ch'effetto poi non ebbe in quattro lustri?

ROSMONDA

    Diede, e diede la figlia ancora in fasce
2355   a l'alpestre donzelle o pur selvagge,
e tra quell'ombre in quell'orror nutrita
la fanciulletta fu d'atra spelunca.

TORRISMONDO

Perché si tacque a la regina eccelsa?

ROSMONDA

    Quel palagio, quell'antro e quelle ninfe,
2360   e quelle antiche usanze, e l'arti maghe
eran sospette a la pietosa madre,
a cui mostrata fui, volgendo il sole
già de la vita mia il secondo corso,
pur come figlia sua, né mi conobbe;
2365   e 'l re fece l'inganno, e 'l tenne occulto.
E per voler di lui s'infinse e tacque
la vera madre mia, che presa in guerra
fu già da lui ne la sua patria Irlanda,
ov'ella nata fu di nobil sangue.

TORRISMONDO

2370   Vive l'altra sorella ancor ne l'antro?

TORRISMONDO

And how was this fear, of so remote an evil,
born in him? Who aroused it?

ROSMONDA

2350   The words of wise nymphs who ever foretell
the eternal fates to men, aroused it.

TORRISMONDO

So, he believed the vain enchantment
that has not had effect in twenty years?

ROSMONDA

He did, and gave the babe still clad in swaddling clothes
2355   to those maidens of the woods and mountains,
and so among those shades and in the gloom
of a dark cave, the child was raised.

TORRISMONDO

Why was this hidden from the lofty queen?

ROSMONDA

That palace, that cavern and those nymphs,
2360   those ancient rites, and the magic arts
were all suspicious to the loving mother
to whom I was shown, when the sun was already
bringing to a close the second year of my life,
yet she did not recognize me as her daughter;
2365   and the king planned the deception and kept it hidden.
And by his will my true mother pretended
and said nothing—she who had been taken by him
a prisoner of war from her native Ireland,
where she was born of noble blood.

TORRISMONDO

2370   And does the other sister live on in the cave?

ROSMONDA

Vi stette a pena infino a l'anno istesso,
e poi d'altri indovini altri consigli
crebbero quel timore e quel sospetto,
talché mandolla in più lontane parti
2375   per un secreto suo fedel messaggio;
né seppi come, o dove.

TORRISMONDO

Il servo almeno
conoscer tu devresti.

ROSMONDA

Io no 'l conosco,
né so ben anco s'io n'intesi il nome;
ma spesso udia già ricordar Frontone,
2380   e 'l nome in mente or serbo.

TORRISMONDO

Il re celato
tenne sempre a la moglie il cambio e l'arte?

ROSMONDA

Tenne sinché 'l prevenne acerba morte,
facendo lui co' Dani aspra battaglia.
Così narrò la mia canuta ed egra
2385   madre languente, e lui seguì morendo.

TORRISMONDO

Cose mi narri tu d'alto silenzio
veracemente degne, e 'n cor profondo
serbar le devi e ritenerle ascoste:
ch'i secreti de' regi al folle volgo
2390   ben commessi non sono, e fuor gli sparge
spesso loquace fama, anzi buggiarda.
A me chiamisi il Saggio, e poi Frontone.

ROSMONDA

She stayed there scarcely till the end of the same year,
and then the counsel of other soothsayers
increased his fear and apprehension
so that he sent her to more distant lands
2375   by a discreet and reliable messenger;
I never did know how or where.

TORRISMONDO

The servant, at least,
you ought to recognize.

ROSMONDA

I do not know him,
nor do I well remember if I heard his name;
but often I heard them speak of one Frontone—
2380   a name that still sticks in my mind.

TORRISMONDO

Did the king keep
the exchange and the fraud always hidden from his wife?

ROSMONDA

He did till he succumbed to untimely death,
while he was in a bitter battle with the Danes.
So my aged and ailing mother told me
2385   on her death-bed, and followed him in death.

TORRISMONDO

These things you are telling me are truly worthy
of utmost silence, and in your deepest heart
you must keep them concealed:
for the secrets of kings are not to be entrusted
2390   to the foolish populace, and often loquacious—
or better, lying—Rumor broadcasts them.
Have the Soothsayer brought before me, then Frontone.

SCENA QUARTA

TORRISMONDO, INDOVINO, CORO.

[TORRISMONDO]

Lasso, quinci Fortuna e quindi Amore
mille pungenti strali ognor m'aventa,
2395   né scocca a voto mai, né tira indarno.
I pensier son saette, e 'l core un segno,
de la vittoria è la mia vita il pregio,
giudici il mio volere e 'l mio destino,
né l'un né l'altro arciero ancora è stanco.
2400   Che fia, misero me? Per caso od arte
quasi mi si rapisce e mi s'invola
una sorella, e d'esser mia ricusa,
e l'altra, oimè, non trovo e non racquisto,
e non ristoro o ricompenso il danno,
2405   e 'l cambio manca ove mancò la fede,
acciocch'offrir non possa al re Germondo
cosa degna di lui, ma vano in tutto
sia come l'impromessa altro consiglio.
Sorella per sorella, o sorte iniqua,
2410   già supponesti ne la culla e 'n fasce,
ed or me la ritogli anzi la tomba,
e l'altra non mi rendi. O speco, o selve,
in cui già la nutrir leggiadre ninfe,
o de la terra algente orridi monti,
2415   o gioghi alpestri, o tenebrose valli,
ove s'asconde? o 'n qual deserta piaggia,
in qual isola tua solinga ed erma,
o gran padre Ocean, nel vasto grembo
tu la circondi? Andrò pur anco errando,
2420   andrò solcando il mare, andrò cercando
non la perduta fede e chi l'insegna,
ma come possa almen coprire il fallo?

CORO

Ecco, signore, a voi già viene il Saggio,

SCENE FOUR

TORRISMONDO, SOOTHSAYER, CHORUS

[TORRISMONDO]

Alas, Fortune and Love on either side
assault me with a thousand piercing darts,
2395 nor do they ever aim or shoot in vain.
Thoughts are the arrows, and my heart the target,
the prize of victory my very life,
the judges are my will and destiny,
and neither archer is yet wearied.
2400 What will befall me, wretched me? By chance or by design
one sister is almost snatched
and stolen from me, she denies that she is mine,
and the other, alas, I cannot find out or recover,
nor can I restore or remedy my loss,
2405 and restitution's missing where faith failed,
so that I cannot offer King Germondo
anything worthy of him, while every other course
is as utterly vain as what was promised.
You substituted a sister for a sister,
2410 O cruel fate, in her cradle and swaddling clothes,
and now you take her from me before the grave,
and do not give the other back. O cave, O forests,
where lovely nymphs once raised her,
O icy, horrid mountains of the earth,
2415 O alpine passes, O mysterious valleys,
where does she hide? On what deserted shore,
in which of your lonely, solitary islands,
O great Father Ocean, in your vast bosom
do you encircle her? Shall I go wandering still,
2420 shall I go furrowing the sea, seeking
not for lost faith and the one who teaches it,
but how at least I may conceal my wrong?

CHORUS

Here he is, Master: the Soothsayer comes before you,

a cui sol fra' mortali è noto il vero
2425   da caligini occulto e da tenebre.

TORRISMONDO

O Saggio, tu che sai (pensando a tutto
quel che s'insegna al mondo o si dimostra)
i secreti del cielo e de la terra,
dimmi se mia sorella è in questo regno.

INDOVINO

2430   Ahi, ahi, quanto è 'l saper dannoso e grave,
ove al saggio non giovi. E ben previdi
ch'io veniva a trovar periglio e biasmo.

TORRISMONDO

Per qual cagion tu sei turbato in vista?

INDOVINO

Lasciami, no 'l cercar, nulla rileva
2435   che 'l mio pensier si scopra o si nasconda.

TORRISMONDO

Dimmi se mia sorella è in questo regno.

INDOVINO

È dove nacque, e dove nacque or posa,
se pur ha posa, e non ha posa in terra.

TORRISMONDO

Dunque in terra non è?

INDOVINO

Non posa in terra,
2440   ma poserà dove tu avrai riposo.

2425 to whom alone among mortals is known the truth
hidden by mists and darkness.

TORRISMONDO

O Sage, you who know (thinking of everything
taught or demonstrable in the world)
the secrets of the heavens and earth,
tell me if my sister is present in this kingdom.

SOOTHSAYER

2430 Alas, alas, how grave and harmful is the knowledge
that is of no use to the knower. Well I foresaw
that I was coming here to find peril and blame.

TORRISMONDO

Why does your countenance look so dismayed?

SOOTHSAYER

2435 Dismiss me, do not seek to know, it matters not
whether my thought be hidden or unveiled.

TORRISMONDO

Tell me if my sister is in this kingdom.

SOOTHSAYER

She is where she was born, where she was born she now
    reposes,
if there can be repose; there's no repose on earth.

TORRISMONDO

She's not on earth, then?

SOOTHSAYER

She has no peace on earth,

2440 she'll find repose where you will find repose.

TORRISMONDO

Quale a gli oscuri detti oscuro velo
intorno avolgi, o quale inganno od arte?
Dimmi se mia sorella è in questo regno.

INDOVINO

Tu medesmo t'inganni. È tua la frode,
2445   perché tu la facesti, e teco alberga.

TORRISMONDO

Se non è il tuo saper vano com'ombra,
discopri tu l'inganno, e tu rivela
se la sorella mia tra Goti or vive.

INDOVINO

Vive tra Goti.

TORRISMONDO

              Ed in qual parte, e come?
2450   È quella forse che stimava, od altra?
S'altra, dove s'asconde o si ritrova?

INDOVINO

È l'altra, ed u' si trova ancor s'asconde,
e la ritroverai da te partendo
e servando la fede.

TORRISMONDO

              Intrichi ancora
2455   gli oscuri sensi di parole incerte,
per accrescer l'inganno, e 'nsieme il prezzo
de le menzogne tue. Parlar conviensi,
talché si scopra in ragionando il falso.

TORRISMONDO

With what dark veil do you envelop
your obscure words, what art or what deception?
Tell me if my sister is in this kingdom.

SOOTHSAYER

It is you who deceive yourself. Yours is the fraud,
2445   because it was you created it; in you it dwells.

TORRISMONDO

Unless your wisdom is as empty as a shadow,
then you shall unveil the fraud, and you shall reveal
whether my sister lives among the Goths.

SOOTHSAYER

She lives among the Goths.

TORRISMONDO

And where, and how?
2450   Is she the one I thought or someone else?
If someone else, where is she hidden, where can she be
    found?

SOOTHSAYER

She is the other, and where she is now, she hides still,
and you will find her when you leave yourself
and keep your promise.

TORRISMONDO

You are still tangling
2455   your dark meaning with doubtful words,
so as to augment the fraud, and with it the price
of your lies. We have need to speak,
so that by speech falsehood may be discovered.

INDOVINO

È certo il tuo destin, la fede incerta.
2460 Ma se quanto oro entro le vene asconde
l'avara terra a me nel prezzo offrissi,
altro non puoi saper, ch'il fato involve
l'altre cose, che chiedi, al nostro senso,
e lor nasconde entro profonda notte.
2465 Ma pur veggio nascendo il gran Centauro
saettar fin dal cielo e tender l'arco,
e la belva crudel, ch'irata mugge,
con terribil sembianza uscir de l'antro,
e paventare il Vecchio, e 'l fiero Marte
2470 oppor lo scudo e flammeggiar ne l'elmo,
e con la spada e fulminar con l'asta.
Veggio, o parmi veder, del vecchio Atlante
appresso il cerchio, e 'l gran Delfino ascoso,
e stella minacciar più tarda e pigra.
2475 E la Vergine io veggio amica a l'arti
turbata in vista, e la celeste Libra
con men felici e men sereni raggi.
E cader la Corona in mezzo a l'onde.
Né dimostrar benigno e lieto aspetto
2480 chi scote da le nubi il ciel tonando,
o pur la mansueta e gentil figlia.
Ma 'l superbo guerrier la mira e turba.
E i lascivi animali ancora io sguardo,
a cui vicino è Marte, e vibra il ferro;
2485 e i duo Pesci lucenti il dorso e il tergo
l'uno a Borea inalzarsi e l'altro scendere
a l'Austro, e di tre giri e di tre flamme
acceso il cielo, e da quel nodo avinto
tre volte intorno e minacciando, appresso,
2490 il fero dio che regge il quinto cerchio;
e, pien d'orrore ogni altro e di spavento,
de' segni o de gli alberghi empio tiranno
girando intorno ir con veloce carro,
o signoreggi a sommo il cielo, o caggia.

SOOTHSAYER

Your destiny is certain, your faith uncertain.
2460 But if you offered me the worth of all the gold
which the miserly earth hides in its veins,
I could not tell you more, for fate conceals
from our understanding the other things you ask,
burying them with the deepest night.
2465 But now I see the great Centaur, rising,
shoot from the sky, and bend his bow,
and the cruel beast, bellowing in wrath,
with fearsome aspect issue from the cave,
and frighten old Aquarius, and fierce Mars
2470 brandish his shield, all fiery in his helmet,
and threaten with his sword and with his spear.
I see, or seem to see, old Atlas' circle
next, and the great hidden Dolphin,
and, threatening, the slowest, laziest star.
2475 And I see Virgo, friend to the arts,
of turbid aspect, and celestial Libra
with less serene and less auspicious rays,
and the Crown drop into the waves.
Nor does he who shakes the sky with thunder
2480 from the clouds show a glad and favorable aspect,
and neither does his meek and gentle daughter.
But the proud warrior watches and confounds her.
And I also see the wanton animals
near whom is Mars, hurling his iron weapon;
2485 and the two Pisces with their glistening backs,
one rising toward Boreas, the other descending
to Auster, and the sky lit with three circles
and three flames and three times wound around
with that knot, and menacing close behind
2490 the proud god who rules the fifth heaven;
and, filling all the others with fear and horror,
that cruel tyrant of the signs and their houses
go wheeling round in his swift chariot,
now dominating the highest sky, now falling.

CORO

2495   Vero o falso che parli, ei solo intende
       le sue parole, e 'l suo giudicio è incerto
       non men del nostro. E se l'uom dar potesse
       per sapienza sapienza in cambio,
       aver potrebbe accorgimento e senno
2500   quanto bastasse a ragionar co' regi.

TORRISMONDO

       Lasciamlo. Or trovi le spelunche e i monti,
       ove nulla impedir del ciel notturno
       gli pò l'aspetto. Ivi a sua voglia intenda
       a misurarlo, a numerar le stelle,
2505   e con danno minor se stesso inganni,
       se così vuole.

INDOVINO

                 Anzi ch'al fine aggiunga
       una di quelle omai fornite parti
       de le cui note ho questo legno impresso,
       a cui la stanca mia vita s'appoggia,
2510   i miei veri giudìci or presi a scherno,
       o superba Aarana, o reggia antica
       ch'or da te mi discacci, a te fian conti.

SCENA QUINTA

FRONTONE, TORRISMONDO.

[FRONTONE]

       Qual fortuna o qual caso or mi richiama
       dopo tanti anni di quiete amica
2515   a la tempesta del reale albergo?
       La qual sovente ella perturba e mesce.
       O felice colui che vive in guisa

CHORUS

2495 Whether he speaks the truth or lies, only he comprehends
his words, and his judgment is uncertain
no less than ours. And if a man could give
knowledge in exchange for knowledge,
he could obtain sagacity and wisdom
2500 enough to converse with kings.

TORRISMONDO

We'll let him be. Let him find out the caves
and peaks where nothing can impede his view
of the nocturnal sky. Let him there attempt
to measure it, and number all the stars,
2505 and with less injury deceive himself,
if he so wishes.

SOOTHSAYER

Before one of those cycles
which are about to end, and which I sculpted
on this staff, which sustains my weary life,
reaches its culmination, the truth
2510 of my predictions, now reviled,
O proud Arana, O ancient royal seat,
that now cast me away, will be known to you.

SCENE FIVE

FRONTONE, TORRISMONDO

[FRONTONE]

What fortune or what chance calls me back,
after so many years of welcome peace,
2515 to the tempest of the royal dwelling?
That fortune which often troubles and confuses.
Happy the man who so lives as to be able

ch'altrui celar si possa o 'n alto monte,
o 'n colle o 'n poggio o 'n valle ima e palustre.
2520 Ma dove ella non mira? ove non giunge?
qual non ritrova ancor solinga parte?
Ecco mi tragge pur da casa angusta
e mi conduce al re. Sia destra almeno
questa che spira a la mia stanca etade
2525 aura de la fortuna, e sia tranquilla.
Al vostro comandare or pronto io vegno,
invitto re de' Goti.

TORRISMONDO

Arrivi a tempo
per trarmi fuor d'inganno. Or narra il vero.
Questa, che fu creduta, è mia sorella?

FRONTONE

2530 Non nacque di tua madre.

TORRISMONDO

E in questo errore
ella tanti anni si rimase involta?

FRONTONE

Così piacque a tuo padre, e piacque al fato.

TORRISMONDO

Ma, dapoi ch'ebbe me prodotto al mondo,
altri produsse? o stanca al primo parto
2535 steril divenne ed infeconda madre?

FRONTONE

Steril non già, ch'al partorir secondo
fece d'una fanciulla il re più lieto.

to hide from others—either on a high mountain,
or on a hill or knoll or in a deep and marshy vale.
2520   But where does fortune not spy? Where does it not extend?
What place so lonely that it fails to reach?
Here fortune drags me from my narrow home
and brings me to the king. Let at least
this wind of fortune blowing on my tired age
2525   be favorable and tranquil.
I'm here and ready to do your bidding,
indomitable king of the Goths.

TORRISMONDO

You arrive in time
to save me from a deception. Now speak the truth.
Is this my sister, as she was thought to be?

FRONTONE

2530   She is not your mother's daughter.

TORRISMONDO

And did she remain
shrouded in this mistake for so many years?

FRONTONE

So did it please your father, and please fate.

TORRISMONDO

But after she brought me into the world,
did she bear other children? Or did she, weary from that
        first delivery,
2535   become a barren and a sterile mother?

FRONTONE

Not sterile, no, for with her second childbirth,
she made the king still happier with a daughter.

TORRISMONDO

Che avenne di lei?

FRONTONE

Temuta in fasce
fu per fiero destin dal padre istesso.

TORRISMONDO

2540   E qual d'una fanciulla aver temenza
re forte e saggio debbe?

FRONTONE

Avea spavento
del minacciar de le nemiche stelle.
Ché, lei crescendo di bellezza e d'anni,
a te morte predisse, a noi servaggio
2545   il fatal canto de l'accorte ninfe
che pargoletta la nutrir ne l'antro.

TORRISMONDO

Chi lunge la portò dal verde speco?

FRONTONE

Io: così volle il padre e volle il cielo.

TORRISMONDO

In qual parte del mondo?

FRONTONE

Ove non volli,
2550   né 'l re commise. Anzi portati a forza
fummo ella ed io, ch'altro voler possente
è più di quel de' regi, ed altra forza.

TORRISMONDO

What happened to her?

FRONTONE

Because of a cruel destiny,
while still an infant she was feared by her own father.

TORRISMONDO

2540   And what fear of a little child
could a strong and wise king have?

FRONTONE

He feared
the menace of the hostile stars.
For, as she grew in years and beauty,
the fateful song of the far-sighted nymphs
2545   who raised her in the cavern as a child
predicted death for you and servitude for us.

TORRISMONDO

Who took her far away from the green cave?

FRONTONE

I did: as your father and heaven willed it.

TORRISMONDO

To what part of the world?

FRONTONE

To where I did not wish
2550   and the king never ordered. Rather, we were both
taken there forcibly, she and I, for another will
and another force is more powerful than a king's.

TORRISMONDO

Ma dove la mandava il re mio padre?

FRONTONE

Sin nel regno di Dacia. Ed ivi occulta
2555   si pensò di tenerla al suo destino.
Ma fu presa la nave il terzo giorno,
ch'ambo ci conducea per l'onde salse,
da quattro armati legni, in cui, turbando
del profondo oceano i salsi regni,
2560   gian con rapido corso e con rapace
i ladroni del mar fieri Norvegi.
E fu divisa poi la fatta preda,
ed io ne l'uno, ella ne l'altro abete
fu messa; io tra prigioni, ella tra donne;
2565   io di catene carco, ella disciolta.
E rivolgendo in ver Norvegia il corso,
in un seno di mar trovammo ascosi
molti legni de' Goti, anch'essi avezzi
di corseggiare i larghi ondosi campi,
2570   da' quali a pena si fuggì volando,
come alata saetta, il leggier legno
ov'era la fanciulla, e fu repente
preso quell'altro ove legato io giacqui.
E 'l duce allor di quelle genti infide
2575   pur in mia vece ivi rimase avinto.

TORRISMONDO

Ma sai tu qual rifugio o quale scampo
avesse il legno il qual portò per l'onde
troppo infelice e troppo nobil preda?

FRONTONE

In Norvegia fuggì, se 'l ver n'intesi
2580   da quel prigione.

TORRISMONDO

But where did my father the king send her?

FRONTONE

Far off, to Dacia's kingdom. And there he thought
2555 to keep her hidden from her destiny.
But on the third day the ship that was carrying
us both through the salt waves was captured
by four armed vessels, in which, churning
the deep ocean's salt realm,
2560 with a swift, rapacious course
proud Norwegians, thieves of the sea, sailed.
And then the conquered booty was divided,
and I was put on one ship, she on another,
I with the prisoners, she with the women,
2565 I bound in chains, she free.
But, as we turned our route towards Norway,
hidden in an inlet of the sea, we found
many ships of the Goths, also accustomed
to preying on the vast fields of the waves,
2570 from whom the swift ship which carried the girl
barely escaped, flying like a winged arrow,
while the other, where I was lying bound,
was quickly seized. Whereupon the captain
of that traitorous crew
2575 was shackled in my place.

TORRISMONDO

But do you know what shelter or escape
may have met the ship that carried
such an unhappy and noble victim over the waves?

FRONTONE

It fled to Norway, if I heard correctly
2580 from that captive.

TORRISMONDO

E che di lei divenne?

FRONTONE

Questo non so. Perch'in quel tempo stesso
il re prevento fu d'acerba morte,
e nove morti appresso e novi affanni
turbar de' Goti e de' Norvegi il regno.

TORRISMONDO

2585   Ma del ladro marin contezza avesti?

FRONTONE

L'ebbi di lor. Perché fratelli entrambi
furo, e di nobil sangue, e 'n aspro essiglio
cacciati a forza. E prigionier rimase
Aldano, e lunge si ritrasse Araldo.
2590   Ma quel che vi restò, fra noi dimora.

SCENA SESTA

MESSAGGERO, CORO, TORRISMONDO, FRONTONE.

MESSAG[GERO]

Questa del nostro re matura morte
affrettar dee, non ritardar le nozze.
Perch'egli, il giorno avanti, a sé raccolse
i duci di Norvegia e i saggi e i forti,
2595   e lor pregò ch'a la sua figlia Alvida
serbassero la fede e 'nsieme il regno
di cui fatta l'avea vivendo erede.
Talché lo mio venir non fia dolente,
ma lieto, o di piacer temprato almeno.
2600   Perocch'il bene al male ognor si mesce,

TORRISMONDO

And what happened to her?

FRONTONE

This I do not know. For at that time
the king was struck down by untimely death,
and later other deaths and other sorrows
beset the kingdom of the Goths and the Norwegians.

TORRISMONDO

2585   But, did you discover who the pirates were?

FRONTONE

Of them I did have news. For they were brothers
and both of noble blood, forcibly driven
into bitter exile. Aldano was taken prisoner,
while Araldo fled away.
2590   But the one who stayed lives here among us.

SCENE SIX

MESSENGER, CHORUS, TORRISMONDO, FRONTONE

[MESSENGER]

The long expected death of Norway's king
must hasten, not delay, the wedding.
For the day before he died, he called before him
the princes of Norway and the wise and strong,
2595   and besought them that they should keep their pledge
to his daughter Alvida and to the kingdom
to which, while living, he had made her heir.
So let not my arrival bring you pain,
but happiness, or tempered at least with pleasure.
2600   Since good is always mixed with ill

e 'l male al bene. E con sì varie tempre
il dolore e la gioia ancora è mista.
Ma dove fia la bella alta regina,
figlia de la fortuna e figlia ancora
2605   del re già morto? a cui l'amiche stelle
or fan soggetti i duo possenti regni
che 'l spumante ocean circonda e bagna,
e 'l terzo, se vorrà, d'infesto, amico.
Imparerò da voi la nobil reggia
2610   del re de' Goti invitto, e dove alberghi
la sua regina?

CORO

Ecco il sublime tetto:
ella dentro dimora, e fuor si spazia
il re nostro signore.

MESSAG[GERO]

Siate sempre felice e co' felici,
2615   o degnissimo re d'alta regina.

TORRISMONDO

E tu, che bene auguri, e ne sei degno
per buono augurio ancor. Ma sponi e narra
qual cagion ti conduca o che n'apporti.

MESSAG[GERO]

Non rea novella a questo antico regno,
2620   a questa alta regina, a queste nozze,
e buona a voi, cui tanto il cielo arrise.

TORRISMONDO

Narrala.

MESSAG[GERO]

A la regina io sono il messo.

and ill with good. And in such a varied order
pain and joy are forever mixed.
But where is the beautiful and noble queen,
daughter of fortune and still the daughter
2605 of the dead king? The friendly stars
now subject to her the two mighty kingdoms
which the foaming ocean surrounds and bathes,
and, if she will, the third, once hostile, now friendly.
Will you tell me how to find the royal palace
2610 of the undefeated king of the Goths, and where
his queen is lodged?

CHORUS

There is the lofty roof:
she lives within, and our master the king
paces outside.

MESSENGER

Be ever happy among the happy,
2615 O most worthy king of an august queen.

TORRISMONDO

And to you also, you who wish us well, you who are worthy
of our best wishes. But speak and narrate
what reason brings you or what news you bring us.

MESSENGER

Not evil news I bring this ancient kingdom,
2620 to this high queen, and to these nuptials,
but good for you, on whom heaven has smiled.

TORRISMONDO

Tell it to me.

MESSENGER

My message is for the queen.

TORRISMONDO

Quello ch'a me si spone, a lei si narra,
perché nulla è fra noi distinto e sevro.

MESSAG[GERO]

2625 La Norvegia lo scettro a lei riserba.

TORRISMONDO

Perché? Non regna ancora il vecchio Araldo?

MESSAG[GERO]

Non certo; ma 'l sepolcro in sé l'asconde.

TORRISMONDO

È dunque Araldo morto?

MESSAG[GERO]

Il vero udisti.

TORRISMONDO

L'uccise lungo od improviso assalto
2630 de la morte crudel che tutti ancide?

MESSAG[GERO]

Tosto gli antichi corpi il male atterra.

TORRISMONDO

Ha ceduto a natura iniqua e parca,
che la vita mortal restringe e serra
dentro brevi confini, e troppo angusti
2635 quando è la vita assai minor del merto.

MESSAG[GERO]

A lei suo corpo, a voi concede il regno.

TORRISMONDO

Whatever you relate to me, you tell to her,
for there is nothing not in common between us.

MESSENGER

2625   Norway reserves its sceptre for her.

TORRISMONDO

Why, does old Araldo rule no more?

MESSENGER

Surely not; for the grave hides him.

TORRISMONDO

Then, is Araldo dead?

MESSENGER

You heard the truth.

TORRISMONDO

Was he slain by a lingering or a swift assault
2630   of cruel death who slays all in the end?

MESSENGER

Illness soon overcomes old bodies.

TORRISMONDO

He yielded to unjust and niggard Nature,
which restrains and encloses mortal life
within brief confines, all too narrow yet,
2635   when life is so much shorter than our merits.

MESSENGER

To death his body, to both of you he cedes his kingdom.

FRONTONE

Signor, quest'è pur quello ond'or si parla,
ché l'antica memoria ancor non perdo
de' sembianti e del nome.

TORRISMONDO

Ei giunge a tempo.
2640   Ma riconosce ei te, se lui conosci?

FRONTONE

D'avermi visto ti rimembra unquanco?

MESSAG[GERO]

Non mi ricordo.

FRONTONE

Io ridurollo a mente,
e di quel che non sa farollo accorto,
e ben so ch'ora il sa. Sovienti, amico,
2645   d'aver con quattro legni un legno preso,
che del mar trapassava il dubbio varco,
ed a' liti di Gozia in occidente
conversi, rivolgea l'eccelsa poppa,
avendo i Dani e i lor paesi a fronte?
2650   Io fui preso in quel legno: or mi conosci?

MESSAG[GERO]

Si cangia spesso la fortuna e 'l tempo,
e spesso alta cagion di nostre colpe
stata è l'avara e la maligna sorte.

FRONTONE

Ma che facesti de la nobil preda,
2655   de la vergine dico? È muto, o morto.
Non sai ch'abbiamo il tuo fratel non lunge?
Egli parli in tua vece, o tu ragiona.

FRONTONE

My lord, this is the man that we were speaking of,
for I have not yet lost my old remembrance
of his features and his name.

TORRISMONDO

His arrival is timely.
2640   But does he recognize you, if you recognize him?

FRONTONE

Do you remember ever seeing me?

MESSENGER

I do not remember.

FRONTONE

I will stir his memory,
make him aware of what he does not know,
and well I know he knows. Do you remember, friend,
2645   how you captured with four vessels a ship
that was crossing the perilous sea
with her lofty stern turned in the direction
of Gothland's shores facing towards the West,
having the Danes and their lands before her?
2650   I was captured on that ship: do you recognize me now?

MESSENGER

Fortune is often mutable, and so is time,
and often avaricious, spiteful chance
is the deep reason for our faults.

FRONTONE

But what did you do with your noble captive—
2655   with the girl, I mean? He is mute or dead.
Do you not know we have your brother not far off?
Let him speak for you, or speak yourself.

MESSAG[GERO]

De le cose passate il fato accusa.
Fu quella colpa sua, ma nostro il merto
2660   ch'a la vergine diè sì nobil padre.

TORRISMONDO

Oimè, ch'io tardi intendo, o troppo intendo,
e di conoscer troppo ancor pavento.
Ma 'l conoscer inanzi empio destino
è solazzo nel male. Or tu racconta
2665   il ver, qualunque sia: ch'alta mercede
suol ritrovare il ver, non che perdono.

MESSAG[GERO]

Diedi la verginella al re dolente
per la sua morta figlia, e die' conforto
che temprasse il suo lutto e 'l suo dolore:
2670   sì che figlia si fé la cara ancilla,
che di Rosmonda poi chiamata Alvida
fu co 'l nome de l'altra, ed or s'appella.
L'istoria a pochi è nota, a molti ascocsa.

TORRISMONDO

Oimè, che troppo al fin si scopre, ahi lasso!
2675   Qual ritrovo o ricerco altro consiglio?

SCENA SETTIMA

GERMONDO, TORRISMONDO.

[GERMONDO]

Altro dunque è fra noi più caro mezzo,
che s'interpone e ne ristringe insieme,
o ne disgiunge? e non potrà Germondo

MESSENGER

Blame fate for all past deeds.
That was the fault of fate, ours was the merit
2660   which gave such a noble father to the girl.

TORRISMONDO

Alas! Too late or too much I now understand,
and still I fear to know more.
But to know cruel destiny beforehand
2665   is a solace to grief. Now tell the truth,
whatever it may be: for truth is wont
to find a high reward, besides forgiveness.

MESSENGER

I gave the infant to the king, still grieving
for the death of his own daughter, and gave him comfort
to alleviate his mourning and his sorrow:
2670   thus the dear maid became a daughter to him:
and, once Rosmonda, she was named Alvida,
with the other's name, the name that now she bears.
The story, known to few, is hid to many.

TORRISMONDO

Alas, too much is finally revealed, oh woe is me!
2675   What other course of action can I seek or find?

SCENE SEVEN

GERMONDO, TORRISMONDO

[GERMONDO]

Is there, then, a dearer intermediary between us,
which stands between, and joins us both together,
or keeps us two apart? Cannot Germondo

2680
saper quel ch'in sé volge il re de' Goti
da lui medesmo?

TORRISMONDO

Il re de' Goti è vostro,
signor, come fu sempre, e vostro il regno.
Ma l'altrui stabil voglia, e 'l vostro amore,
e la sua dura sorte, il fa dolente.

GERMONDO

2685
Perturbator a voi di liete nozze
non venni in Gotia, e se 'l venir v'infesta.
altrui colpa è 'l venire, e nostro errore,
e torno indietro, e non ritorno a tempo,
né duo gran falli una partenza emenda.

TORRISMONDO

2690

2695
Fortuna errò, che volse i lieti giochi
in tristi lutti e inaspettata morte,
per cui, se di tal fede il messo è degno,
Norvegia ha 'l re perduto, Alvida il padre.
Voi se cedete i mesti giorni al pianto
e fuggite il dolor nel primo incontro,
io non v'arresto; e non vi chiudo il passo
s'al piacer vostro di tornar v'aggrada.

GERMONDO

2700
Così noto io vi sono? al vostro lutto
io potrei dimostrare asciutto il viso?
Io mai sottrar le spalle al vostro incarco?
Se 'l mio pianto contempra il vostro duolo,
verserò 'l pianto; e se vendetta, il sangue.

TORRISMONDO

Io conobbi, Germondo, il valor vostro,
che splendea com'un sole: or più risplende,
né sono orbo al suo lume. Empia fortuna

know from the sovereign of the Goths himself
2680   what he is thinking of?

TORRISMONDO

The king of the Goths is yours,
my lord, as he was always, and yours is his kingdom.
But another's firm will, your love,
and his hard destiny, cause him to grieve.

GERMONDO

I did not come to Gothland to disrupt your marriage;
2685   and if my coming irks you
the blame is someone else's, and the error ours;
if I go back, by now it is too late,
and one departure can't correct two faults.

TORRISMONDO

The fault is Fortune's, that changed our happy games
2690   into sad mourning and unexpected death,
whereby, if the messenger is trustworthy,
Norway has lost its king, Alvida her father.
If you surrender these sad days to tears
and avoid the sorrow of the first encounter
2695   I will not stop you; nor will I bar your way
if you wish to return to your enjoyment.

GERMONDO

Do you know me so little? Could I show
dry eyes before your mourning?
Could I refuse my shoulders to your burden?
2700   If my tears can relieve your sorrow,
I will shed tears; and, if revenge, my blood.

TORRISMONDO

I knew, Germondo, well I knew your valor,
that shone like a sun: now it shines still more,
nor am I blind to its light. Cruel fortune

2705   farmi l'alba potrà turbata e negra,
  e l'ocean coprir d'oscuro nembo,
  o pur celarmi a mezzo giorno il cielo;
  ma non far ch'io non veggia il vostro merto
  e 'l dever mio. Volli una volta, e dissi;
2710   or non muto il voler, né cangio i detti.
  È vostra Alvida e di Norveggia il regno,
  e sarà s'io potrò. Ma più vi deggio.
  Perché non perdo il mio, né spargo e spando,
  come far io devrei, la vita e l'alma.

  (IL FINE DEL QUARTO ATTO)

CORO

2715   Qual arte occulta o qual saper adempie
  da le celesti sfere
  d'orror gli egri mortali e di spavento?
  Vi sono amori ed odii e mostri e fere
  là sù spietate ed empie,
2720   cagion di morte iniqua o di tormento?
  Vi son là sù tiranni? E l'aria e 'l vento
  non ci perturban solo, e i salsi regni,
  co' feri aspetti, e la feconda terra,
  ma più gli umani ingegni?
2725   Tante ire e tanti sdegni
  movono e dentro a noi sì orribil guerra?
  o son voci onde il volgo agogna ed erra;
  e ciò che gira intorno
  è per far bello il mondo e 'l cielo adorno?

2730   Ma, se pur d'alta parte a noi minaccia
  e da' suoi regni in questi
  di rea fortuna or guerra indìce il fato,
  Leon, Tauro, Serpente, Orse celesti,
  qui dove il mondo agghiaccia,

2705 can make my dawn troubled and black,
   and cover the ocean with a dark cloud,
   or hide the sky at noontide from my eyes;
   but it will never make me blind to your worth
   and my duty. I willed it once, and swore it;
2710 now I do not change my mind, or words.
   Alvida is yours and Norway's kingdom,
   and will be as long as I am able. But still I owe you more.
   I never forfeited my kingdom, and I did not shed and spill,
   as I was bound to do, my life and soul.

   (END OF ACT FOUR)

      CHORUS

   [Human valor is celebrated, which triumphs over the in-
   fluence of the stars and subdues nature.]

2715 What hidden art or what knowledge
   of the celestial spheres
   fills languishing mortals with horror and dismay?
   Are there loves and hates and are there monsters
   and ruthless ravening beasts on high,
2720 the cause of cruel death or torment?
   Are there tyrants on high? Who not only vex
   the air and wind, the salty kingdom
   and the fertile earth with their fierce aspects,
   but even more our human minds?
2725 Does so much rage and do so many grudges
   wage so fierce a war within us?
   Or are they only names to fool the erring masses;
   and is all that revolves around us
   meant to give beauty to the world and to adorn the sky?

2730 But even if fate threatens us from above,
   and from its realms against our own
   declares a war of evil fortune
   with Leo, Taurus, Scorpio, the celestial Bears,
   here where the world is ice,

2735　　e gran Centauro ed Orione armato,
　　　　non si renda per segno in ciel turbato
　　　　l'animo invitto, e non si mostri infermo,
　　　　ma co 'l valor respinga i duri colpi:
　　　　ché 'l destin non è fermo
2740　　a l'intrepido schermo.
　　　　Perch'umana virtù nulla s'incolpi,
　　　　ma de l'ingiuste accuse il ciel discolpi,
　　　　sovra le stelle eccelse
　　　　nata, e scesa nel core, albergo felse.

2745　　Che non lece a virtù? Nel gran periglio
　　　　chi di lei più sicura
　　　　e presta aspira al Cielo e 'n alto intende?
　　　　Chi più, là dove Borea i flumi indura,
　　　　l'arme ha pronte e 'l consiglio,
2750　　o dove ardente sol l'arene accende?
　　　　Non la bruma o l'ardor virtute offende,
　　　　non ferro o flamma o venti o rupi averse
　　　　o duri scogli a lei far ponno oltraggio:
　　　　perché navi sommerse
2755　　siano, ed altre disperse
　　　　mandi procella infesta al gran viaggio,
　　　　e 'n ciel s'estingua ogni lucente raggio.
　　　　E co' più fieri spirti
　　　　sprezza fortuna ancor tra scogli e sirti.

2760　　Virtù non lascia in terra o pur ne l'onde
　　　　guado intentato o passo,
　　　　od occulta latebra o calle incerto.
　　　　A lei s'apre la selva e 'l duro sasso,
　　　　e ne l'acque profonde
2765　　s'aperse a' legni il monte al mare aperto.
　　　　Al fin d'Argo la fama oscura e 'l merto
　　　　fia di Giason: ch'a più lodate imprese
　　　　porteranno altre navi i duci illustri.
　　　　Avrà sue leggi prese
2770　　l'ocean, che distese

2735   and the great Centaur, too, and armed Orion,
let not the unvanquished soul yield to the signs
in the sky and let it show no weakness;
but with valor counter the bitter blows:
for fate is not immutable
2740   before a dauntless defense.
Born above the highest stars, human virtue,
not to be blamed, but to exonerate
heaven of unjust accusations,
descended into man's heart and made it her home.

2745   What can virtue not do? In times of crisis,
who surer and swifter than she
aspires to Heaven and sets her gaze on high?
And here, where Boreas hardens the rivers,
or where the scorching sun inflames the sand,
2750   who is better prepared with arms and counsel?
No mist or heat can ever affect virtue,
nor steel nor flame nor winds nor opposing cliffs,
no jagged rocks can harm it:
even though ships are sunk
2755   and others thrown off course
by hostile storms on their great journeys,
and every shining star extinguished in the sky.
She, with the most intrepid spirits,
still scorns the gale amid the reefs and shoals.

2760   Virtue leaves, on earth or on the waves,
no ford or passage unexplored,
no hidden place untrodden, or hazardous path.
Before her the forests and the mountain rocks arc opened,
just as in deep waters
2765   the mountain was opened up to ships down to the open
        sea.
At length the fame of the Argonauts will be obscured,
and the glory of Jason: for more famous captains
will sail their ships on more praiseworthy ventures.
The ocean, which once spread wide
2770   its arms around the world

le braccia intorno. E già volgendo i lustri
averrà che lor gloria il mondo illustri,
come sol, che rotando
caccia le nubi e le tempeste in bando.

2775   Virtù scende a l'Inferno,
passa Stige secura ed Acheronte,
non che l'orrido bosco o l'erto monte.
Virtude al Ciel ritorna,
e, dove prima nacque, al fin soggiorna.

will have received its laws. And soon with the passing of
   the years
their glory will illuminate the world,
like the sun, which, as it circles the earth,
drives clouds and storms into exile.

2775   Virtue descends to Hell,
and safely crosses Styx and Acheron,
not just the frightful wood and the steep mountain.
Virtue returns to Heaven,
and, where it was first born, there finally it dwells.

ATTO QUINTO

ALVIDA, NUTRICE.

[ALVIDA]

2780 In qual parte del mondo or m'ha condotta
la mia fortuna, e fra qual gente avversa,
o dei sommi del cielo?

NUTRICE

Ancor temete
e vi dolete ancor.

ALVIDA

Io più non temo,
né posso più temer, ché 'l male è certo,
2785 e certo il danno e la vergogna e l'onta.
Già son tradita, esclusa, anzi scacciata,
perch'è morto in un tempo il re mio padre
e del marito mio la fede estinta.
Egli da l'una parte a tutti impone
2790 ch'a me si asconda l'improvisa morte,
da l'altra ei mi conforta, e mi comanda
ch'io pensi a novo sposo o a novo amante,
e mi chiama sorella, e mi discaccia
con questo nome.
2795 O mar di Gotia, o lidi, o porti, o reggia
che raccogliesti le regine antiche,
dove ricovro, ahi lassa, o dove fuggo?

ACT FIVE

SCENE ONE

ALVIDA, NURSE

[ALVIDA]

2780 To what part of the world has my fortune
now brought me, and among what hostile people,
O highest gods of heaven?

NURSE

You are still afraid,
you are still grieving.

ALVIDA

I fear no longer,
I can fear no more: for the evil is certain,
2785 and certain is the harm, the shame and the disgrace.
I'm already betrayed, excluded, nay, cast out,
for at the same time the king my father is dead
and my husband's faith extinguished.
He, on the one hand, compels everyone
2790 to keep the sudden death hidden from me,
and, on the other, comforts me and commands me
to think about a new husband or a new lover,
and calls me sister, thus repudiating me
with this name.
2795 O sea of Gothland, O shores, O ports, O royal palace,
the resting place of ancient queens,
where shall I take refuge, alas, where shall I flee?

Dove m'ascondo più? Nel proprio regno
u' l'alta sede il mio nemico ingombri
2800   perch'io vi serva? o 'n più odiosa parte
spero trovar pietà tradita amante,
anzi tradita sposa?

NUTRICE

È possibil giammai che tanto inganno
alberghi in Torrismondo e tanta fraude?

ALVIDA

2805   È possibile, è vero, è certo, è certa
la sua fraude e 'l mio scorno e l'altrui morte;
anzi la violenza è certa, e 'nsieme
la mia morte medesma, oh me dolente!

NUTRICE

Certa la fate voi d'incerta e dubbia
2810   or facendovi incontra al male estremo;
ma pur non fu tanto importuna unquanco
l'iniqua, inesorabile, superba,
né con tanto disprezzo e tanto orgoglio
perturbò a' lieti amanti un dì felice.
2815   Ma son tutti, morendo il padre vostro,
seco estinti gli amici e i fidi servi
e i suoi cari parenti? e spente insieme
l'onestà, la vergogna e la giustizia?
né secura è la fede in parte alcuna?
2820   Già tutte siam tradite e quasi morte,
se non è vano il timor vostro e 'l dubbio.

ALVIDA

O morì la giustizia il giorno istesso
co 'l giustissimo vecchio, e seco sparve,
e fé seco volando al Ciel ritorno.
2825   E la forza e la fraude e 'l tradimento
presero ogni alma ed ingombrar la terra.
Non ardisce la fede erger la destra

where can I ever hide? In my own kingdom
where my enemy will occupy the high throne
2800   so that I may serve him? Or do I, a betrayed lover
or better a betrayed bride, hope to find pity
in a still more hateful place?

NURSE

Is it possible that such deceit
and such fraud should ever dwell in Torrismondo?

ALVIDA

2805   It's possible, it's true, it's certain; certain is
his fraud as well as my disgrace and my father's death;
indeed, violence is certain and with it
my own death, oh wretched me!

NURSE

What is uncertain and doubtful you make certain,
2810   even exposing yourself to the ultimate evil;
and yet never was fortune so importune,
that wicked, inexorable and haughty dame,
nor with such scorn and pride did she
disturb a happy day for cheerful lovers.
2815   But with your father's death, are all
his friends, faithful servants and dear relatives
extinct with him? And extinct too
are honesty, shame and justice?
and is faith nowhere secure?
2820   We are all already betrayed and might as well be dead
if your fear and doubt are not without foundation.

ALVIDA

Either that, or justice died the very day
that most righteous old man died, and vanished with him,
and, flying with his soul, returned to Heaven.
2825   And force and fraud and treachery
took over every soul and ruled the earth.
Faith does not dare raise her right hand

e l'onor più non osa alzar la fronte.
E la ragione è muta, anzi lusinga
2830   la possente fortuna. Al fato averso
cede il senno e 'l consiglio, e cede al ferro
maestà di temute antiche leggi,
mentre a guisa di tuono altrui spaventa
e d'arme e di minacce alto ribombo.
2835   È re chiamato il forte. Al forte il regno,
altrui mal grado, è supplicando offerto,
e ciò che piace al più possente è giusto.
Io non gli piaccio, e 'l suo piacer conturbo
io sola; e de' Norveggi or preso il regno,
2840   la regina rifiuta il re sublime
de' magnanimi Goti.

NUTRICE

A detti falsi
forse troppo credete; e 'l dritto e 'l torto
alma turbata e mesta, egra d'amore,
non conosce sovente, e non distingue
2845   dal vero il falso, e l'un per l'altro afferma.

REGINA*

Siasi de la novella e del messaggio
e de la fé norvegia e del mio regno
e de gli ordini suoi turbati e rotti
ciò che vuol la mia sorte o 'l mio nemico:
2850   basta ch'ei mi rifiuta; e 'l vero io ascolto
del rifiuto crudele. Io stessa, io stessa
con questi propi orecchi udii pur dianzi:
"Alvida, il vostro sposo è 'l re Germondo,
non vi spiaccia cangiar l'un re ne l'altro
2855   e l'un ne l'altro valoroso amico,
ed al nostro voler concorde e fermo
il vostro non discordi". In questo modo
mi concede al suo amico, anzi al nemico
del sangue mio. Così vuol ch'io m'acqueti

---

*Alvida

and honor is afraid to raise its head.
And reason is mute—or rather, flatters
2830 powerful fortune. Wisdom and counsel
surrender to adverse fate, and the majesty
of feared and ancient laws surrenders to the sword,
while as if by a thunder roll mankind is terrified
by the deafening din of arms and threats.
2835 The strong man is called king; to him is imploringly
offered
the kingdom, though others may object;
whatever pleases the strongest is right.
He does not like me, and I alone trouble his pleasure;
and now that the kingdom of the Norwegians has been
seized,
2840 the sublime king of the magnanimous Goths
repudiates Norway's queen.

NURSE

Perhaps you give excessive credit
to false rumors; for a troubled and sad soul,
languishing from love, often does not know
right from wrong, and does not distinguish
2845 true from false, taking one instead for the other.

QUEEN (ALVIDA)

So be the news, so be the messenger,
Norwegian loyalty, my kingdom,
my kingdom's order upset and destroyed,
as my fate and my enemy would have it be;
2850 it's enough for me that he refuse me, and I am sure
I hear the truth of this cruel refusal. I myself, I myself,
with these very ears just heard him say:
"Alvida, your bridegroom is King Germondo;
do not refuse to exchange one king for another,
2855 one valorous friend for another,
and let your will not dissent from ours,
which is firm and concordant." This is the way
he gives me to his friend—rather, to the enemy
of my race. This is how he wants me to resign myself

2860 nel voler d'uno amante e d'un tiranno.
Così l'un re mi compra e l'altro vende,
ed io son pur la serva, anzi la merce,
fra tanta cupidigia e tal disprezzo.
Udisti mai tal fede? udisti cambio
2865 tanto insolito al mondo e tanto ingiusto?

NUTRICE

Senza disprezzo forse e senza sdegno
è questo cambio. Alta ragione occulta
dee movere il buon re. Ché d'opra incerta
sovente il buon consiglio altrui s'asconde.

ALVIDA

2870 La ragion ch'egli adduce è finta e vana
e in me lo sdegno accresce, in me lo scorno,
mentre il crudel così mi scaccia, e parte
prende gioco di me. "Marito vostro"
mi disse "è 'l buon Germondo, ed io fratello."
2875 Ed adornando va menzogne e fole
d'un rapto antico e d'un'antica fraude.
E mi figura e finge un bosco, un antro
di ninfe incantatrici. E 'l falso inganno
vera cagione è del rifiuto ingiusto,
2880 e fia di peggio. E Torrismondo è questi,
questi, che mi discaccia, anzi m'ancide,
questi, ch'ebbe di me le prime spoglie,
or l'ultime n'attende; e già se 'n gode;
e questi è 'l mio diletto e la mia vita.
2885 Oggi d'estinto re sprezzata figlia
son rifiutata. O patria, o terra, o cielo,
rifiutata vivrò? vivrò schernita?
Vivrò con tanto scorno? Ancora indugio?
Ancor pavento? E che? La morte, o 'l tardi
2890 morire? ed amo ancora? ancor sospiro?
Lacrimo ancor? Non è vergogna il pianto?
Che fan questi sospir? Timida mano,
timidissimo cor, che pur agogni?
Mancano l'arme a l'ira, o l'ira a l'alma?

2860 to the will of a lover and a tyrant.
Thus one king buys me and another sells me,
and I'm the servant—or rather, the merchandise—
in the midst of so much greed and such contempt.
Did you ever hear of a faith like this? Did you ever hear
2865 in all the world of a bargain so unusual and unjust?

NURSE

This exchange is perhaps without contempt
and without disdain. Some high hidden reason
must motivate the good king. For often the good sense
of a doubtful deed is concealed from others.

ALVIDA

2870 The reason he gives is feigned and empty
and increases the anger and the shame in me,
while thus the cruel man drives me away,
and at the same time makes fun of me. "Your husband"
he said "is the good Germondo; I am your brother."
2875 And he adorns his lies and fables
with an old abduction and an old deception.
And he describes and depicts for me a forest, a cavern,
the dwelling place of faery nymphs. But false deceit
is the true reason for his unjust refusal,
2880 and maybe worse. And this is Torrismondo!
It is he who sends me away, or rather kills me;
he who had the first spoils of me
now can't wait for the last; and already he rejoices;
and this man is my delight and all my life.
2885 Today, the despised daughter of a deceased king,
I am rejected. O native land, O earth, O Heaven,
shall I live rejected? Shall I live scorned?
Shall I live with such shame? Do I still delay?
Am I still afraid? Of what? Of death, or of dying too late?
2890 Do I still love? Am I still sighing?
Still weeping? Is it not a disgrace to weep?
Why all these sighs? Timid hand,
most hesitant heart, what are you waiting for?
Is anger lacking weapons, or the soul anger?

2895 Se vendetta non vuoi, né vuole Amore,
basta un punto a la morte. Or mori, ed ama
morendo; e se la morte estingue amore
l'anima estingua ancor, ché vera morte
non saria, se vivesse amore e l'alma.

NUTRICE

2900 Deh, lasciate pensier crudele ed empio.
Niun vi sforza ancora o vi discaccia;
ma v'onora ciascuno, ed ancor donna
sete di voi medesma, e di noi tutte
sete e sarete sempre alta regina.

SCENA SECONDA

REGINA

2905 Dopo tanti anni e lustri un dì sereno,
un chiaro e lieto dì fortuna apporta.
Ogni cosa là dentro è fatta adorna
e ridente, e di gemme e d'or riluce.
Duo lieti matrimoni in un sol giorno,
2910 duo regi e due regine aggiunte insieme,
duo figli, anzi pur quattro; e quinci e quindi
pur con sangue real misto il mio sangue,
e bellezza e valore e gloria e pompa
e molte in una reggia amiche genti
2915 e doni e giostre e cari e lieti balli
oggi vedrò contenta. Ahi nostra mente,
chi ti contenta o chi t'appaga in terra,
se non si può d'empio destin superbo
mutar piangendo la severa legge,
2920 né sua ragion ritorre a fera morte?
'Lassa, non questa fronte essangue e crespa,
o questa coma che più rara imbianca,
o gli umeri già curvi e 'l piè tremante

2895   If you do not wish vengeance, and Love does not wish it,
all death requires is a moment. Die, then, and love
while dying; and if death extinguishes love,
let it extinguish also the soul, for it would not be
real death if love and the soul should live on.

NURSE

2900   Ah, put aside this cruel and impious thought.
No one is forcing or casting you away as yet;
but everyone honors you, and you are still mistress
of yourself, and you are and always will be
the high queen of us all.

SCENE TWO

QUEEN MOTHER

2905   After so many years, so many lusters, fortune brings
a tranquil, clear and happy day.
Everything within the palace has been adorned
and made cheerful, shining with jewels and gold.
Two happy weddings on a single day,
2910   two kings and two queens joined together,
two children, or rather four; and on both sides
I shall be happy to see my blood mixed
with other royal blood, and beauty and strength
and glory and pomp and a host of friends
2915   in one royal palace, and gifts and jousts
and pleasant carefree dances. Ah, mind of man,
who can satisfy you or who can please you on earth,
if our tears cannot alter the stern law
of pitiless proud destiny,
2920   nor rescue his just deserts from cruel death?
Wretched me! Neither this bloodless and wrinkled
     forehead
nor this hair now turning white and thin
nor my bent shoulders and my unsure feet

scemano il mio piacer. Ma tu sol manchi,
2925   o mio già re, già sposo, a queste nozze,
o de' figliuoli miei signore e padre.
Deh, se rimiri mai dal Ciel sereno
de' tuoi diletti e miei l'amato albergo,
e se ritorni a consolarmi in sonno,
2930   sii presente, se puoi. Risguarda i figli,
o padre, e di famosa e chiara stirpe
lieto l'onor ti faccia, amico spirto.

SCENA TERZA

ROSMONDA sola.

Ancor mi vivo di mio stato incerta,
ancor pavento e spero e bramo e taccio,
2935   e del parlar mi pento e de l'ardire,
e poi del mio pentire io mi ripento.
Quel che sarà non so, ché non governa
queste cose mortali il voler nostro,
ma 'l voler di colui che tutto regge.
2940   Però questo solenne e lieto giorno
visiterò devota i sacri altari
ed offrirò queste ghirlande al tempio
di vergini viole e d'altri fiori,
persi, gialli, purpurei, azzurri e bianchi,
2945   ch'in su l'aurora io colsi, e poi contesti
gli ho di mia mano. Or degni il Re del Cielo
gradir la mia devota e pura mente,
ed al Settentrion gli occhi rivolga
pietosamente e con benigno sguardo.

can lessen my pleasure. But you alone are absent from
    this wedding,
2925   you, once king, once bridegroom to me,
you, father and master of my children.
Oh, if you ever from bright Heaven look down
on the beloved home of your pleasures and mine,
and if you ever return to comfort me in my dreams,
2930   be present, if you can. Look upon your children,
O father, and may the honor of a famous
and illustrious race bring you joy, O friendly spirit.

SCENE THREE

ROSMONDA (alone)

I still live on uncertain of my state;
I fear and hope and long and still keep silent,
2935   and I regret having spoken and been daring,
then I repent having repented.
What will happen I do not know, for it is not our will
that rules these mortal things
but the will of the One who rules all things.
2940   Yet, on this solemn and happy day
devoutly I shall visit the sacred altars
and offer to the temple these garlands
of virgin violets and other flowers,
deep purple, yellow, crimson, blue and white,
2945   which at dawn I gathered and then plaited together
with my own hand. Now may the king of Heaven
deem my devout and chaste mind worthy of his
    acceptance,
and may He turn his eyes to this our North
pityingly and with a benevolent glance.

SCENA QUARTA

CAMERIERO, CORO.

[CAMERIERO]

2950   O Gotia, o d'Aquilone invitto regno,
    o patria antica, oggi è tua gloria al fondo,
    oggi è 'l sostegno tuo caduto e sparso,
    oggi fera cagion d'eterno pianto
    a te si porge.

CORO

           Ahi, che dolente voce
2955   mi percote gli orecchi e giunge al core!
    Che fia?

CAMERIERO

         Misera madre e mesto giorno,
    reggia infelice, e chi vi more e vive
    infelice egualmente. Orribil caso!

CORO

    Narralo, e dà principio al mio dolore.

CAMERIERO

2960   Il re doglioso a la dolente Alvida
    già detto avea ch'al suo fedel Germondo
    esser moglie devea, con brevi preghi
    stringendo lei ch'in questo amor contenta,
    come ben convenia, quetasse il core,
2965   ché l'altre cose poi saprebbe a tempo,
    Ma del suo padre l'improvisa morte,
    per occulta cagion tenuta ascosa,
    accrebbe in lei sospetto e duolo e sdegno
    ch'in furor si converse e 'n nova rabbia,
2970   pur come fosse già schernita amante

SCENE FOUR

STEWARD, CHORUS

[STEWARD]

2950 O Gothland, O unconquered Northern kingdom,
O ancient native land, today your glory is at its lowest ebb;
today your chief support is fallen and laid low;
today a stern reason for eternal grief
is offered you.

CHORUS

Oh, what sorrowful voice
2955 strikes my ears and reaches my heart!
What can it be?

STEWARD

Wretched mother and sad day,
unhappy palace, and no less unhappy they who die
and live in it! Horrible happenings!

CHORUS

Tell me, and let my sorrow begin.

STEWARD

2960 The unhappy king had already told
grieving Alvida that she must be the wife
of his faithful friend Germondo, with brief prayers
compelling her, as it was fitting, to calm
her heart, happy with this love,
2965 for she would know the rest in due course of time.
But her father's sudden death,
kept secret for some hidden reason,
increased her suspicion, pain and anger,
which then turned into fury and new rage,
2970 as if she were already a mocked lover

data in preda al nemico, onde s'ancise,
passando di sua man co 'l ferro acuto
il suo tenero petto.

CORO

2975   Ahi froppo frettolosa! Ahi cruda morte,
estremo d'ogni male!

CAMERIERO

Il male integro
non sapete anco. Il re se stesso offese
nel modo istesso, e giace appresso estinto.

CORO

Ahi, ahi, ahi, crudel morte e crudel fato!
Quale altro più gravoso oltraggio o danno
2980   può farci la fortuna o 'l cielo averso?

CAMERIERO

Non so. Ma l'un dolore aggiunge a l'altro,
l'una a l'altra ruina. E 'n forte punto
oggi è la stirpe sua recisa e tronca.

CORO

Misera ed orba madre, ove s'appoggia
2985   la cadente vecchiezza, e chi sostienla?

CAMERIERO

L'infelice non sa d'aver trovato
oggi una figlia e due perduti insieme,
e forse lieta ogni passato affanno
in tutto oblia, non sol consola e molce,
2990   e di gioia e piacere ha colmo il petto.

CORO

Or chi le narrerà l'aspro destino
de' suoi morti figliuoli?

given as trophy to her enemy. Wherefore she killed herself,
with her own hand plunging a pointed blade
into her tender breast.

CHORUS

Oh far too hasty! Oh cruel death,
2975   the ultimate of evils!

STEWARD

But still you do not know
the full brunt of the evil. The king wounded himself
in the same way, and lies lifeless next to her.

CHORUS

Alas, alas, cruel death and cruel fate!
What other graver outrage or harm
2980   can fortune or hostile heaven inflict upon us?

STEWARD

I do not know. But one sorrow is added to another,
one disaster to another. And in one fell swoop
today his line is severed and cut off.

CHORUS

Wretched and bereaved mother, on what
2985   is her failing old age to lean, and who sustains her?

STEWARD

The unhappy mother does not know that today
she has found a daughter and lost two children at once,
and, happy perhaps, she not only finds relief and comfort
for all past anxieties, but utterly forgets them,
2990   and her breast is swelled with joy and pleasure.

CHORUS

Now who shall reveal to her
the harsh fate of her dead children?

CAMERIERO

Io non ardisco
con questo aviso di passarle il core.
Ma già tutto d'orrore e di spavento
2995   là dentro è pieno il suo reale albergo,
e risonare i tetti e l'ampie logge
s'odono intorno di femineo pianto,
e di battersi il petto a palma a palma,
e di meste querele e di lamenti:
3000   tanto timor, tanto dolore ingombra
le femine norvegie. E men dolenti
sarian, se fatte serve in cruda guerra
fossero da nemici infesti ed empi
e temessero omai di morte e d'onta.
3005   E l'altre sconsolate e meste donne
consolarle non ponno, anzi piangendo
parte, pianger fariano un cor selvaggio
del suo dolore, e lacrimar le pietre.

CORO

E noi, che parte abbiamo in tanto danno,
non sapremo anco più distinti i modi
3010   d'una morte e de l'altra?

CAMERIERO

Il re trovolla
pallida, essangue, onde le disse: "Alvida,
Alvida, anima mia, che odo, ahi lasso,
che veggio? Ahi qual pensiero, ahi qual inganno,
3015   qual dolor, qual furor così ti spinse
a ferir te medesma? Oimè, son queste
piaghe de la tua mano?" Allor gravosa
ella rispose con languida voce:
"Dunque viver devea d'altrui che vostra,
3020   e da voi rifiutata?
e potea co 'l vostro odio e co 'l disprezzo,
se de l'amor vivea?
Assai men grave è il rifiutar la vita,

STEWARD

I do not dare
to pierce her heart with this news.
But, there within, her royal palace is already
2995   filled with horror and fright,
and its roofs and broad galleries
are heard to ring with women's weeping,
and with the sound of hands striking their breasts,
as well as mournful outcry and lament:
3000   such fear, such sorrow weighs
on the Norwegian women. And they would feel less grief
if in a savage war they had been made
slaves by fierce and pitiless enemies
and were now in fear of death and shame.
3005   And the other disconsolate and sad women
cannot comfort them; rather, their weeping
would cause the hardest heart to mourn
at their sorrow, and the rocks to shed tears.

CHORUS

And we, who have a share in so much grief,
3010   shall we not know in greater detail the manner
of the one death and the other?

STEWARD

The king found her
wan, deadly pale, wherefore he said: "Alvida,
Alvida, my soul, what do I hear, alas,
what do I see? Oh what thought, oh what deceit,
3015   what sorrow, what fury drove you
to wound yourself? Oh me, are these
wounds by your own hand?" Then, death-encumbered,
with a weak voice she answered:
"And did you expect me to live as someone else's,
3020   and rejected by you?
And could I have lived with your hate and your contempt,
if I lived for your love?
It's much less grievous to reject life,

e men grave il morire.
3025 Già fuggir non poteva in altra guisa
tanto dolore".
Ei ripigliò que' suoi dogliosi accenti:
"Tanto dolore io sosterrò vivendo?
o 'n altra guisa io morrei dunque, Alvida,
3030 se voi moriste? Ah, no 'l consenta il Cielo!
Io vi potrei lasciare, Alvida, in morte?
Con le ferite vostre il cor nel petto
voi mi passaste, Alvida.
E questo vostro sangue è sangue mio,
3035 o Alvida sorella,
così voglio chiamarvi". E 'l ver le disse,
e confermò giurando e lagrimando
l'inganno e 'l fallo de l'ardita destra.
Ella parte credeva, e già pentita
3040 parea d'abbandonar la chiara luce
nel flor de gli anni, e rispondea gemendo:
"In quel modo che lece io sarò vostra
quanto meco potrà durar questa alma,
e poi vostra morrommi.
3045 Spiacemi sol che 'l morir mio vi turbi,
e v'apporti cagion d'amara vita".
Egli pur lagrimando a lei soggiunse:
"Come fratello omai, non come amante,
prendo gli ultimi baci. Al vostro sposo
3050 gli altri pregata di serbar vi piaccia,
ché non sarà mortal sì duro colpo".
Ma in van sperò: perché l'estremo spirto
ne la bocca di lui spirava, e disse:
"O mio più che fratello e più ch'amato,
3055 esser questo non pò, ché morte adombra
già le mie luci".
Dapoi ch'ella fu morta, il re sospeso
stette per breve spazio; e muto e mesto,
da la pietate e da l'orror confuso,
3060 il suo dolor premea nel cor profondo.
Poi disse: "Alvida, tu sei morta, io vivo
senza l'anima?" E tacque.

and less grievous to die.

3025   In no other way could I escape
such pain."
He continued his sorrowful words:
"Can I bear such sorrow and remain alive?
or would I want to die some other way, Alvida,

3030   if you died thus? Oh, let Heaven not allow it!
Could I leave you alone, Alvida, in death?
With your wounds you pierced
my heart, Alvida.
This blood of yours is my blood,

3035   O Alvida, my sister,
for so I wish to call you." And he spoke the truth to her,
and confirmed, solemnly swearing and weeping,
the misunderstanding and mistake that forced her bold
     hand.
In part she believed him, and already

3040   she seemed sorry to leave the bright light of day
in her first bloom, as, moaning, she replied:
"I will be yours
so long as this soul of mine will last,
and, later, still yours, I will die.

3045   My only regret is that my death grieves you,
and gives you cause for a bitter life."
Still weeping, this, too, he said to her:
"As a brother now, not as a lover,
I take my last kisses. I beg you,

3050   keep the others for your bridegroom,
for the blow, however cruel, will not be mortal."
But he hoped in vain: for, breathing her last breath
into his mouth, she said:
"O more than brother and more than lover,

3055   this cannot be, for death dims
my eyes already."
As soon as she was dead, the king stood
hesitant a moment, speechless and sad;
dazed with pity and horror,

3060   he pressed his pain deep down into his heart.
He said then: "Alvida, now you are dead, will I still live
without my soul?" And he spoke no more.

E scrisse questa lettra, e la mi porse
dicendo: "Porteraila al re Germondo,
3065   e quanto avrai di me sentito e visto,
tutto gli narra, e scusa il nostro fallo".
Così disse. E mentre io pensoso attendo,
dal suo fianco sinistro ei prese il ferro
e si trafisse con la destra il petto,
3070   senza parlar, senza mutar sembianza,
pur come fosse lieto in far vendetta.
Io gridai, corsi, presi il braccio indarno,
non anco debil fatto. Ei mi respinse
con quel valor che non ha pari al mondo,
3075   dicendo: "Amico, al mio voler t'acqueta,
e ne la tua fortuna. A te morendo
lascio il più caro officio e 'l più lodato,
un signor più felice, un re più degno,
e la memoria mia.
3080   Ch'ognun la cara vita altrui pò torre,
ma la morte, nessuno".

SCENA QUINTA

GERMONDO, CAMERIERO.

[GERMONDO]

Qual suon dolente il lieto dì perturba?
e di confuse voci e d'alte strida
qual tumulto s'aggira? e di temenza
3085   son questi, o di gran doglia incerti segni?
Forse è dentro il nemico, o pur s'aspetta?
Ma sia che può, non sarò giunto indarno;
e dar non si potrà Norvegio o Dano
del suo fallace ardir superbo vanto.
3090   Qual pazzia sì gli affida, o quale inganno,
se Torrismondo ha 'l fido amico appresso?

He wrote this letter, and gave it to me,
saying: "Bring it to King Germondo,

3065   and what you have heard and seen of me,
tell him in detail, and excuse my fault."
These were his words. And while I waited plunged in
    thought,
he seized the sword from his left side
and pierced his heart with his right hand,

3070   without saying one word, without changing expression,
as if he were happy to take revenge.
I shouted, ran, I took his arm in vain,
which had not yet become weak. He pushed me back
with that fortitude that has no equal on earth,

3075   saying: "Friend, resign yourself to my will,
and to your destiny. Dying, to you I bequeath
the dearest, most praiseworthy of all tasks,
a happier lord, a worthier king,
and my memory.

3080   Anyone can take another's precious life;
no one can take his death."

SCENE FIVE

GERMONDO, STEWARD

[GERMONDO]

What doleful sound troubles this happy day?
and what turmoil of confused voices
and piercing shrieks do I hear? And are these

3085   the uncertain signs of great sorrow or of fear?
Perhaps an enemy is within, or is expected?
Whatever it be, I will not have arrived in vain;
and no Norwegian or Dane shall be able to boast
of his deceitful, proud boldness.

3090   What madness or what deceit gives them such impudence,
if Torrismondo has his faithful friend beside him?

CAMERIERO

Oimè, che Torrismondo altro nemico
non ebbe che se stesso e la sua fede.

GERMONDO

Qual nemicizia intendi, o che ragioni?

CAMERIERO

3095   Ei, signor, la vi spone, e qui la narra.
Perché questa è sua carta, io fido servo.

GERMONDO

Oimè, quel ch'io leggo e quel ch'intendo!
Odi le sue parole, e 'l mio dolore.
"Scrivo inanzi al morire, e tardi io scrivo,
3100   e tardi io muoio. Altri m'è corso inanzi,
e la sua morte di morir m'insegna,
perch'io muoia più mesto e più dolente,
una donna seguendo, e sia l'estremo
chi 'l primo esser devea spargendo il sangue,
3105   non per lavar, ma per fuggir la colpa,
ch'or porterò come gravoso pondo
per questa ultima via. Morrò lasciando
di moglie in vece a voi canuta madre:
perché la mia sorella a me la fede
3110   o 'l poterla osservare, a sé la vita,
a voi se stessa ha tolto. O vero amico,
se vero amico mi può far la morte
vero amico sono io. Prendete il regno,
non ricusate or la corona e 'l manto
3115   e d'amico fedele il nome e l'opre.
Siate a cadente vecchia alto sostegno
in vece mia. Non disprezzate i preghi,
non disdegnate in su l'orribil passo
che tal mi chiami e di tal nome onori
3120   l'acerba morte mia, che tutto solve,
fuorché l'obbligo mio ch'a voi mi strinse.

STEWARD

Alas, Torrismondo had no enemy
except himself and his own loyalty.

GERMONDO

What enmity do you mean, what are you saying?

STEWARD

3095 He himself, my lord, explains it, and here recounts it.
For this is his letter, and I his faithful servant.

GERMONDO

Alas, what things I read, what things I hear!
Listen to his words, and to my grief:
"I write on the point of death, and I write too late,
3100 just as I die too late. Another sped on ahead,
and her death teaches me to die,
so that I might die more sad and sorrowful,
following a woman, and so that I should be last,
who should have been the first to spill my blood,
3105 so as to avoid the guilt, not purge it once committed,
the guilt which now I shall bear with me like a heavy
        burden
for what's left of my journey. I will die leaving to you,
instead of a wife, my grey-haired mother,
for my sister took away my faith
3110 or my ability to keep it, her own life from herself,
herself from you. O my true friend,
if death can make me a true friend,
a true friend is what I am. Take the kingdom,
do not refuse now the crown and mantle
3115 or the name and deeds of a loyal friend.
Be a staunch support to a weak old woman,
in my place. Do not scorn my prayers,
do not disdain that at this horrid moment
I should so call myself and honor with such a name
3120 my untimely death, which resolves everything
save the obligation that bound me to you.

Vivete voi, che 'l valor vostro è degno
d'eterna vita, e l'amicizia e 'l merto.
Io chiedo questa grazia a voi morendo."
3125   0 dolente principio, o fin dolente!
Ma che pensa? dov'è? non vive ancora?

CAMERIERO

Visse, lasciò la moglie, or lascia il regno;
e l'uno è tuo, l'altro pur volle il fato.

GERMONDO

Oscuro è quel che narri, e quel ch'accenna
3130   il tuo signor.

CAMERIERO

Ei riconobbe Alvida
la sua vera sorella, e poi s'uccise,
come credo io, per emendare il fallo
in voi commesso.

GERMONDO

Era sorella adunque?

CAMERIERO

Era, e saprete come.

GERMONDO

Ahi, troppo a torto
3135   tanto si diffidò nel fido amico,
che la mia fede, e non la sua, condanna
con la sua morte. Oimè, qual grave colpa
non perdona amicizia o non difende?
Meno offeso m'avria volgendo il ferro
3140   contra il mio petto. Anzi io morir devea,
ch'a lui diedi cagion d'acerba morte.
Ahi fortuna, ahi promesse, ahi fede, ahi fede,

Live, for your valor, your friendship
and your merit are worthy of eternal life.
Dying, I ask this grace of you."
3125   O painful beginning, o sorrowful end!
But what is he thinking of? Where is he?
Is he still alive?

STEWARD

He lived, he left a wife, now leaves a kingdom;
the one is yours, the other was claimed by fate.

GERMONDO

3130   What you tell me is as obscure as your master's
allusions.

STEWARD

He recognized Alvida
as his true sister, then he killed himself,
so I believe, to amend his trespass
against you.

GERMONDO

She was his sister, then?

STEWARD

She was, as you will learn.

GERMONDO

Oh, too wrongly, then,
3135   he mistrusted his faithful friend,
so that he condemns my loyalty, not his,
with his death. Alas, is there such a grievous fault
that friendship cannot forgive or excuse?
He would have offended me less had he turned his sword
3140   against my breast. I should have died instead,
if it was I who caused his bitter death.
O Fortune, O Promises, O Faith, O Faith,

così t'osserva, e così dona il regno?
Così me prega?

CAMERIERO

Il ciel fé scarso il dono,
e la sua Parca e la fortuna aversa,
3145   non l'ultimo voler: ché tutto ei diede
quanto darvi potea.

GERMONDO

Tutto ei mi tolse
togliendomi se stesso. Amor crudele,
tu sei cagion del mio spietato affanno,
3150   tu mi togli l'amico e tu l'amata,
e tu gli uccidi, e mi trafiggi il petto
con duo colpi mortali. Io tutto perdo
poiché lui perdo. Oimè dolente acquisto,
dannoso acquisto, in cui perde se stessa
3155   la nova sposa, e 'l re se stesso e gli altri,
e 'l suo figliuol la madre, e 'l vero amico
l'amico suo, né ritrovò l'amante;
la milizia l'onor, ch'orba divenne;
questo regno, il signore; io, la speranza
3160   d'ogni mia gloria e d'ogni mio diletto.
Perdere ancora il cielo il sol devrebbe,
e 'l sole i raggi, e la sua luce il giorno,
e per pietà celar l'oscura notte
il fallo altrui co 'l tenebroso manto;
3165   perdere il mare i lidi, e l'alte sponde
gli ondosi fiumi, e ricoprir la terra
ingrata, or che non sente e non conosce
il danno proprio e non s'adira e sterpe
faggi, orni, pini, cerri, antiche querce,
3170   alti sepolcri, e d'infelice morte
dolente e mesto albergo, o pur non crolla
questa gran reggia e le superbe torri,
e non percote i monti a' duri monti,

is this the way he keeps his faith, the way he gives his
    kingdom?
Is this the way he pleads with me?

STEWARD

        It was Heaven made the gift inadequate,
3145   and Fate, and hostile Fortune,
not his last wish: for he gave all
that he could give.

GERMONDO

        He took everything away,
taking himself away from me. Cruel Love,
you are the cause of my pitiless anguish,
3150   you take my friend and the woman I loved from me
and you kill them both, and pierce my heart
with two mortal blows. I lose all
in losing him. O mournful gain,
injurious gain, in which the new bride
3155   loses herself, and the king loses himself and others,
and the mother her son, and the true friend
his friend, without finding his beloved;
the army loses its chief and is then stripped of glory;
this kingdom, its master; I, every hope
3160   of glory and delight.
The sky should lose the sun,
the sun its rays, the day its light,
and out of pity the dark night should hide
man's fault in its gloomy cloak;
3165   the sea should lose its shores, the flowing rivers
their high banks, and inundate the ungrateful earth,
since it fails to feel and recognize
its own loss, and, possessed with anger, does not uproot
beeches, ashes, pines, holms and ancient oaks,
3170   lofty tombs, and unhappy death's
sorrowful and sad dwellings, and does not raze to the
    ground
this great palace and the haughty towers,
and fling mountains against hard mountains,

e non rompe i lor gioghi, e i gravi sassi
3175   da l'aspre rupi non trabocca al fondo,
e nel suo grembo alta ruina involve
di mete, di colossi e di colonne,
perché sia non angusta e 'ndegna tomba;
e da valli e da selve e da spelunche
3180   con spaventose voci alto non mugge,
per far l'essequie con l'estremo pianto,
che darà al mondo ancor perpetuo affanno.

SCENA SESTA

REGINA, CAMERIERO, GERMONDO, ROSMONDA, CORO.

[REGINA]

Deh, che si tace a me, che si nasconde?
Sola non saprò io, schernita vecchia,
3185   di chi son madre, o pur se madre io sono?

CAMERIERO

Regina, oggi la sorte il vero scopre
ch'a tutti noi molti anni occulto giacque.
Però non accusar nostro consiglio,
ch'a te non fu cagion d'alcuno inganno;
3190   ma qui si mostri il tuo canuto senno.

REGINA

Se pur questa non è mia vera figlia,
qual altra è dunque?

and break their backs, and pitch
3175   huge boulders from the rough cliffs to the valley bottom,
        and in the valley's depths enfold high ruins
        of pillars, of colossi, of columns,
        so as to make it a capacious and worthy tomb,
        and from valleys, woods and caverns
3180   why does the earth not roar loudly with a thousand
            dreadful voices,
        making their obsequies with utmost wailing,
        spreading perpetual panic through the world?

SCENE SIX

QUEEN MOTHER, STEWARD, GERMONDO, ROSMONDA,
CHORUS.

[QUEEN MOTHER]

Oh, what am I not being told? What is being hidden
    from me?
Will I, a despised old woman, be the only one not to
    know
3185   whose mother I am, or even if I am a mother?

STEWARD

Queen, today fate uncovers the truth
that for many years was hidden from us all.
But do not blame our decision,
which did not lead to any misunderstanding on your part;
3190   but here let your mature wisdom be shown.

QUEEN MOTHER

If this is not my real daughter,
what other is then?

CAMERIERO

Partoristi un'altra,
prima Rosmonda e poi chiamata Alvida,
del buon re tuo marito e signor nostro;
3195   ma per sua poi nudrilla il re norvegio.

REGINA

Tanto dolor per ritrovata figlia
e trovata sorella? Altro pavento
che disturbate nozze. Altro si perde.

CAMERIERO

Oimè lasso!

REGINA

Qual silenzio è questo?
3200   Ov'è la mia Rosmonda?

CAMERIERO

Ov'ella volse.

REGINA

E Torrismondo?

CAMERIERO

In quel medesmo loco,
ov'egli volle.

GERMONDO

Altre percosse in prima
hai sostenute di fortuna aversa;
ora questi soffrir più gravi colpi,
3205   che già primi non sono, al fin convienti,
o mia saggia regina e saggia madre.

STEWARD

You gave birth to another,
named first Rosmonda, and then Alvida,
by the good king your husband and our master;
3195   but afterward she was raised by the Norwegian king as his
daughter.

QUEEN MOTHER

So much sorrow for a daughter found again
and for a sister found? I fear something far worse
than an interrupted wedding. Something else is lost.

STEWARD

Oh wretched me!

QUEEN MOTHER

What is this silence?
3200   Where is my Rosmonda?

STEWARD

Where she wished to be.

QUEEN MOTHER

And Torrismondo?

STEWARD

In the same place,
where he wished to be.

GERMONDO

Other blows
of hostile fortune you have sustained before;
now these graver blows,
3205   which are not the first, you must suffer finally,
O my wise queen and wise mother.

Ché s'altri figli avesti, or son tuo figlio:
non mi sdegnar, benché sia grave il danno.

REGINA

Ahi, ahi, ahi, dice: "Avesti"; io non gli ho dunque?
3210   Non respiran più dunque
i miei duo cari figli?

GERMONDO

Ahi, che non caggia!
Deh quinci Torrismondo e quindi Alvida,
quinci vera amicizia e quindi amore
fanno de gli occhi miei duo larghi fonti
3215   d'amarissimo pianto, e 'l core albergo
d'infiniti sospiri. E 'n tanto affanno
e fra tanti dolori ha sì gran parte
la pietà di costei. Misera vecchia,
e più misera madre! Oimè, quel giorno
3220   ch'ella sperava più d'esser felice,
è fatta di miseria estremo essempio.
Io sarò suo conforto, anzi sostegno.
Io farò questo, lagrimando insieme,
dolente sì, ma pur dovuto officio
3225   e pieno di pietà. Consenta almeno
ch'io la sostegna.

ROSMONDA

Oh foss'io morta in fasce,
o 'n questo giorno almen turbato e fosco,
mentre egli fu sì lieto e sì tranquillo.
Bello e dolce morire era allor quando
3230   io fatto non l'avea dolente e tristo.
Io misera il perturbo, e l'alta reggia
io riempio d'orrore e di spavento.
Io la corona atterro e crollo il seggio.
Io d'error fui cagione, or son di morte
3235   al mio signore. Or m'offrirò per figlia
a questa orba regina ed orba madre,

For, though you had other children, now I am your son;
do not disdain me, though the loss is heavy.

QUEEN MOTHER

Oh, oh, oh, you say: "You had"; I do not have them, then?
3210   Are my two dear children, then,
breathing no more?

GERMONDO

Oh, see that she does not fall!
Oh, on the one side Torrismondo and on the other Alvida,
on one side true friendship and love on the other,
make of my eyes two copious streams
3215   of most bitter tears, and my heart a dwelling place
of endless sighs. And in such anguish
and among so many griefs compassion for this lady
has such a great part. Wretched old woman,
and oh, more wretched mother! Alas, on the very day
3220   that she hoped to know her greatest happiness
she has become an extreme example of misery.
I shall be her comfort, her support.
Weeping together, I shall perform
this sorrowful but no less dutiful task,
3225   full of the utmost compassion. May she agree at least
that I should be her stay.

ROSMONDA

Oh, would I had died in swaddling clothes,
or at least on this day, now dark and troubled,
while it was still so happy and so calm.
It would have been fair and sweet to die
3230   before I made the day sorrowful and sad.
It is I, alas, who trouble it, and fill the lofty palace
with dread and horror.
I overthrew the crown and shook the throne.
I was the cause of error, now of the death
3235   of my master. Now I will offer myself as a daughter
to this bereaved queen, bereaved mother,

la qual pur dianzi ricusai per madre.
E ricusai, misera me, l'amore,
e ricusai l'onore,
3240	serva troppo infelice,
ch'era pur meglio ch'io morissi in culla
innocente fanciulla.

CORO

A piangere impariamo il vostro affanno
nel comune dolor che tutti afflige.
3245	Al signor nostro omai quale altro onore
far possiam che di lagrime dolenti?
Al signor nostro, il qual fu lume e speglio
di virtute e d'onor, chi nega il pianto?

REGINA

Ahi, chi mi tiene in vita?
3250	O vecchiezza vivace,
a che mi serbi ancora?
Non de' miei dolci figli
a le bramate nozze,
non al parto felice
3255	de' nepoti mi serbi.
Al duolo amaro, al lutto,
a la morte, a la tomba
de' miei duo cari figli,
or mi conserva il fato.
3260	Ahi, ahi, ahi, ahi,
ch'io non gli trovo, e cerco,
misera me dolente,
pur di vederli in vano.
Ahi, dove sono?
3265	Ahi, chi gli asconde?
O vivi, o morti,
anzi pur morti.
Oimè,
oimè!

whom a short while ago I rejected as a mother.
And, wretched me, I rejected love,
rejected honor,
3240   unhappy servant that I am,
it would have been better had I died,
an innocent babe in my cradle.

CHORUS

We learn to weep for your misery
in the common sorrow that afflicts all.
3245   To our lord, now what other honor
can we give save our sorrowful tears?
To our master, who was the light and mirror
of virtue and honor, who will deny tears?

QUEEN MOTHER

Oh, who keeps me alive still?
3250   O lively old age,
what do you hold in store for me?
Not the longed-for wedding
of my sweet children,
not the happy birth
3255   of grandchildren do you hold in store.
For bitter pain, for mourning,
for death, for the tomb
of my two dear children,
now my fate preserves me.
3260   Oh, oh, oh, oh, oh,
I cannot find them, and I seek,
Oh wretched me,
in vain to see them.
Oh, where are they?
3265   Oh, who hides them?
Living, or dead,
ah, surely dead.
Oh me,
oh me!

GERMONDO

3270   Quetate il duol, ché tutto scopre il tempo.

REGINA

Signor, se dura morte
i miei figlioli estinse,
ché non me 'l puoi negare,
e certo non me 'l nieghi,
3275   ma co'l pianto il confermi
e co' mesti sospiri,
abbi pietà, ti prego,
di me: passami il petto,
e fa ch'io segua omai
3280   l'uno e l'altro mio figlio,
già stanca e tarda vecchia
e sconsolata madre
meschina.

GERMONDO

S'io potessi, regina, i figli vostri
3285   con la mia morte ritornare in vita,
sì 'l farei senza indugio, e 'n altro modo
creder non posso di morir contento.
Ma, poi che legge il nega aspra e superba
di spietato destin, vivrò dolente
3290   sol per vostro sostegno e vostro scampo.
E saran con funebre e nobil pompa
i vostri cari figli ambo rinchiusi
in un grande e marmoreo sepolcro:
perché questo è de' morti onore estremo;
3295   benché ad invitti re, famosi in arme,
sia tomba l'universo e 'l Cielo albergo.
A voi dunque vivrò, regina e madre:
voi sarete regina, io vostro servo
e vostro figlio ancor, se troppo a sdegno
3300   voi non m'avete. A voi la spada io cingo,
per voi non gitto la corona o calco,

GERMONDO

3270   Calm your grief, for time uncovers all.

QUEEN MOTHER

My lord, if cruel death
snuffed out my children—
for you cannot deny this
and you certainly do not deny it,
3275   but with tears and with sad sighs
confirm it—
I beg you, have pity on me:
pierce my heart,
and let me follow
3280   my daughter and my son,
weary that I am, a slow old woman,
a poor disconsolate
mother.

GERMONDO

If, O Queen, with my own death
3285   I could restore your children back to life,
I would do it without delay, for I believe
I could not die happy in any other way.
But, since the stern and proud law
of ruthless destiny denies it, I will live, though in tears,
3290   only for your support and safety.
And with funereal and noble pomp
your children will both be enclosed
in a great marble sepulcher:
for this is the final honor of the dead;
3295   though to unvanquished kings, famous in war,
the universe is tomb and Heaven home.
For you then I will live, my queen and mother:
you will be queen, I will be your servant
and your son also, if you do not hold me
3300   in too great disdain. I wear my sword for you,
for you I refrain from casting off the crown or treading on
      it,

non spargo l'arme sì felici un tempo,
e non verso lo spirto e spando il sangue.
Pronto a' vostri servigi, al vostro cenno,
3305   sinché le membra reggerà quest'alma,
sarà co 'l proprio regno il re Germondo.

REGINA

Oimè, che la mia vita
è quasi giunta al fine,
ed io pur anco vivo
3310   perché l'amara vista
mi faccia di morire
via più bramosa
co' dolci figli,
ahi, ahi, ahi, ahi!

GERMONDO

3315   Oimè, che non trapassi. O donne, o donne,
portatela voi dentro, abbiate cura
che 'l dolor non l'uccida o tosco o ferro.
O mia vita non vita, o fumo, od ombra
di vera vita, o simolacro, o morte!

(IL FINE DEL QUINTO ATTO)

CORO

3320   Ahi lacrime, ahi dolore:
passa la vita e si dilegua e fugge,
come giel che si strugge.

Ogni altezza s'inchina, e sparge a terra
ogni fermo sostegno
3325   ogni possente regno
in pace cadde al fin, se crebbe in guerra.
E come raggio il verno, imbruna e more
gloria d'altrui splendore;

from laying my once so welcome arms aside,
from breathing my last breath or spilling my blood.
Ready to do you service, to do your bidding
3305   as long as this soul sustains my limbs,
King Germondo will be ready, and all his kingdom.

QUEEN MOTHER

Oh me, my life
has almost reached its end,
and still I live
3310   so that this bitter sight
may make me
even more eager to die
along with my sweet children—
oh, oh, oh, oh!

GERMONDO

3315   Alas, don't let her die. O women, o women,
take her inside, and see
that pain does not kill her, nor poison nor sword.
O my life, no life at all, but smoke, the shadow
of a real life, O counterfeit, O Death!

(END OF ACT FIVE)

CHORUS

[A lament for the mutability and vanity of all things.]

3320   Oh, tears, oh, grief:
life passes, vanishes and flies,
like melting ice.

Every height bows low, and scatters
every firm support to the ground,
3325   every powerful kingdom
in peace finally fell, if in war it grew.
And as a wintry beam, the glory
of man's radiance darkens and dies.

e come alpestro e rapido torrente,
3330 come acceso baleno
in notturno sereno,
come aura, o fumo, o come stral, repente
volan le nostre fame, ed ogni onore
sembra languido flore.

3335 Che più si spera o che s'attende omai?
Dopo trionfo e palma,
sol qui restano a l'alma
lutto e lamento e lagrimosi lai.
Che più giova amicizia o giova amore?
3340 Ahi lagrime, ahi dolore!

And like a swift alpine torrent,
3330   like lightning
on a clear night,
like a breeze or like smoke, or like an arrow, swiftly
our reputations fly, and every honor
seems like a wilting flower.

3335   What else is there to hope for, what can we expect?
After triumph and victory,
here nothing remains for the soul
but mourning and wailing and tearful laments.
What avails friendship? What avails love?
3340   Oh tears, oh grief!

NOTES TO THE TRANSLATION

In preparing these notes I have consulted the following five annotated editions of *Il re Torrismondo*: Torquato Tasso, *Opere,* a cura di E. Mazzali (Naples: Fulvio Rossi, 1962); Torquato Tasso, *Opere* II a cura di Bruno Maier (Milan: Rizzoli, 1964); *Opere di Torquato Tasso* a cura di Bortolo Tommaso Sozzi (Turin: Unione Tipografico-Editrice Torinese, 1964); *Il Teatro Italiano II: La tragedia del Cinquecento,* Tomo Secondo, a cura di Marco Ariani (notes by Roberto Bigazzi) (Turin: Giulio Einaudi, 1977); Torquato Tasso, *Teatro,* a cura di Marziano Guglielminetti (Milan: Garzanti, 1983).

12	Maier's edition explains "fortuna" as "social condition."
45–46	As one of those mythical giants who tried to climb to the sky, using as steps Pelion, Ossa, and Mount Olympus: mountains of Greece.
65	Araldo, King of Norway, was believed by Alvida to be her father. Alvida swore to him that she would give her love only to the man who would avenge her brother's death, killed by Germondo, King of Sweden—a death left unavenged.
76–77	Alvida's brother's birthday coincided with the day her father celebrated his crowning as king of Norway.
82–83	The original lines "Io del piacer di quella prima vista / così presa restai" recall the words of Dante's Francesca: "mi prese del costui piacer sì forte" (*Inferno,* V, 104)

99   In Sozzi's standard critical edition, reproduced by
all the others, we read "Arane" on line 99 of the
Italian text, "Arana" on line 918, and "Aarana" on
line 2511. In my translation I have consistently
used the spelling "Arana." Arana or Arane is the
royal palace near Lake Venus, found as Aarane in
Olaus Magnus, *Historia de gentibus septen-
trionalibus* (Westmead, Farnbrough, Hants.,
England: Gregg International, 1971), XI, 21. Olaus
Magnus' text was translated into German, Swedish,
French, and English: *A Compendious History of
the Goths, Sweeds, Vandals, and Other Northern
Nations* (London: J. Streater, 1658). All references
to Olaus Magnus are from Ariani's edition, which is
based on the Italian version: *Storia d'Olao Magno
Arcivescovo d'Upsali, De' Popoli Settentrionali,*
translated by Remigio Fiorentino (Turin: Vincenzo
Bona, 1958).

114   The original wording recalls Dante's "conosco i
segni dell'antica fiamma" (*Purgatorio* XXX, 48).

138   the king of Sweden: Germondo.

139–40   The reason for postponing the wedding: the arrival
of Germondo, the man who had killed her brother,
offends Alvida.

146   Olma is described by Olaus Magnus, XI, 28, as: "città
regia, e notabilmente fortificata da l'arte, e da la
natura" (a royal city, remarkably fortified by art
and nature).

159   Maier explains "pungente ferro" (piercing iron) as
"chastity belt," but Olaus Magnus, extolling the
chastity of Nordic women, claims that new brides
would place a sword in bed between them when
they were first married.

162   The wording recalls the suicide Pier della Vigna's
"disdegnoso gusto" in Dante's *Inferno* XIII, 70.

175   In the Italian text, the Nurse addresses Alvida as

"figlia" (daughter), instead of "regina"(queen), I.1, 125. See also Act III, Scene 6, line 1866.

182   The Nurse, who has been speaking to Alvida with the formal "voi," suddenly shifts to the familiar "tu."

234   A note in the Italian editions (with the exception of Guglielminetti's) explains "Tana" as a Norwegian river; I believe that Tasso is thinking of the Tanais (the Don, in Russia), which is often mentioned along with the Rhine and the Danube in Latin poetry. Also, in Petrarch's *Rime* (CXLVIII 3, 4), these three rivers are mentioned together.

235–36   The unfriendly sea has been variously explained as the Barents Sea (Maier and Sozzi) and the Black Sea (Ariani and Guglielminetti). The Red Sea and the Caspian appear together in Petrarch's *Rime* CCX 3: "dal lito vermiglio a l'onde caspe."

258–59   The original verse recalls, in a "tragic" register, Petrarch's sonnet "Solo et pensoso."

259–60   The Ercinian Forest extended into the Black Forest as far as Harz in Germany.

261   The Hyperborean Mountains are in the extreme north.

269   The original verse echoes Petrarch's "me sconsolato et a me grave pondo" (*Rime* CCCXXXVIII, 4).

276   Maier, Sozzi, and Ariani explain "squille" (bells) as the church bells ringing the Ave Maria, which is rung at dawn and dusk (as in Petrarch's *Rime* CIX, 6).

279   Cerberus and Scylla: famous monsters of the Classical tradition.

282   Hydra in Lerna: a snake with seven heads in the swamp of Lerna (in Greece), killed by Hercules.

313–14   Torrismondo's words recall those of Dante's

Francesca: "Nessun maggior dolore / che ricordarsi del tempo felice / nella miseria; . . ." (*Inferno* V, 121–123).

346–47   The Tartars and Muscovites were inhabitants of those regions that we know today as Russia. Olaus Magnus speaks of these people in his *Historia de gentibus septentrionalibus* (XI).

350   For the history of these northern regions see Olaus Magnus (I, I).

353   The seven stars of the Great Bear.

385–91   The original lines echo the words of Ulysses in Dante's *Inferno:* né dolcezza di figlio, né la pietà / del vecchio padre, né'l debito amore / lo qual dovea Penelope far lieta, / vincer poter dentro da me l'ardore / ch'i'ebbi a divenir del mondo esperto (XXVI, 94–98).

470   my father-in-law: the king of Norway.

473   The subject is the king of Norway.

477   Alvida, that is.

496   See again the words of Dante's Francesca: "Amor, ch'a nullo amato amar perdona" (*Inferno* V, 103).

504   whirling wind: This atmospheric phenomenon is described by Olaus Magnus (I, II).

509–10   all the others: winds, that is: Boreas and Auster: which blow from north and south; Zephyr, which blows from the west; Eurus, which blows from the east.

513–14   The original lines echo Virgil's: "Eripiunt subito nubes caelumque diemque / Teucrorum ex oculis; ponto nox incubat atra" (*Aeneid* I, 88–89).

532   Olaus Magnus (II, 10) describes the force of the Northern winds and how tree trunks end up in the sea, causing the destruction of ships.

544   The original wording is a direct quotation from Virgil's *Aeneid,* I, 118, on which the whole description is based.

546   our ship: Torrismondo's and Alvida's.

550–54   Olaus Magnus (II, 27) has a description of these ports on windy and stormy days.

561   The topos of night being friendly to furtive lovers appears often in Tasso's *Gerusalemme Liberata:* "E la notte i suoi furti ancor copria, / ch'a i ladri amica ed a gli amanti uscia" (VI, 89), and "Ma quando l'ombra co' silenzi amici / Rappella a i furti lor gli amanti accorti" (XVI, 27).

564   The original line is modelled on the words of Dante's Francesca: "ma solo un punto fu quel che ci vinse" (*Inferno* V, 132).

579   Furies: the mythological Megaera, Tisiphone, and Alecto.

667   The three heroes (Hercules, Achilles, and Alexander) were examples of famous lovers.

756   The original line echoes the word play of Pier della Vigna's suicide: "ingiusto fece contra me giusto" in Dante's *Inferno* (XIII, 72).

769   oblique: a reminiscence of "l'oblico cerchio" in Dante's *Paradiso* (X, 13).

809   The original line echoes Petrarch's *Triumphus Cupidinis* (III, 66) and Ariosto's *Orlando Furioso* (XXVIII, 98).

823   The original line echoes Petrarch's *Rime* (CCCXXXII, 70).

827   This first chorus, like the other choruses at the end of each act, are lyric poems with a fixed alternation of long and short lines. ABbCACeADEeDDEfF is the scheme in this case (where a capital letter signifies an eleven-syllable line, a small letter a line of seven

syllables, and identical letters, capital or small, a rhyme). The model is the Petrarchan *canzone*. To facilitate the reader's understanding of the chorus at the end of each Act, I translated the brief summaries as found in Guglielminetti's edition. Wisdom is identified as Minerva or Athena, born from the head of Jove or Jupiter.

831   Lake Avernus is located in the underworld.

832   Acheron: one of the infernal rivers.

833   black Styx: the infernal swamp surrounding the city of Dis (See Dante's *Inferno* VII, 103.)

839–40   The Roman Empire, transferred from Rome to Byzantium.

841   this part of the earth: Gothland.

868   terrible trace: the barbarian invasion of Alarico's Goths in the sack of Rome of 410.

869   that proud one: Constantinople, capital of the Byzantine Empire.

877   other giants: giants different from those of classical mythology (see note 45–46); the giants described in Olaus Magnus' account of the northern regions (V, I).

904   Thule: Europe's most distant northern land.

907–8   In our soil no olive tree grows. (Wisdom is here identified with Pallas Athena, to whom the olive was sacred.)

956–61   These lines could be glossed with Shakespeare's *Macbeth,* "There is no art to find the mind's construction in the face."

997   Sisyphus: mythical lord of Corinth, whose soul in Hell was eternally condemned to push a rock uphill.

1017–18 Unless the queen, Torrismondo's mother, can convince Rosmonda to marry Germondo (in place of Alvida).

1037	Rosmonda knows that she is not Torrismondo's real sister.
1038	The image of the soul as a white bird trapped in the black mud of life is a common image in Giovanni Della Casa's poetry.
1047–53	Rosmonda is secretly in love with Torrismondo.
1060	The Italian "occulto" (hidden) and its synonyms are key words throughout the play.
1066	queen-bride: Alvida.
1120	Beauty is its own ornament.
1129	our unvanquished guest: Germondo.
1141	greater crown: a queen's crown, not just that of a princess.
1147	in honest freedom: free from the bonds of marriage.
1179	The Queen has an almost sacred remembrance of her marriage. The line "per me sempre onorata e sempre acerba," echoes Virgil's "Semper acerbum, semper honoratum" (*Aeneid* V, 49–50).
1183–84	The original Italian echoes Petrarch's *Rime* (XVI, 5, 6): "indi trahendo poi l'antiquo flanco / per l'extreme giornate di sua vita."
1196	The original "memoria innamorata" echoes Petrarch's *Rime* (LXXI, 99).
1197	my duty: the Queen's duty is to convince Rosmonda to marry Germondo.
1203–4	The Queen declares that her thoughts were the same as those of her husband.
1230–50	These lines also echo Petrarch.
1247–49	The original lines could be autobiographical. They recall the gloomy, pessimistic attitude of the poet in his letters from Sant'Anna.

1284   mighty Ancient Mother: The earth (an echoe of Petrarch's *Triumphus Mortis* I, 89).

1297–1309   Rosmonda would like to be a traditional Amazon (like Virgil's Camilla or Tasso's Clorinda). Olaus Magnus tells us about northern women who were warriors and pirates.

1332   The original echoes Ovid's *Tristia* (I, ix, i: "Detur inoffenso vitae tibi tangere metam").

1359–63   Italian editors note that Tasso probably intended to omit these bracketed lines. They are, however, necessary to understand what follows.

1366   the other: the other light, i.e., Rosmonda.

1371–72   The wedding of Torrismondo to Alvida and that of Germondo to Rosmonda.

1399   Torrismondo's description of the proposed festivities is heavily dependent on Olaus Magnus' account of Scandinavian customs.

1400   castle: Olaus Magnus (I, 23) describes how young men engage in the construction of castles of snow and decorate them with flags (in black or other colors); he adds that afterwards, these young men divide themselves in different groups, some guard the walls, others assault the walls. This is how they train for war.

1407–9   Olaus Magnus (XV, 14–15) describes how these young men keep themselves in shape: racing, jumping, and hurling rocks. He describes a race with horses or with skis.

1411   Olaus Magnus gives an account of exploding weapons.

1413–17   These games are described by Olaus Magnus as part of war training (XV, 6).

1421–27   In the *Aeneid* V, Virgil describes similar games for the anniversary of Anchises' death (boxing is included with these games).

1424–41	Similar games are described by Olaus Magnus (XV, 23, 24).
1442–47	For the dance of fire, see Olaus Magnus (XV, 27).
1448–50	Olaus Magnus tells us about horse races on ice in two different chapters (I, 24; XI, 35–37).
1454–57	Olaus Magnus recalls tourneys for happy events (XV, 18).
1466–68	Olaus Magnus describes metal steeds with fire coming out of their mouths (IX, 4).
1489	Hippolyta: queen of the Amazons (women warriors who dwelt in Asia on the banks of the river Thermodon).
1491	In order to draw the bow easily, the Amazons had their right breasts removed.
1493	she: Rosmonda.
1496	Hercules and Theseus fought against the Amazons. Theseus married Hippolyta.
1498	Unlike Hippolyta, Rosmonda will not be conquered unless she will bend to love.
1505	Arcturus is the main star in the northern constellation of Bootes.
1507	The original line echoes Petrarch's *Rime* (XXXVII, 24) "per vie lunghe e distorte."
1509–12	Although the horse-drawn chariot of the sun strays far from these Northern countries, he can still admire these people's valor.
1513–18	The Chorus ends this invocation with the wish that Rosmonda will marry Germondo.
1528–29	The Counselor alludes to Torrismondo's victories.
1544	the king: Germondo.
1564	Of the ancient Goths, Torrismondo is the worthiest (a verbal echo of Tasso's *Rinaldo* XI, 83).

1568	this king: Torrismondo.
1576	The four horses which pull the sun's chariot.
1655–57	Vulturnus is the east wind, Auster is the south wind, Boreas is the north wind.
1658	The Italian "Calpe" is one of the promontories on either side of the Straits of Gibraltar and in classical mythology one of Hercules' columns.
1659	Hercules' other column is Abila on the African coast.
1668	Lethe: one of the rivers of the underworld, whose waters had the power to make one forget the past.
1704–6	Germondo considers the kingdom of the entire world inferior to serving Alvida.
1707–8	Listed are rivers of Asia (Euphrates, Tigris, Orontes, and Ganges), of India (Hydaspes), of Greece (Acheloos), and of Africa (the Nile).
1709	The mountains of Athos, Parnassus, and Olympus in Greece, Mount Taurus in Asia, and Mount Atlas in Africa.
1718–19	An echo of Ovid's "Materiam superabat opus" (*Metamorphoses,* II, 5) and of Tasso's *Gerusalemme Liberata* (II, 93 and XVI, 2).
1730–31	Alvida is depicted in Swedish costume.
1732–33	A symbolic representation of Germondo's love for Alvida.
1736	myrtle: symbolic of love.
1738	arrows and knots also symbolize love.
1742–45	Her brother's blood. Alvida understands that the unknown warrior was Germondo, who is now in love with her. Germondo offers Alvida the glory he gained by killing her brother (the crown is depicted under her feet).

1775–76   the ferocious / enemy: Germondo.

1782   the mighty warrior: Germondo.

1786   the proud winner: Germondo.

1802   Nicosia: a city in Norway.

1822   Germondo defeats the winner.

1840   Since Germondo did not reveal himself, he did not gain glory from the deed.

1987   in Heaven or on earth.

1998   friendship: the friendship of Torrismondo for Germondo.

2007   neither passion: neither love nor friendship.

2023   your renown: the fame of Germondo and Torrismondo.

2026–27   Thule: modern Greenland. It is the geographical antithesis of the river Bactrus (in the extreme eastern part of the world), where Bactra was situated.

2039   A defense as ineffective as a fragile tower would provide.

2052   One toward the west, the other toward the east.

2053   divided: each on his own path.

2068   Pannonia: an ancient Roman province, north of Dalmatia (it coincides in part with modern Hungary).

2073   The three great kingdoms are Gothland, Sweden, and Norway.

2078   Two kingdoms are already united: Gothland and Norway, because of the marriage between Torrismondo and Alvida.

2085–86   this new / and dear knot: Germondo's marriage to Rosmonda.

2113   The original echoes Petrarch's *Rime* (XLVIII, 1–3).

2127   The original echoes Petrarch's *Rime* (LIII, 86).

2134   Add one marriage to the other: to Alvida and Torrismondo's wedding, add your wedding to Rosmonda.

2148   quit the battlefield: by renouncing Alvida.

2150–51 Germondo's future will be decided by Torrismondo.

2153   The original wording echoes the phraseology of Dante (*Inferno* V, 90).

2158   Hymen: the god of matrimony, carrying a burning torch. See Ovid's *Metamorphoses* (IV, 758).

2168   The original echoes Petrarch's *Rime* (XII and LXI, 1–2).

2185   Alvida's disdain of accepting Germondo to be her husband.

2194   The original echoes Petrarch's *Rime* (CXXV, 57).

2203   sister: Germondo has a sister whom he could give as wife to Torrismondo.

2216   your refusal: to marry Germondo.

2231   Rosmonda had two brothers (2270).

2245   By revealing the truth Rosmonda would lose her royal position.

2299   Rosmonda will find her freedom by fulfilling her mother's vows.

2350–51 Olaus Magnus (II, 10) mentions nymphs who predict the future.

2371   the same year: the one in which the false Rosmonda was brought to the royal palace.

2393–96 The theme of Love and Fortune echoes Petrarch's *Rime* (CXXIV; LXXVI, 2; CCLXX, 104; CXXII, 9).

2405   I do not have a sister to substitute for Alvida.

2422   How can I find my lost sister in order to give her
        as a bride to Germondo?

2423   From this point on, the reminiscence of Sophocles'
        Oedipus Rex become more pronounced.

2459   your faith uncertain: your loyalty to Germondo.

2465   Centaur: the zodiacal sign of Sagittarius.

2467   the cruel beast: the zodiacal sign of Taurus.

2469   "il Vecchio" (the Old Man): the zodiacal sign of
        Aquarius.

2472   old Atlas: the earth.

2473   the Dolphin: a northern constellation.

2474   laziest star: the constellation of Bootes (see l. 1505).

2475   Virgo: another sign of the Zodiac that takes its
        name from Pallas Athena or Minerva, goddess of
        the arts.

2478   the Crown: a northern constellation.

2479   the one who shakes the sky: Zeus, Jove, or Jupiter.

2481   daughter: identified by some commentators as
        Venus (Maier, Sozzi) and by others as Diana
        (Ariani).

2483   animals: Aries and Capricorn.

2487–94 Mars is the subject.

2491   others: the other zodiacal signs.

2492   cruel tyrant: in opposition to proud god (2490);
        signs: the zodiacal signs; houses: their seat.

2506   cycles: astral combinations.

2508–9 Olaus Magnus (I, 34) mentions such canes and
        calendars.

2586	of them: of the two brothers (Aldano and Araldo, as will be explained in 2588–89).
2591	The tragedy continues to be reminiscent of Sophocles and brings forth a Messenger with the news of the death of the king of Norway (believed by Alvida to be her father).
2608	the third once hostile: Sweden (Norway's enemy).
2626	old Araldo: king of Norway (not the Araldo of 2589).
2645–49	The ship was crossing the dangerous waters between the Western coast of Gothland and the coast of Denmark.
2656	your brother: Aldano (see 2586).
2674	Unlike Oedipus, Torrismondo immediately understands the incestuous nature of his love.
2686	someone else: Torrismondo (who promised him Alvida).
2688	two errors: my error and the error of those who misinformed me.
2689–90	The original Italian reminds us of Dante's *Inferno* XIII, 69 "che' lieti onor tornaro in tristi lutti."
2693–95	If you ... stop you: if you leave Alvida to mourn her father's death, and if you wish to avoid meeting her during these days of sorrow, you are free to go.
2701	my blood: if revenge can relieve your sorrow, I will shed my blood.
2718–19	monsters ... beasts: the constellations were believed to influence human actions.
2733–35	These constellations are divided into the Northern Zodiac ("here where the world freezes," 2734) and the Southern Zodiac (the Centaur and Orion depicted with a sword), as in Petrarch's *Rime* XLI, 10.
2745	Virtue: fortitude.

2748	Boreas: the northern wind that turns rivers into hard ice (see 914). The line recalls Tasso's *Gerusalemme Liberata* XIV, 34 and Ovid's *Tristia* III 13–14: "nix iacet, et iactam . . . Indurat Boreas."
2766	Argonauts: Jason's companions on the mythical ship Argus.
2775–76	Styx Acheron (see note 832–33). (The lines echo Dante, *Inferno* IX, 80–81).
2802	hateful place: Sweden, where she would be Germondo's wife.
2823	old man: the King of Norway (whom Alvida believed to be her father).
2882	first spoils: virginity.
2924	Her regret for her dead husband continues to characterize the Queen (as in 1178) along with the hope of seeing her future grandchildren born of the marriages of both her children (1336).
2929	The original echoes Petrarch's *Rime* CCL, 1 "Solea lontana in sonno consolarme" and CCLXXXII, 2.
2939	the One: God (the original wording echoes Dante's *Paradiso* I, 1: "La gloria di colui che tutto move").
2983	his line: Torrismondo's. I follow Guglielminetti and Ariani's interpretation. Sozzi and Maier interpret the "line" to be the descendants of the Queen.
3038	Her mistake of wounding herself, thinking that Torrismondo did not love her.
3050	bridegroom: Germondo.
3077	praiseworthy of all tasks: the task of carrying out my will.
3078	a . . . king: Germondo.
3100	Another: Alvida.
3126	The original reminds us of Cavalcante's questions

to Dante (see *Inferno* X, 68). A similar question with a similar echo is in 3209.

3128   and one: the kingdom; the other: Alvida.

3177   colossi: majestic statues and other ancient Roman constructions.

3209   See note 3126.

3229   The original echoes Tasso's *Aminta* (III, ii, 1430) and Petrarch's *Rime* CCCXXXI, 43.

3239   honor: the title of queen.

3250   lively: because is prolonging life.

3318   The original recalls Petrarch's *Rime* CLVI, 4.

3321   The original echoes Tasso's *Gerusalemme Liberata*: "Così trapassa al trapassar d'un giorno / De la vita mortale il fiore e 'l verde;" (XVI, 15), and Petrarch's *Rime*: "altri, chi 'l prega, si delegua et fugge;" (CV, 28).

3327–28   Sozzi's error in the division of the stanzas of this chorus is reproduced by Mazzali and Maier, but not by Ariani and Guglielminetti.

BIBLIOGRAPHY

Alfieri, Vittorio. *Rime,* a cura di Rosolino Guastella, nuova presentazione di Cesare Bozzetti. Florence: Sansoni, 1963.

Arce, Joaquin. *Tasso y la poesía española.* Barcelona: Editorial Planeta, 1973.

Ariani, Marco. "Tra Manierismo e barocco: Il Torrismondo di Torquato Tasso," *Tra Classicismo e manierismo. Il teatro tragico del Cinquecento.* Florence: Olschki, 1974, 231–87; and "Il discorso perplesso: 'parlar disgiunto' e 'ars oratoria' nel *Torrismondo* di Torquato Tasso," *Paradigma* 3 (1980), 51–89.

I Barbari, Testi dei Secoli IV–XI scelti, tradotti e commentati da Elio Bartolini. Milan: Lagonesi, 1970.

Bigazzi, Roberto. "La dibattuta storia di Torrismondo," *MLA* 98 (1983); and in Marco Ariani's *Torquato Tasso: Torrismondo,* in *Il teatro italiano, II: La Tragedia del Cinquecento,* II.

Black, John. *Life of Torquato Tasso with an Historical and Critical Account of His Writings,* Vol. I. Edinburgh: John Murray, 1810.

Boulting, William. *Tasso and His Times.* London: Methuen, 1907.

Bowra, Cecil Maurice. *From Virgil to Milton.* London: Macmillan, 1945.

Brand, Charles Peter. *Torquato Tasso: A Study of the Poet and His Contribution to English Literature.* Cambridge, England: Cambridge UP, 1965.

Calderón de la Barca, Pedro. *Four Plays,* translated and with an introduction by Edwin Honig. New York: Hill and Wang, 1961.

Cambon, Glauco. *Ugo Foscolo, Poet of Exile.* Princeton, N.J.: Princeton UP, 1980.

Carducci, Giosuè. "Il Torrismondo," *Opere,* XIV. Bologna: Zanichelli, 1954.

Cerbo, Anna. *Il teatro dell'intelletto. Drammaturgia di tardo Rinascimento nel Meridione.* Naples: Istituto Universitario Orientale, 1990.

Chambers, E. K. *The Elizabethan Stage.* Oxford: The Clarendon, 1923.

Chatfield-Taylor, H. C. *Goldoni: A Biography.* New York: Duffield, 1913.

Chiodo, Domenico. "Il mito dell'età aurea nell'opera tassiana sul tragico." *Studi tassiani* 37 (1989): 31–58.

————. "Il Re Torrismondo e la riflessione tassiana sul tragico." *Studi tassiani* 37 (1989): 37–63.

Cochrane, Eric. *The Late Italian Renaissance, 1525–1630.* New York, Evanston, London: Harper Torchbooks, 1970.

Cremante, Renzo, ed. *Il teatro del 500,* I: *La tragedia.* Milan/Naples: Ricciardi, 1988.

Dalibray, Charles Vion. *Le Torrismon du Tasse Tragédie.* Paris: Denis Houssaye, 1636.

Daniele, Antonio. "Sul linguaggio tragico del Cinquecento e il Torrismondo del Tasso," *Atti dell'Istituto Veneto di Scienze Lettere ed Arti* 132 (1973–4): 425–56; reprinted in *Capitoli tassiani.* Padua: Antenore, 1983, 242–56.

Da Pozzo, Giovanni. *Torquato Tasso.* Florence: La Nuova Italia, 1921.

Della Terza, Dante. "La corte e il teatro: il mondo del Tasso," in *Tradizione ed esegesi. Semantica dell'innovazione da Agostino a De Sanctis.* Padua: Liviana, 1987, 61–70.

Di Benedetto, Arnaldo. "Agnizioni di lettura e note critiche sul Tasso," *Studi Tassiani* 18 (1968): 5–21; reprinted as "Sul Re Torrismondo" in *Tasso, minori e minimi a Ferrara.* Pisa: Nistri-Lischi, 1970, 95–101; and as "Per una valutazione del Re Torrismondo" in *Stile e Linguaggio.* Rome: Bonacci, 1974, 136–41, and as "Per una valutazione del Re Torrismondo" in *Tasso, minori e minimi a Ferrara* (2nd edition). Turin: Genesi, 1989.

Donadoni, Eugenio, and Richard Cody. *The Landscape of the Mind: Pastoralism and Platonic Theory in Tasso's Aminta and Shakespeare's Early Comedies.* Oxford and New York: Oxford UP, 1969.

D'Ovidio, Francesco. "Due tragedie del Cinquecento," *Studi sul Petrarca e sul Tasso.* Rome, 1926.

Ermini, Filippo. *L'Italia Liberata di Giangiorgio Trissino.* Rome: Tipografia Editrice Romana, 1895.

Flora, Francesco. *Storia della Letteratura Italiana,* II, "Il Quattrocento e il primo Cinquecento." Milan: Arnoldo Mondadori, 1972.

Foscolo, Ugo. *Saggi di Letteratura Italiana,* I, edizione a cura di Cesare Foligno. Florence: Felice Le Monnier, 1958.

From Marino to Marinetti: An Anthology of Forty Italian Poets, translated into English verse and with an introduction by Joseph Tusiani. New York: Baroque, 1974.

Getto, Giovanni. "Dal Galealto al Torrismondo," in *Malinconia del Tasso.* Naples: Liguori, 1979, 187–226.

————. *Interpretazione del Tasso.* Naples: Edizioni Scientifiche Italiane, 1951, 205–49.

Gilbert, Allan H. *Literary Criticism: Plato to Dryden.* Detroit: Wayne State UP, 1982.

Godfrey of Bulloigne: a critical edition of Edward Fairfax's translation of Tasso's Gerusalemme Liberata, together with Fairfax Original Poems. Oxford: Clarendon, 1981.

Godfrey of Bulloigne, or The Recoverie of Hierusalem: an heroical poem written in Italian by Seig. Torquato Tasso and translated into English by Richard Carew, Esquire, with an introduction by Werner von Koppenfels. Hildesheim: Gerstenberg Verlag, 1980.

Goethe, Johann Wolfgang von. *Torquato Tasso,* translated by John Prudhoe. Manchester: Manchester UP, 1979.

Goudet, Jacques. "La Nature du tragique dans *Il Re Torrismondo* du Tasse," in *Revue des études italiennes* 8 (1961): 146–68.

———. "Johannes et Olaus Magnus et l'intrigue de *Il Re Torrismondo,*" *Revue des études italiennes* 13 (1966): 61–67.

Guastavini, G. *Il re Torrismondo di Torquato Tasso.* Genoa: Bartoli, 1587.

Guglielminetti, Marziano. "Introduzione," Torquato Tasso, *Teatro.* Milan: Garzanti, 1983, vii–xlii.

Herrick, Marvin T. *Italian Tragedy in the Renaissance.* Urbana: U of Illinois P, 1965.

Hoole, J. *Jerusalem Delivered, an Heroic Poem.* Newburyport, Mass.: Edward Little, 1763.

Incanti, Cinzia. "Dal Galealto al Torrismondo. Note sul teatro del Tasso," *Misure critiche* 8 (luglio–dicembre 1978).

Horne, P. R. *The Tragedies of Giambattista Cinthio Giraldi.* London: Oxford UP, 1962.

Istoria della Volgar Poesia, II. Venice: Basegio, 1730.

Kates, Judith A. *Tasso and Milton: The Problem of Christian Epic.* Lewisburg, Pa.: Bucknell UP, 1983.

Manso, G. B. *Vita di Torquato Tasso.* Venice: Gamba, 1825.

Migiel, Marilyn. *Gender and Genealogy in Tasso's Gerusalemme Liberata.* Lewiston, N.Y.: Mellen Press, 1993.

Milton, John. *The Latin Poems.* New Heaven: Yale UP, 1930.

———. *The Poetical Works of John Milton,* II. Oxford: Clarendon, 1966.

Minesi, Emanuela. "Osservazioni sul linguaggio del Torrismondo," *Studi Tassiani* 28 (1980): 73–112.

Musumarra, Carmelo. *La poesia tragica italiana nel Rinascimento.* Florence: Olschki, 1972.

———. "Imitazione poetica e realtà di vita nella tragedia rinascimentale," *Critica letteraria* 16 (1988): 627–39.

Neri, Ferdinando. *La tragedia italiana del Cinquecento.* Florence: Galletti and Cocci, 1904.

Nichols, Fred J., ed. and trans. *An Anthology of Neo-Latin Poetry.* New Haven: Yale UP, 1979.

Olao Magno Gotho Archiepiscopo. *Historia de gentibus septemtrionalibus.* Westmead, Farnborough, Hants., England: Gregg International, 1971.

Paratore, Ettore. "Nuove prospettive sull'influsso del teatro classico nel '500," in *Il teatro classico nel Cinquecento.* Rome: Accademia dei Licei, 1971, 9–95

Peacock, Roland. *Goethe's Major Plays.* Manchester: Manchester UP, 1959.

Pierce, Glenn. "What is Tragic about Torrismondo?" *Quaderni d'italianistica* 12 (1991): 173–89.

Pieri, Marzia. "Interpretazione teatrale del Torrismondo," *Rassegna della letteratura italiana* 90 (1986): 397–413.

Praz, Mario. *The Flaming Heart.* Gloucester, Mass.: Peter Smith, 1966.

Prince, Frank Templeton. *The Italian Element in Milton's Verse.* Oxford: Claredon Press, 1954.

Racine, Jean. *The Best Plays of Racine,* translated by Lacy Lockert. Princeton, N.J.: Princeton UP, 1964.

———. *Britannicus,* edited by H. J. Chaytor. Cambridge: Cambridge UP, 1950.

Ramat, Raffaello. "Il Re Torrismondo," in *Torquato Tasso.* Milan: Marzorati, 1957, 365–413; reprinted in *Saggi sul Rinascimento.* Florence: La Nuova Italia, 1969, 218–71.

Renda, Umberto. "Il Torrismondo di Torquato Tasso e la tecnica del Cinquecento," *Rivista Abruzzese di Scienze, Lettere ed Arti* 20 (1905): 85–100, 179–203, 363–77, 422–33, 525–38, 626–40; also in *Rivista Abruzzese* (1906): 248–60, 509–18, 570–81, 651–61.

Rhu, Lawrence F. *The Genesis of Tasso's Narrative Theory. English Translations of the Early Poetics and a Comparative Survey of Their Significance.* Detroit: Wayne State UP, 1993.

Scianatico, Giovanna. "Le Tasse et le maniérisme." *Revue de Littérature Comparée* 4 (1988): 545–57.

Scrivano, Riccardo. "Tasso e il teatro," in *La norma e lo scarto. Proposte per il Cinquecento letterario italiano.* Rome: Bonacci, 1980.

Sells, Lytton A. *The Italian Influence in English Poetry* (from Chaucer to Southwell). Bloomington: Indiana UP, 1955.

Sellstrom, A. Donald. "Corneille and Tasso: An Unacknowledged Link." *Revue de Littérature Comparée* 62 (1988): 477–82.

Seneca. *The Complete Roman Drama,* edited with an introduction by George E. Duckworth, II. New York: Random, 1942.

Serassi, Pierantonio. *Vita di Torquato Tasso.* Bergamo, 1785.

Simpson, Joyce. *Le Tasse et la Littérature et l'art Baroque en France.* Paris: Librairie A. G. Nizet, 1962.

Solerti, Angelo. *Vita di Torquato Tasso,* I: La Vita. Rome: Ermanno Loescher, 1895.

Sophocles. *The Complete Plays of Sophocles.* New York: Bantam, 1982.

Sozzi, B. T. "Per l'edizione critica del Torrismondo," and "Le correzioni autografe al Torrismondo," in *Studi sul Tasso.* Pisa: Nistri-Lisci, 1954, 77–171.

―――. "Il Torrismondo," in *Nuovi studi sul Tasso.* Bergamo: Centro Tassiano, 1963, 116–20.

Spitzer, Leo. "L'effet de sourdine dans le style classique: Racine," in *Etudes de style.* Paris, 1970, 208–335.

Storia della Letteratura Italiana, VII. Modena: Società Tipografica, 1972.

Storia D'Olao Magno Arcivescovo D'Upsali, De' Costumi De' Popoli Settentrionali, tradotta da Remigio Fiorentino. Turin: Vincenzo Bona, 1958.

Tasso, Torquato. *Aminta,* introduzione di Mario Fubini, note di Bruno Maier. Milan: Biblioteca Universale Rizzoli, 1963.

―――. *Dialogues: A Selection, with the Discourse on the Art of the Dialogue.* Translated with an Introduction and Notes by Carnes Lord and Dain A. Trafton. Berkeley, Los Angeles, London: U of California P, 1982.

―――. *Discourses on the Heroic Poem.* Translated with notes by Mariella Cavalchini and Irene Samuel. Oxford and New York: Oxford UP, 1973.

―――. *Jerusalem Delivered.* Being a translation into English verse by Edward Fairfax of Tasso's *Gerusalemme Liberata.* With an introduction by John Charles Nelson. New York: Capricorn, 1963.

―――. *Jerusalem Delivered,* translated into verse and with an introduction by Joseph Tusiani. Cranbury, N.J.: Associated UP, 1970.

―――. *Jerusalem Delivered.* An English Prose Version. Translated and Edited by Ralph Nash. Detroit: Wayne State UP, 1987.

―――. *Opere,* a cura di Bruno Maier II. Milan: Rizzoli, 1964.

―――. *Prose,* a cura di Ettore Mazzali con una premessa di Francesco Flora. Milan: Riccardo Ricciardi, 1959.

―――. *Prose Diverse.* Florence: Editore G. Guasti, 1875.

―――. *The Creation of the World,* translated into English verse with an introduction by Joseph Tusiani, annotated by Gaetano Cipolla. Binghamton, N.Y.: Medieval and Renaissance Text and Studies, 1982.

Il Teatro Italiano, II: La Tragedia del Cinquecento. Turin: Giulio Einaudi, 1977.

Teatro di Torquato Tasso, edizione critica a cura di Angelo Solerti con due saggi di Giosuè Carducci. Bologna: Ditta Nicola Zanichelli, 1895.

Thomas, Calvin. *Goethe's Torquato Tasso*. Boston: D. C. Heath, 1906.

Three Renaissance Pastorals: Tasso-Guarini-Daniel, edited and annotated by Elizabeth Story Donno. Binghamton, N.Y.: Medieval and Renaissance Text and Studies, 1993.

Trissino, Giangiorgio. *La Sofonisba* con note di Torquato Tasso, edite a cura di Franco Paglierani. Bologna: Gaetano Romagnoli, 1884.

Varese, Claudio. *Torquato Tasso: epos-parola-scena*. Messina: G. D'Anna, 1976.

Vazzoler, Franco. "Approssimazioni critiche per la tragedia italiana del Cinquecento." *L'immagine riflessa* 2 (1978): 84–94.

Venturini, Giuseppe. "La genesi dell'Alfeo di Orazio Ariosti e il Torrismondo del Tasso," *Studi Urbinati* 43 (1969).

———"Il Torrismondo," in *Saggi Critici. Cinquecento minore: O. Ariosti. G. M. Verdizotti e il loro influsso nella vita e nell'opera del Tasso*. Ravenna: Longo, 1970.

Verdino, Stefano. "Funzione drammatica e testo profondo: il racconto della tempesta nel Torrismondo di Torquato Tasso," *Rivista italiana di drammaturgia* 15–16 (1980).

———. "Organizzazione della tragedia in *Il re Torrismondo*." In Aldo Agazzi, ed. *Studi in onore di Bartolo Tommaso Sozzi*. Bergamo: Centro di studi tassiani, 1991, 117–50.

Vincent, E. R. *Ugo Foscolo An Italian in Regency England*. Cambridge: Cambridge UP, 1953.

Weinberg, Bernard. *A History of Literary Criticism in the Italian Renaissance*, II. Chicago: U of Chicago P, 1961.

Wellek, René. *Concept of Criticism*. New Haven: Yale UP, 1963.

Wilkins, Ernest Hatch. *A History of Italian Literature*. Cambridge Mass.: Harvard UP, 1974.